1000 THINGS YOU NEVER LEARNED IN BUSINESS SCHOOL

Other books by William N. Yeomans:

Jobs, a series of six books, the latest of which is *Jobs 82–83.*

1000 THINGS YOU NEVER LEARNED IN BUSINESS SCHOOL

HOW TO GET AHEAD OF THE PACK & STAY THERE

William N. Yeomans

McGraw-Hill Book Company

New York
St. Louis
San Francisco
Bogotá
Guatemala
Hamburg
Lisbon
Madrid
Mexico
Montreal
Panama
Paris
San Juan
São Paulo
Tokyo
Toronto

1 2 3 4 5 6 7 8 9 DOC DOC 8 7 6 5 4

ISBN 0-07-072274-9

LIBRARY OF CONGRESS CATALOGING IN PUBLICATION DATA

Yeomans, William N.
1000 things you never learned in business school.
1. Psychology, Industrial. 2. Vocational guidance.
3. Communication in management. 4. Personnel management.
I. Title. II. Title: One thousand things you never
learned in business school.
HF5548.8.Y46 1985 650.1 84-7180
ISBN 0-07-072274-9

Book design by M.R.P. Design.

To my wife, Kay, who makes all things possible and who has given me invaluable advice and assistance with this book.

With special thanks to Melanie Kavanaugh, who, after typing first drafts for several of my books, has finally deciphered my handwriting.

Contents

Building a Team / 139

Harnessing the Organization / 181

Managing Your Career

1. **Starting Up:** How to Use This Book

Al: Did you hear about Fred's new job?

Sue: Yeah. I'm so happy for him. He sure has himself on a fast track.

Al: I don't know what he's got, but I sure wish I had some of it.

Overheard in the Accounting Dept.
Greenwich Gridlock Corp.

How's your career going? Is it moving along as well as you think it should? Are you doing work as important as you'd like to be? Are you confident about your future?

Or do you have some doubts? Maybe you sometimes wonder if, when it's all over, you'll have been just another Joe or Jane, pressing along day after day, doing good work but never really making a mark, never getting out ahead of the pack, never realizing the satisfactions and rewards that can come from reaching your potential.

Lots of people are concerned about their careers, and with good reason. It's the worry of the decade. Just about everything we knew about success and getting ahead in the world has changed in the last few years, and the new rules are a lot tougher than the old.

For one thing, many organizations are not growing the way they were in the sixties and early seventies. Back then thousands upon thousands of jobs were created every year just by expansion. Not so today. In business, government, universities—everywhere you look—breakneck growth has been replaced with "productivity": getting more out of less. Markets are saturated; competition is fierce; money is tight; new facilities, equipment, and people cost too much; expansion has slowed, and with it promotional opportunity. Many of us who were hired ten, fifteen, or twenty years ago looked forward to advancement opportunities that just don't exist today.

If that weren't enough, the baby boomers, now middle-aged (or fast getting there), are clogging up all kinds of career pipelines because there are so many of them: 77 million, in fact, or about a third of our whole population. In 1970 they made up only 15 percent of the work force; today they are half, and their sheer numbers make advancement harder for everyone, including themselves. There will never be enough top jobs to accommodate them all, and many are already frustrated, stalled in their careers. And things won't brighten up in a hurry. If there are ten people competing for each management job today, by 1990 there will be twenty.

As if to make sure the problem stays around even longer, too many new college graduates flood into the labor market each year—way more than the jobs available. Many new graduates have to take jobs in which their training and skills are underutilized. Others, who do find work in their chosen fields, soon discover they are blocked by a ton of baby boomers just ahead of them.

All that has probably affected you in one of two ways. Either you have:

1. Lowered your aspirations and decided to settle for less, to hold on to what you've got; or you are
2. Struggling to get an advantage, to find some way to get ahead in this fiercely competitive work environment.

If you have chosen the latter, you know you can't rely on the old standbys for success like native ability, luck (being in the right place at the right time), hard work, drive and initiative, or even a good education. There are too many others with those same attributes competing with you for too few jobs.

You must have something extra to stand out from the crowd, to be special, to grab hold of that larger responsibility.

You can get that something extra. You can get it by honing and polishing key skills that will help you improve your performance dramatically, give you wider visibility in your organization, and get you on a faster track to becoming what you want to be.

These are today's skills—and tomorrow's—for getting ahead, for succeeding, for playing the game and winning under the new rules. I call them *Upward Bound* skills.

For the most part these are not classic business-school skills. Planning, leading, organizing, and controlling are important, and you must know them to survive in your job. But they are not *Upward Bound* skills because everyone else knows them, too, either through school or experience on the job.

Upward Bound skills are special skills you can pile on top of what you already have. They are neglected skills that top executives all across the nation tell us are lacking in their people and sorely needed to keep their key employees growing in today's environment, and their organizations alive and well in the years ahead.

Maybe you've neglected them too. They are everyday skills you probably haven't done much to develop or refine because you haven't had the opportunity or haven't recognized their importance.

Make no mistake. These are powerful, no-nonsense skills. They are highly impressive, visible skills. A little improvement in any one of them will help . . . it will be noticed. Growth in several can have an explosive effect on your career, way beyond any effort you put in, and can spell the difference between a good career and a great one. That's why I call them *Upward Bound* skills.

And here they are.

Managing your career. How to take charge and not just let your career happen to you. How to recognize what career options you have . . . and you have more than you think you do.

Thinking up. How to make your attitude and outlook work for you. How to think in new and broader ways as a top executive should. How to develop your capacity for innovation, for coming up with new ways of seeing things and with original solutions . . . a skill that is rapidly coming into demand.

Communicating. How to be a crackerjack communicator: speaker, writer, meeting leader. It takes more than just "good" today. Organizations of all kinds are crying for top-notch communicators—and you can be one.

Getting what you want. How to develop and use a problem-solving approach to negotiation that will get what you want *and* improve relationships at the same time.

Building a team. How to pick good players, how to turn them on, how to get them to work together as a team; and, a vital but badly misunderstood team skill, how to listen.

Harnessing the organization. How to manage the climate you work in, including managing the person who counts most—your boss.

Doing it right. How to recall names, facts, and figures accurately when you need them, how to make decisions, and how to get more done in less time.

Keeping cool. How to control stress and make it work for you—even with the extra pressure you put on yourself to get out ahead of the pack.

There they are.

I have identified, refined, modified, and pinpointed these skills, one by one, over twenty years in which I have plowed through truckloads of books and articles on behavior, management, career development, and success; interviewed successful people in all kinds of jobs in a variety of organizations, and met with training and development experts all across the country. I have spent two decades observing managers doing well in their jobs, others getting stalled and sidetracked, and I have spent a good chunk of time personally directing the training and development of thousands of managers at all organizational levels for one of the nation's largest corporations. I have spent a working lifetime thinking about, researching, speaking, and writing about careers, personal development, and success. During that time it has become evident to me that there are certain skills that, if perfected, contribute mightily to success, and I have crystallized them into the *Upward Bound* skills.

In presenting these skills to you, ***1000 Things You Never Learned in Business School*** is the best of what is found in high-powered training today, compressed into one book you can work through at your own pace. You don't have to wait years and spend a small fortune (yours or your organization's) to get yourself trained. You can get a fast start on it all right here.

All this probably conjures up images of big promotions, more money, bigger offices, lots of people to boss around, power, fame, and other trappings of success like mahogany wastebaskets. Those are important, there's no doubt about it, and this book will help you get them.

But there's another part to being successful: being the very best in your present job, being so good at what you do that you command attention and respect throughout your whole organization.

There are very special people around who aren't rich, aren't famous, and still have tin wastebaskets, but are happy doing what they are doing and proud that they're doing it well. Those people may not be on space shots to the chairman's job, but they know they have solid futures ahead of them. And if they have to stay in their present jobs longer than they had planned, they are happy and fulfilled anyhow because they are tops at what they do.

And that, as you work your way up, step by step, can be very satisfying and rewarding too.

That, in fact, may be the *only* way you can work your way up today. To get to that next level you have to be outstanding at what you are doing now. You won't get promoted just to fill openings or because you happen to be pretty good. The field of selection for most jobs is too great. There are too many people to choose from. To be selected, you've got to stand head and shoulders above everyone else.

Probably you are working hard at your present job and doing it well. That's an absolute must, but it may not be enough. Sharpening up your *Upward Bound* skills can give you the extra edge you need.

Here are some things you should know about ***1000 Things You Never Learned in Business School.***

1. The book will help you most if you are seriously interested in doing better at work and willing to get up out of your recliner and go for it. Just as you can't get skinny reading diet books, you can't get ahead reading books on achievement. So make up your mind now. If you want to read this book for fun and forget it, fine. If you want to make it work for you, promise yourself you will make a reasonable effort to follow the guidance in the chapters. Note the word "reasonable." I'm not asking you to change your whole lifestyle or work until you drop. With some additional effort and discipline, you can make improvements in your performance dramatic enough to help you move ahead. They don't have to be giant steps. The distance between a good performer and a pro is slight—and often is based on many small things that make a real difference.
2. ***1000 Things You Never Learned in Business School*** will help you if you are an executive or a manager, scientist, administrator, engineer, government worker, military officer, teacher, or other professional. It will help you if you are a student thinking about a future career, a trainee just starting out, or someone returning to work after many years out of the labor force. But it will be especially helpful to you if you are looking for a new start, if you have years of experience and know your job but feel that you should be doing better. It is for those on the plateau, stuck in the middle, for anyone seriously interested in achieving or getting ahead faster.

3. This is not an inspirational book. At least it's not meant to be. If it gets you all juiced up, fine, but that's not its intent. It is designed to be a series of powerful personal-development programs, covering a wide range of often neglected skills. It does not contain a lot of fuzzy theories, but usable, tested approaches and techniques you can use to do better at your job.
4. While ***1000 Things You Never Learned in Business School*** covers standout skills such as managing your boss, problem solving, and writing skills, it does not cover such skills as manipulating people, bullying and pulling rank, deceit, passing the buck, playing politics, and buttering people up. If you want to use any or all of those skills, go ahead. They can work sometimes, usually in the short run, but I don't discuss them in this book.
5. Watch out. By improving a few *Upward Bound* skills just a little, you will begin to be recognized as someone a cut above the rest. That means you will have extra demands placed on you and people will expect more of you. Once you have given a first-class front-of-the-room presentation, for instance, you are more likely to be asked to give other presentations . . . and you'll be expected to do them all just as well as the first. The net effect will be that you'll be doing more work, more responsible work; you will be more visible and play a larger leadership role in your organization.
6. *Upward Bound* skills will have a dramatic impact on your career, and they will also help you in other ways: off the job, as you deal with family, civic groups, church activities, charity work, hobbies, sports, and other activities. They have wide application, and you'll find yourself using them in all kinds of situations.
7. ***1000 Things You Never Learned in Business School*** is written in highlights. If you are eager to get going, you don't have the time to wade through a river of background material on all these subjects. So I have done a lot of wading for you and fished out the best of what I have found over the years on how to develop these skills.
8. ***1000 Things You Never Learned in Business School*** is easy to use. It is not written like some somber treatise that's as much fun as a root canal. Achievement is serious enough as it is, fraught with frustration, anxiety, Excedrin, and Gelusil, and you don't need anything to make it seem any heavier. So I have tried to write in a style light enough to help you feel more relaxed about the whole thing. Don't be misled, though. The underlying message is very serious, the advice genuine and highly functional.

Throughout the book there are anecdotes, quotes, and stories in which I fearlessly name names, places, and dates . . . every sordid detail. They are all fictitious, made up by me. But all are very close to actual events that have happened or easily could have.

9. There is not much philosophy or theory in ***1000 Things You Never Learned in Business School.*** It is a "how to" book. The emphasis is on doing. That's the way adults learn. You can watch reruns of the winter Olympics all day, but until you slide off the chair lift on top of the mountain and know the terror of starting off down the perpendicular drop to the bottom of the world, you haven't started to learn how to ski. In the same way, you can't learn to run a super meeting, use your time better, or negotiate for what you want until you actually get out and do it.

10. At the end of the book, I've included a list of books and articles I think are especially good on the subject of each chapter. In some cases, I have also listed seminars to attend or other resources for obtaining additional information.

    This book is a distillation, and by its nature cannot deal in great depth with any of the subjects covered. I would urge you to explore further any area that particularly interests you or in which you need additional help or insight. Many of the resources I have listed are classics in their field and are worth your attention.

    I have not listed complete or exhaustive bibliographies. I know you don't have time to pick titles out of several pages of listings. So I have done that for you by listing only those that I feel are the most helpful.

11. In this book there are many charts to help you organize your thinking, set priorities, and map out strategies. Because of page-size limitations in a book of this sort, most will not be large enough to use as they are. You'll have to copy those charts on larger paper. Where you want to do your most creative and high-powered thinking, use the biggest sheet of paper you can find, so small narrow columns won't restrict your imagination or tempt you to leave things out. The charts are "tools" you can use immediately to help you get started building your skills. One problem with any kind of learning is that you can get excited about it when it is going on, but then you quickly get tied up in day-to-day pressures back on the job and never get around to using it. If you put these aids to work for you, you will have a better chance of improving.

All right. How do you get started? You have a big book in front of you, with a ton of chapters, seventeen in all, on how to improve your skills.

UPWARD BOUND Priorities

Upward Bound Skills		How Well You Do			Importance to My Career A = Very High, B = Fairly High, C = Medium	Priority
		Just Great	So-So	An Embarrassment		
Managing Your Career	Career Planning (Chapter 2)	Know where I'm going and how to get there. Know my options and how to use them	Not quite sure	Lost	_____	_____
Thinking Up	Attitude (Chapter 3)	Great outlook. Always confident and positive	Sometimes optimistic, sometimes not	Whine a lot	_____	_____
	Creativity (Chapter 4)	Get creative, original ideas that work. See things in new ways.	Mostly come up with ordinary, everyday ideas	Have trouble finding ideas of any kind	_____	_____
Communicating	Writing (Chapter 5)	A regular John Steinbeck	Get my point across but have some trouble with words, speed, clarity	Terminal writer's block	_____	_____
	Speaking (Chapter 6)	Captivating. Words and gestures flow, audience hangs on every phrase	Do as well as most. Able to get up, say my piece, and avoid apoplexy	Sweat and stutter	_____	_____
	Running Meetings (Chapter 7)	Lead skillfully. Meetings go where I want, on time, and get results	Some wandering, side discussions, wasted time. Meetings take too long, at times don't lead to action	Chaos, out of control. Meetings roam in all directions, often end with nothing decided	_____	_____
etting hat You Want	Negotiating (Chapter 8)	Drive a hard bargain. Know how to get what I want	Come out even; win some, lose some	Usually get ripped off	_____	_____

	(Chapter 9)	ways find winners	some duds			
Building A Team	Motivating (Chapter 10)	Keep my team revved up and really producing	Generate some excitement	Barely manage to keep them awake	______	______
	Getting People to Work Together (Chapter 10)	Slick as the '56 Yankees	At times they work like a team	Brawling and running off in all directions	______	______
	Listening (Chapter 11)	Total. Hear and understand everything	Drift in and out. Miss some of what's said	Never-Never Land	______	______
Harnessing the Organization	Knowing What's Important in the Organization (Especially factors not related to work) (Chapter 12)	Know them cold. Make them work for me	Not always sure	Might as well be in a foreign culture	______	______
	Managing the Boss (Chapter 13)	Almost always get him/her to go along. Know how the boss thinks and how to play it	Get through to the boss once in a while	Like talking to a fence post	______	______
Doing it Right	Memory (Chapter 14)	Mind like an Apple (Computer, that is)	Sometimes can't recall facts when I want to	Can't think of my own phone number	______	______
	Problem Solving/ Decision Making (Chapter 15)	A wizard. Most often right	50–50	Where's my Ouija Board?	______	______
	Managing Time (Chapter 16)	Completely in control. Always on top of things	Often need more time, have more to do than I can handle	Climbing through an avalanche	______	______
Keeping It Cool	Handling Stress (Chapter 17)	Cool and calm. Handle calamities without a twitch	Sometimes flustered, tense, worried	Pass the tranquilizers	______	______

How are you going to get through all that and come out better off than when you started? You've already figured out it's impossible to work on all those skills at once. That would be like trying to eat a day's output of your local Burger King at one sitting.

The best way to work your way through ***1000 Things You Never Learned in Business School*** is to decide which skills are most important and go after them first. Then as you master those skills you can move on to the other *Upward Bound* skills, working through the book at your own pace and in the order that will help your career most.

The *Upward Bound* Priorities chart will help you sort things out and decide where you'll get the best and fastest return.

Upward Bound skills are listed on the left-hand side of the chart. Opposite each, in the middle, is a rating scale called "How Well You Do" that you should use to assess your ability. Circle the statement that best describes how well you do. No one is going to see the questionnaire, so be tough on yourself.

Go ahead and fill in that section of the chart now. When you have finished, take a look at where you've put your check marks. If all of them are in the "Just Great" column, you are either a truly amazing person or you have been without oxygen for too long. If you *are* truly amazing, scale this book in the direction of someone who really needs it and get on with your career. You've probably missed two promotions just reading this far. But go back and look again. You may want to move some of your checks to the middle column.

If all your checks are in the "Embarrassment" column, you've probably been too hard on yourself. Think about it more.

Next is a column headed "Importance to My Career." Use this column to estimate how much it would help your career if you made dramatic improvements in each of the skills. Use "A" to indicate great importance—improvement would really help your career. Use "B" to indicate those skills that are important, but not the most important, and "C" for those skills that are of medium importance. Notice you can't rank skills of no importance, because every one of those skills is important to some degree. Even if you do not use the skill in your job now, you should be getting familiar with it, because you'll use it later.

Now for the "Priority" column: Take a long look at where you need help and what is important to your career. Pick the *Upward Bound* skill you should work on first and mark it number 1 in the "Priority" column. Then select number 2 and so on.

When you've established your sequence, you can begin. Start with the chapter you marked priority number 1. Read it. Study it. Think about it. Make a plan (see below). Begin trying out pieces of it on the job or at home. As you become familiar and comfortable with them dig in in earnest and practice. Practice until the skills involved become natural and easy to you: become second nature, part of your everyday routine.

Then go to priority number 2 and do the same thing, and so on, working your way through all the chapters. And you should go through them all, even the ones that are last on your priority list. Remember, these are *Upward Bound* skills and it will be to your benefit to improve even those you think you're pretty good at now. There's always something new to learn—a shortcut, an insight, a new way of looking at something, a way to make it better. And even those skills that are of "C" importance need attention because they are still of *some* importance. Combined with all the others they will give you a powerful and impressive skill package that can't miss being recognized in your organization.

Upward Bound means modifying old habits and learning new skills. That's not always easy. Here is a step-by-step system for changing, learning, and growing. Use it as you work your way through each of the *Upward Bound* skills.

1. Visualize how great it will be after you improve your skill. Picture yourself using the improved skill and dazzling others (and yourself) with it. Think of how proud you'll feel when you get all those compliments on your new behavior.
2. Go at this with a winning attitude. No kidding. It really helps. Tell yourself these are skills you can learn with a little work and that you'll soon be very good at them.
3. Make a plan. Good intentions are fine, but for making things happen, plans are better. First, make some copies of the Plan for Use on the Job chart below. Then, as you work through each of the chapters, use the Plan to outline what you will do to use the skill on the job. Break the skill into specific parts you want to try out and list those in the left-hand column.

   Don't write vague entries like "Do this more" or "Do a better job in this area." They don't mean much and won't help you learn anything. Instead be precise. If you are learning to give presentations, for example, you might want to start your listing like this:

   A. Write a script on the Acme project that is short, but has real interest value for the audience. Put a "grabber" at the beginning.
   B. Design slides and charts to liven up the presentation.
   C. Mark key word and phrases for emphasis.
   D. Practice at least three times out loud, alone. Practice using slides and charts.

Get out from behind the podium

Use gestures

Look up, use eye contact

E. Practice once with a live group of five or more. (Mark, Edna, Alice, Fran, Bob)

Get feedback

Revise presentation

F. Give Presentation

Get feedback

Fill in the times and dates for finishing each action, then, when you are done, complete the analysis portion of the Plan.

4. Do a little bit at a time. When you make your plan, don't try to get everything done in the first week. You won't be able to do it. You'll become discouraged and go right back to doing what you did before without making any progress. Building skills takes time. You may want to plan out six months or longer to complete your most important, high priority skills and another six months to do the rest.

5. Discipline yourself. Stick to your plan, even when you don't feel like it, which will be most of the time. Do a little bit each day, each week, until learning becomes a habit in itself.

6. Practice. Adults learn by doing. Use your new skill as soon and often as possible. Don't ever try to improve a skill you aren't going to use for a long time. If you want to make better presentations, but don't have one coming up until next quarter (and can't invent reasons for giving one next week), skip that chapter until you get closer to the time you can actually use it. Follow your Plan for Use on the Job. When you're tempted to slide back into your old habits, quickly substitute the new.

7. Reward yourself for successes. Even little ones. Tell yourself you knew you could do it. Look back occasionally at where you began, then look at where you are now. You'll be surprised at how far you've come. Don't worry about occasional failures. They'll happen along the way, but you will overcome them.

8. As you begin to use each skill, rehearse in your mind how you'll do it. See yourself doing it well and visualize, step by step, what you'll be doing.

9. Involve others. Tell them you're trying to improve a certain skill. Ask them for feedback. Committing to others is a powerful motivator.

Plan for Use on the Job

Upward Bound Skill ______________________ Priority __________

Date by Which You Will Have Mastered: ______________

What You Plan To Do (Begin with Action verb. Be specific: Indicate amount, who is involved, etc.)	When (Times, dates for completion)	Analysis		
		Did you complete? If so, what happened? If not, why not?	How well did this work? Your reaction? Others?	What did you learn? How can you do better next time?

10. Periodically review what you've done and look at how far you've come. Tell yourself how proud you are, then go out and buy yourself a steak dinner.

Now you're ready to dive into your first priority. Why not begin right now?

I hope you enjoy ***1000 Things You Never Learned in Business School*** and that it will help you grow and change your career and your life. Good luck and have fun out ahead of the pack!

2. Up, Up . . . and Away: How to Manage Your Career

Big Boss: Harvey, it gives me great pleasure to award you this twenty-five year pin. I know that over those many years of loyal service to the company on your way up to your present position, manager of the mail room, you've held many exciting jobs.

Harvey: No, sir, I haven't.

Big Boss: You haven't?

Harvey: No, I came here as manager of the mail room.

Big Boss: You've been manager of the mail room for twenty-five years?

Harvey: Yes, sir.

Big Boss: (Gulp) Well, isn't that terrific.

If you really want to get ahead, you cannot sit around and wait for a career to happen to you. You must get out and actively manage it—make it happen.

Essentially, this whole book is about managing your career. The emphasis in each of the other chapters is on doing that by improving specific *Upward Bound* skills that will put you ahead of the crowd. In this chapter, we'll look at your career itself and help you answer key questions about it:

1. Where are you going?
2. How can you get there?
3. How well is your present job helping you get there?
4. How can you improve your work situation?

Let's look at each.

WHERE ARE YOU GOING?

It's hard to move from where you are now to something better if you don't have a good idea of what that something better is.

If you really want to get your career going, you should have a long-range goal—a pretty clear idea of what your work and your life will look like, say, five years from now. Your career goals should be:

Clear in your mind: Distinct enough so you can write them down in a few sentences. You should be able to picture yourself arriving at your goal, being there, and you should be able to see the steps to get there.

Believable: Would you tell your friends about your goal or would you be afraid they'd fall off their chairs laughing? When *you* think about your goal, do you fall off your chair laughing? If so, pick another goal.

Within your control: At least for the most part. A goal that is completely dependent on outside influences, luck, others' actions and decisions, and things that may happen is not a good one.

Realistic: You should have a reasonable chance to make your goal. It does not have to be easy to make, but it should be possible. Remember, it is simpler to write a goal than to achieve one. Don't pick a goal that is so far out that you have one chance in a thousand of making it. You'll fail and be discouraged.

Detailed enough so you'll be able to tell when you get there. "To improve myself" is a commendable thought, but it's too vague to be a good goal. "To advance two pay levels within five years and have the title of department manager supervising a staff of ten or more people" is a good beginning. It's specific and measurable.

Inspiring: There's nothing worse than a boring goal. Your goal must get you excited just thinking about it and make you anxious to get going to meet it.

Okay, now let's try to write some career goals. Find a nice, quiet place and lock yourself in for an hour or two. Think first, then answer these questions.

1. What's important to you in life? (I know that's a colossal question to spring on you, but try to answer it.) Think in terms of work, family, hobbies, sports, community activities, church, and any other area that's big for you. List them all below, then number them in order of importance, 1 being the most important, 2 next most important, and so on.

2. What does success mean to you as far as your career is concerned? Where do you see yourself in the next five years? Think in terms of how much and what kinds of responsibilities you'll have, how much money you'll be making, how much you'll have learned, how competent you'll be, and how you'll be thought of by the big bosses. Write your goal below:

3. Now that you have written your goal, go back and look at it in light of the priorities you listed in question number 1. Remember, you only have so much space in your life. You can't be everything. Does your

goal still seem realistic? Or will you be taking too much away from other important areas of your life to accomplish it? Also, test your goal against the six criteria outlined above. After considering what's important in your life and criteria for good goals, you may want to revise your goal:

Here are some additional thoughts about goals:

- It may not seem like it, but your goals will change. That's because circumstances change and you'll change. Believe it or not, what you think is gigantically important today will probably not seem so momentous a year or two from now.
- Therefore, setting goals is a continuing affair, not a one-time thing. But even though the five-year goal you write today may not be what you want five years from now, it is important that you have a goal anyhow. You have to have something to dream about, to work toward.
- Be sure your goal is really your goal and not what society dictates. Don't put down that you want to be president of the division just because that's the "American Way." Be sure you really want to do what a division president does—that it balances out against everything else that's important in your life.
- Be sure your goal reflects your interests—what you enjoy doing. You may get lots of rewards from a higher level job, but if you don't enjoy it and it doesn't mesh with your other areas of importance, you won't be happy, and that's not good career planning.

HOW CAN YOU GET THERE?

Using the Goal Chart below, write out specific action steps you will take to accomplish your career goal. Think about changes you'll make in your work and nonwork life, what accomplishments on the job will help, what you'll have to learn (including, of course, your *Upward Bound* skills), and any other actions that will help. Put these down in the left-hand column. Then consider who can help you, and write their names in the middle column. Set target dates for yourself in the right-hand column.

GOAL CHART

GOAL: ____

____

____

____

How to Accomplish

Action Steps:	Who Can Help:	Finish By:

Now, think of everything that will be an obstacle to your doing your action steps and achieving your goal. Include obstacles within yourself (e.g., advanced laziness), obstacles within your work life (confining job, unsupportive boss), obstacles within your nonwork life (too many hobbies and activities, spread too thin). List them all in the left-hand column of the Career Obstacle Chart below.

Then, do some creative problem solving (see Chapter 4 for methods of generating ideas) on how you can clear those obstacles out of your way.

CAREER OBSTACLE CHART

Obstacle	How to Overcome It

HOW WELL IS YOUR JOB HELPING YOU ACCOMPLISH YOUR GOALS?

Let's take a critical look at the work you're doing and the environment you're doing it in, and see how well those will support your long-range goal.

Take a few minutes and fill out the Job Analysis Questionnaire that follows. You may not be up for another questionnaire right now, but getting you to think about your situation is necessary for career planning, and questionnaires are a way to do that. This one will help you think about your work situation in a complete and organized way and help you come to some conclusions about it.

Your present job is, after all, the starting place from which everything else in your future happens.

Some jobs make it easy for you to get ahead, others get in your way. Assessing your present work situation will help you understand better what impact it will have on your efforts and will help you focus on what you can do to make it better.

For each factor in the left-hand column, pick the statement that best describes your situation and place its score in the right-hand column.

Job Analysis Questionnaire

Factor	Super	Pretty good	Fair	Not too hot	Score
Your Work	Exciting, important, challenging. Helps me learn and grow. Score: 5	Has its moments, but sometimes routine. Score: 4	Mostly routine. Score: 2	A chimpanzee could do it. Score: 0	
	Plenty of responsibility and freedom to exercise it. Score: 5	Some responsibility and freedom. Score: 4	Mostly told what to do and how to do it. Score: 2	Straitjacket. Score: 0	
Training	Constantly learning: seminars, project assignments, coaching on the job. Score: 5	Fairly regular opportunities for training. Score: 3	Lots of talk about training. Not much happens. Score: 1	What's training? Score: 0	
Chance for Advancement	Good future. Frequent openings at higher levels. Score: 5	Promotions less than frequent but do happen. Score: 3	Very slow moving up the ladder. Score: 1	Next promotion will come with Social Security. Score: 0	
Promotion from Within	Almost all higher level jobs filled from within. Score: 4	Many are. Score: 3	Some are. Score: 1	Almost all filled from outside. Score: 0	

Job Analysis Questionnaire (*Continued*)

Factor	Super	Pretty good	Fair	Not too hot	Score
Exposure	Work with wide range of higher management often. Plenty of chances to show my *Upward Bound* skills. Score: 3	Fairly good. Score: 2	Some. Score: 1	Buried. Score: 0	2
Recognition	Immediate praise for good work. Score: 3	Good work is sometimes noticed. Score: 2	Good work is expected but not noticed much. Score: 1	No one knows or cares. Score: 0	1
Communication (Downward)	Open and easy. Always know what's going on. Have all the information I need. Score: 3	Have to struggle for some information. Score: 2	Get bits and pieces. Score: 1	Might as well be working on Neptune. Score: 0	2
(Upward)	Often asked for my opinion. Frequent involvement. Score: 4	Sometimes have chance to give my thoughts. Score: 3	Rarely asked. Score: 1	No one asks or wants my opinion. Score: 0	4

Feedback on Performance (Appraisal)	Always know where I stand, where I'm doing well, where I can improve. Score: 3	Sometimes know. Score: 2	Usually in the dark. Score: 1	No one tells me anything. Score: 0	
People at Work	Stimulating and supportive. People I can respect and learn from. Score: 4	Mostly good folks. Helpful. Score: 3	Most I could do without. Score: 1	Dull deadbeats. Score: 0	
Competition for More Responsibility.	Healthy, open, and aboveboard. Score: 3	Mostly good, some backstabbing. Score: 2	Tough, strained relationships. Score: 1	Down and dirty street fighting. Score: 0	
The Boss	Smart and supportive. Helps people get ahead. Score: 4	Better than most. Score: 3	Helps some people. Score: 1	A loser. Holds people back. Score: 0	
Management in General	Sophisticated, high caliber. Bright, long-range thinkers. Big on career and succession planning, interested in development. Score: 4	Most of those. Score: 3	Somewhat muddled. Little emphasis on people development. Score: 1	Keystone Kops. Score: 0	

Job Analysis Questionnaire (*Continued*)

Factor	Super	Pretty good	Fair	Not too hot	Score
Organizational Growth	Doing extremely well. Good growth. Jobs will continue to open up in future. Score: 4	Above average. Score: 3	Stable, nothing dramatic. Score: 1	About to fold, cutting back, jobs disappearing. Score: 0	1
Pay and Benefits	Good for the level I'm at. In line with expectations. Score: 4	Pretty good. Score: 3	Ordinary. Average or below. Score: 1	Stingy. Score: 0	1
How I Feel	Proud of employer and what I do. Feel useful and important. Confident about future. Score: 5	Feel that way most of the time. Score: 3	Sometimes confident, sometimes not. Score: 1	Just thinking about it depresses me. Score: 0	3

Total Score:

Scoring:

60–67 One in a million. Perfect place to start. You're on your way already.

46–59 Good, solid situation. Should help you grow.

23–45 Okay. Most jobs fall here. You can build on this with some work.

9–22 Marginal. Not impossible, but you'll have a tough time going anywhere from this job.

0–8 A job anyone could leave. Maybe you should too.

As a general rule, the lower your score, the more serious you should be about improving your work situation. But any score below 60 indicates you have opportunities to make your job a better springboard for getting out ahead of the pack.

HOW TO IMPROVE YOUR WORK SITUATION

Talk to most people about that and they'll immediately think of quitting and finding another job. Don't fall into that trap, because there are other and better options. Use them first, and if they don't work, you can always quit.

Here are your work-improvement options, in the order you should use them.

1. Change the nature of your present job.
2. Change jobs within your organization.
3. Change employers.

Let's look at each.

1. Change the Nature of Your Present Job

You are probably not as confined in your present job as you think you are. Most bosses will be happy to see you expand and change your job if it helps get the work done well and makes the boss look good. Use the Work Improvement Plan below to help you think about what you like to do and what you are good at. Then use the plan to come up with creative ways of building more of what you identify into your present work.

WORK IMPROVEMENT PLAN

On List A, record what you like to do, both at work and outside of work. For example, if you like to "wheel and deal," put that down. If you like to design things, put that down.

List A
What I Like to Do

____________________ ____________________
____________________ ____________________
____________________ ____________________

Now, on List B, write what you are good at—your best skills. Think of what you did best in school and what you seem to get most praise and recognition for at work.

List B
What I Am Good At

____________________ ____________________
____________________ ____________________
____________________ ____________________

Go back and assign priorities to List A, "What I Like to Do." Make 1 the highest, 2 next highest, and so on.

Now put priorities on the items on list B, "What I Am Good At."

Using List C, enter your top priority from List A in the left-hand column. Then in the middle column come up with creative ways you can build more of that into your present job. (See Chapter 4 for ways to get creative ideas.) Continue on for your next two priorities from List A, then do the top three from List B.

Leave the right-hand column blank for now.

List C

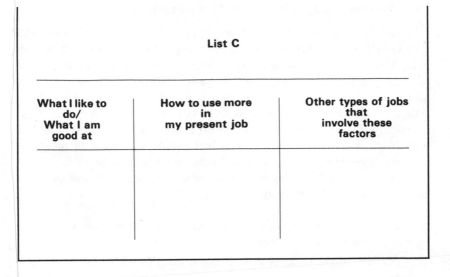

What I like to do/ What I am good at	How to use more in my present job	Other types of jobs that involve these factors

If you have thought of several ways to enhance your present job, stop here for now and try them out. Remember:

Be patient. Changing the work you do within the same job is usually a slow process and happens bit by bit. Don't expect instant satisfaction.

Keep your boss tuned in. You know best if he or she will react better to a discussion of what you plan to do, or an update on what you are doing after you've had some success with it. The point is, make your boss a partner at some point.

Don't scare your boss. Even though you may have a master plan for changing the content of your job, don't talk to your boss in those terms. That will scare the hell out of most bosses. Just lay out a thing or two at a time. "Here's a new approach I've been trying. It's been working out really well . . ."

Don't grab off everyone else's work. Change your job to do your work in a better and more interesting way and to do work that is not being done right now. Don't try to use this option as a takeover tactic.

Improve your present job. Improving your present job should be a constant effort on your part, no matter how great your job is. Keep finding ways to change it, make it better, make it more rewarding to you, and more helpful in accomplishing your career goal.

Have an alternative plan. If you have given this option, changing the nature of your present job, your best shot and it's not working, go on to option number 2 below.

2. Change Jobs within Your Organization

Go back to your Work Improvement Plan and complete it. In the right-hand column, list other jobs inside your organization that might provide what's important to you and utilize your interests and skills more than the one you now have. If you are not sure, talk to people who work in areas you might be interested in and would like to know more about. Don't be hesitant to ask. People love to talk about what they do.

Ideally, the next thing you should do is talk with your boss. This can be very tricky, because some bosses feel people who want to move out of their departments are traitors and tend to treat them as such.

You will have to assess your own situation, and you will probably size it up in one of these ways:

1. Your boss would be open and receptive to a discussion of possible career moves into other areas.
2. Your boss might be agreeable or might not. You don't know.
3. Your boss would kill you.

If you think your boss would be open and receptive, go to it. Be as complimentary as you sincerely can about the boss and the work, but explain that your real interests lie elsewhere. Ask if the boss feels a move to another area is feasible, and, if so, can he or she help make it happen.

If you don't know, you can still have a discussion with your boss but go about it in a less direct way. Arrange time to talk with the boss about your career. Ask what he or she sees happening in your immediate future and what areas of the company that might involve. Depending on the boss's reaction to that question, you can decide whether to spell out your specific wants or to just state that you'd like to broaden yourself and are always ready for something new. Then let that sink in for a while before you get more specific. But do come back and continue the conversation.

Incidentally, with most bosses, you will have to initiate this kind of discussion. Don't wait around for the boss to ask. Chances are, the boss won't. The boss is worried enough about his or her own future without taking on your problems, too.

If you believe your boss would have a "You're a Traitor" response, you still have courses of action, none of them great:

- Go talk to the boss anyhow and face the consequences—you may have to leave the company anyhow, so what do you have to lose?
- Go to the boss's boss and state your case. Tell him that you don't feel your immediate supervisor would be terribly happy about a career-

change discussion because he or she is so dedicated to your department (or some such noncritical approach). Be ready for trouble when going over your boss's head.

- Go to the personnel department and state your case. Maybe they know of a job opening that is just right for you and can arrange a transfer. There's a chance they can help, but don't count on it.
- Go to Option 3 below: Quit and go somewhere else.

Three thoughts about trying to change jobs within your organization.

1. Remember, your boss's ego is at stake. Be positive in discussing your present job and don't say anything to imply his or her leadership is anything but great. There's nothing wrong with the boss or the department—it's just you. Your compass is pointing in another direction.
2. Don't threaten anybody with anything. Don't ever say, "If I can't get a transfer, I'll just have to quit and go somewhere else." Some bosses will react by saying, "Okay, tomorrow would be fine."
3. Changing jobs within your organization will be much easier if you have lots of mentors, and a word about them is in order. For a while there, people were racing around looking for mentors . . . inviting executives to lunch and saying, "Will you be my mentor?" "No? Have you got a friend?"

   There's no question that someone in a high place who likes you can help your career. Millions of people have been pulled and pushed along in their careers by mentors—almost anyone who has gotten anywhere has.

   But mentors can't be arranged like dates. Your best mentors will come from among people who have seen you in action, seen you using your *Upward Bound* skills, and have been impressed. They are the ones who will think of you when an opening occurs. They are the ones who will be receptive to your inquiries about moving into their department. Rather than trying to pin down *a* mentor, think of everyone who has clout as a potential mentor and take every opportunity to show each of them that you're worth mentioning. Use your *Upward Bound* skills to collect all the mentors you can get.

3. Quit and Find a New Employer

When you are absolutely sure there is no hope of improving your situation where you are, get out and go someplace else. You've probably thought about this from time to time already. Maybe you've already changed employers. You're not unusual. Thousands do every year. In fact, we're a nation of job changers. On the average, we make six job changes over a lifetime, and about half of all college graduates are not with their original employers after five years.

My guess is that a large percentage of all those job changers feel afterward that they are no better off or even worse off. The problem is, there are certain realities of work life that exist everywhere and are inescapable. If you are frustrated and discouraged with something where you work now, chances are you will run into something equally bad at a new employer. There are no perfect jobs and no perfect employers.

I am not suggesting that frustrations are not real or important, or that you should just stay with your present employer no matter what. There are times when changing employers is necessary and should be done. But don't do it thinking you will get away from aggravation, stagnation, and everything else that makes you want to drive your fist through the wall. Because you won't. Go out and find another job only when your present job is so bad that there is no hope of it helping you become *Upward Bound.*

Here are some thoughts on quitting:

- The right way is to find a new employer, *then* quit. Never leave a job, if you can help it, until you have another lined up. It is easier to bargain (for salary, job responsibilities, benefits) when you are safely employed than when you are desperate and without a paycheck. Also, employers are always more comfortable stealing you from someone else than saving you from unemployment. There's something a little suspect about a person without a job—especially someone who quit a perfectly good job just to look around.
- If you decide to find another job, don't wait. Begin right away. Don't worry about the old maxim that says stay on any job at least a year. That was made up by employers who had a lot of people quitting after six months. Forget it. If you are in a truly impossible situation, why prolong it for some arbitrary length of time? Get out as fast as you can.
- When you decide to change, don't tell anybody. Even your friends—word gets around. Not until you have found another job and are ready to resign. Some employers get very edgy about having "malcontents" hanging around and may invite you to leave before you are ready.
- When you do resign, make it an upbeat experience. Telling your boss what to do with the job won't get you much except a temporary high, and it may hurt you a lot. People will be checking back in with your

boss all throughout your career for one reason or another and the better memories he or she has of you the better. Tell your boss you really liked working with him or her and with the organization and appreciated all the help he or she gave you (even if the boss didn't give you any and rated zero on the Job Analysis Questionnaire). Explain that this new offer "came along" and it was so good and so much in line with your interests that you couldn't turn it down. If you have an "exit interview" in the personnel department, keep it positive, too, and say the same things.

- Give up to a month's notice, or whatever you and your boss agree is right, to wind up important projects and help your present organization make a smooth transition.
- Be sure to find out about termination provisions regarding insurance plans and settlements on stock, savings and retirement plans.

Here is a simple six-step approach to changing jobs:

1. Start earlier than you think you should; in fact, as soon as you decide to leave. Job hunting takes a long time.
2. Update your resume. Add your most recent employer and your significant accomplishments, being as specific and as complimentary to yourself as you can in one sentence per accomplishment. Then go back to your Work Improvement Plan, List B. Pick out what you do best and incorporate some of those skills in your resume. Also add some of your most impressive personal characteristics:

   Successful manager and motivator of people

   Burning desire to grow and get ahead

   Brute determination to succeed

   Good old common sense

   Natural ability to get along

   Talent for persuading, selling

   Good writing and speaking skills

   Affinity for detail and accuracy

   Well-defined goals

   LOVE OF HARD WORK (emphasized because employers *really* love this one)

   Just pick a few, don't copy the whole list. Give brief examples showing how you've used your talents in real-life situations.

3. Use all the resources you have to contact employers.
    - If you are a recent graduate, check in with your college career-planning and placement center. Many have alumni services and can help you. Also, they have much information on employers. If you are close by, a visit would be worthwhile.
    - Contact everyone you know who has a good job—in an emergency contact anyone who has any job at all—and ask for their advice and any leads they might have. Most people will be happy to help. Be sure to network. See anyone who will talk to you about what they do, even if they don't have a job opening. Ask for names of their contemporaries you can contact and do the same with them. Somewhere along the line, you'll run into a job opening. Personal contact is the best and easiest way to find a new job. Use it.
    - Search the help-wanted ads in the classified section and other parts of the newspaper that have display ads—especially the Sunday edition.
    - Send out letters and resumes. Check your library reference section for lists of employers: Dun & Bradstreet's *Million Dollar Directory,* Moody's *Industrial Manual,* and Standard & Poor's *Corporation Records and Industrial Index* are good places to start. For government jobs, contact your nearest Federal Job Information Center.
    - Also, when all else fails, you can try using employment agencies (watch this, there's money involved and it might be yours). You can also contact executive search firms, but unless they have a search that involves a job you're looking for, they'll be of no help to you. And too, search firms really like to dig up their own candidates.
    - Contact trade associations and professional societies—many of them have job referral services.
4. Practice interviewing. THIS IS EXTREMELY IMPORTANT. By yourself, with a friend, or with a tape recorder. Any way you can. Even if you have had many interviews, you'll never have as much experience as the person who interviews you. You should be able to answer the interviewer's questions easily and with confidence.
5. Do your homework. Before your interview, study the employer. Read the annual report. Dig out newspaper and magazine articles. Ask around. Never go into an interview without knowing something about the employer and without having questions to ask.
6. Follow up. After your interview, write a thank you letter expressing interest in the job and confidence you can do it well. If you don't hear after that, follow up with a phone call. Be polite, but persistent. Most employers like "go-getters," people who are assertive without being obnoxious.

To summarize, here are some final key thoughts on managing your career:

- Always take the long view. Don't react to short-term problems.
- Remember that problems exist everywhere and you can't escape them by changing jobs.
- Don't expect to find *the* one right career. There are no perfect careers, but you probably could be happy at several.
- Try to improve your present situation before making a change.
- Always protect your boss's ego. Like it or not, he or she will always be part of your background and will be asked for opinions on you.
- You have to manage your own career—no one will do it for you. Good careers don't just happen to people; people make them happen.

Thinking Up

3. **Attitudes Anonymous:** How to Develop a Winning Attitude

Person #1:	I really need your help to get approval for this program. Oh, I guess it isn't the best one we've ever come up with, and I know the boss will hate it. It may not even work, but . . .
Person #2:	Say, listen. Let me think it over and get back to you.

Overheard in the hallway,
Corporate headquarters,
North Carolina Narcolepsy Corp.

The way you act or react in a situation tells people a lot about you. They can't know what you think and feel deep inside, but they can and do pick up what bubbles to the surface. And what you allow others to see is important.

Almost always, you have a choice as to what attitude to adopt. There is nothing in any normal work situation that dictates you must react one way or another. If you feel angry about something that happens, for instance, that's how you choose to feel. Nothing in the event itself makes it absolutely necessary for you to feel that way. It is your choice. And since you do have a choice, most of the time you'll be better off if you choose to react in a positive rather than a negative way. Sound like morning exercises for the Campfire Girls? Let me tell you something about attitudes.

Negative thinkers make things tough on themselves. When was the last time you got enthused about working with a negative person? Not ever, I'll bet. People like upbeat thinkers better than those who moan a lot; they like to be around them, and they have confidence in them. The simple truth is you can get a lot more done through other people, faster and more easily, if you are a positive person.

See how you feel about the attitudes of these two people:

Lynn	Michael
That's not a good idea. It's just not going to work.	Let's kick that idea around and see what we can do with it.
It's all screwed up. We really blew it.	Let's not make the same mistake twice. What can we learn from this?
Things are going from bad to worse.	We can turn this around. Let's get to work and find a way to do it.
International Gumball really aced us out of that contract.	We're better than they are. Let's figure out how to get that business back again.
This program is no good at all. They never give us anything we can use. I'm going to call Ed and give him a piece of my mind.	Let's fix this up so we can use it and then get on with it.

What about Lynn and Michael? Which would you rather work with? Which gives the better impression? Which are you most like? Think a minute before you answer the last.

People who listen to tapes of themselves in conversations and meetings are horrified at the amount of negative thinking they do. Many are distressed to find they're really more like Lynn than Michael, even though they think of themselves as open and supportive.

Chances are you aren't as positive as you think you are either. Developing a positive viewpoint doesn't just come with the territory. It is an *Upward Bound* skill that has to be developed like any other. It takes conscious effort, work, and practice. You have to discipline yourself to look at each new situation and ask yourself, "Since I can choose to react any way I want, what is the most positive stance I can take?"

"Positive" can help you in your career; "negative" will almost certainly hurt you.

Here are some positive thoughts on positive thinking:

Get help. It's hard to control attitudes all by yourself. Ask your friends to let you know when you start being overly negative, so you'll know when you're doing it. It helps to get their viewpoint, because what you think is a positive comment may sound very destructive to others. Maybe they'll want to join up, too, and you can help each other.

Take it one day at a time. You can't change your whole outlook and approach to life overnight. Like everyone else, you've been conditioned to find things wrong and to focus on the negative. Remember school? Where did the teacher put the red checks? By the stuff you got wrong. Think about work. When does the boss make the most noise? When you louse up, right? No wonder you look at the negative first. You have a lot of tradition to overcome to become a positive thinker. But you can do it. Tell yourself, "Just for today, I'm going to postpone negative thinking, and look on the positive side. I will concentrate on how to make it work rather than the fact that it's broken. I'll think about how to make it better rather than how it got so bad in the first place. I'll stay open to new ideas and suggestions."

Be positive. After a time, as you consciously try to be more positive, people will see you as more confident and, since confidence gives the impression of success, more successful. Then, you'll start seeing yourself that way too. One will build on the other and the whole thing will start to snowball.

Be realistic. Having a positive attitude doesn't mean that you just accept everything that comes along with a big, cheery smile. It does mean you look at each situation and pick the best way to react to it.

Often, taking the positive view is just looking at the situation in another way. Remember Lynn and Michael? She said, "It's all screwed up. We really blew it." Michael didn't disagree with that, he just didn't want to dwell on it. It's screwed up, but that's the way it is right now. What can we learn from it so we can fix it and so we don't do it again? That's the positive approach.

Let's see what goes into developing the kind of positive outlook that will get you admired, respected, and *Upward Bound*.

HAVING A VISION

Every person who wants to get ahead should have a realistic view of how things are and a long-range vision of how they should be. Anyone who is not thinking beyond the status quo, who does not have a strong desire to make things better on a grand scale, is not using an important *Upward Bound* skill.

Stand for something. Have a vision and let everyone know what that vision is, direct a great deal of your energy at moving toward that vision, and stick to it over a long period of time.

What is your vision? What would be a state of perfection for your operation, your department, or your job?

A friend of mine works as a fund raiser for a nonprofit organization. Here's his vision: To raise enough money so that the entire organization can be run on the interest from investment. Since that would take $4 million and his organization currently has investments of $100,000, his is a pretty lofty goal. But first the dream, then the reality.

Another friend of mine who works in production management has this vision: "To produce all products to the highest quality standards without defects."

Still another acquaintance, who sells a product that is now twelfth in sales volume in her territory, has this vision: "To be number one in sales in the territory."

Visions are like the Ten Commandments. You may never achieve them, but by trying, you'll raise the level of everything you do. Having a vision gives you something to shoot for, something to stand for, and creates a positive, strong image for you.

Your vision should be:

- Long-range and comprehensive. No one will be impressed with a vision of things to do on Thursday. Since you'll want to stick with your vision over a long period of time, you have to pick a good one to begin with.
- Sensible enough so there may be a wild shot at attaining it.
- Far out enough so there's plenty of stretch in it, so that reaching it would require extraordinary effort and even some blind luck.
- Something that you have a large degree of control over. In other words, something *you* can make happen.
- Well-known by everyone (meaning you've communicated it well) and closely identified with you. It is your vision and everyone knows it.
- So desirable a state that everyone wants it to happen and is uplifted when they hear it.

In the space below, work out your vision: (Start with your own area of responsibility at work, think of how it is now and how, ideally, it should be. Later, you may also want to have visions for your department, your career, your marriage, or even your hobbies and outside interests.)

____

____

Once you've formed your vision, remember to tell everyone about it. Find ways to work it into your conversations, memos, and into meetings so that everyone knows of it. Your peers may think you're nuts, but your boss and your boss's boss will see you as a broad thinker, someone with a purpose.

Also remember to stick with it. Don't come up with a new vision each week. Plan your work so that each day you do at least one thing that will move you toward attaining your vision, and, little by little, over a long period of time, you'll make real progress.

Having a vision can separate you from all the others who just plod along day to day without thinking about how great things could be. It can set you apart as someone who has a leadership contribution to make to the long-term future of the organization.

THINKING "CORPORATE"

People on the way up take the broadest possible view of what they do and think of their work in terms of how it affects the total organization as well as their own area.

This isn't easy for most, and it may not be for you, because sometimes what is good for the organization is not particularly good for you. It's like the state building a highway through your backyard. It will save countless people millions of hours in travel time, but it won't do much for your Sunday afternoons in the hammock.

Thinking "corporate" does not mean you don't fight for what's best for your area, because you must. It does mean that you take an extra long view of everything and evaluate its effect beyond your own area.

If you weigh your decisions against what is good for the organization (and let people know you do that) and, if you are willing to make some sacrifices when it is clearly in the interest of the organization to do so, you will be noticed by people at higher levels because you will be acting the way they would (or think they would) if they were in your situation. And they'll like that.

Here are some points to consider:

If you supervise people, do you think of them as your people? They aren't, they're the organization's people. When an opportunity for one of them comes up in another department, do you rush around finding ways to hold on to that person? Normally, you shouldn't. There may be some extreme situations where losing a person would devastate your department, but there's a big difference between that and a temporary annoyance.

If you are really thinking corporate, you should be thinking in terms of what's best for your area, but also what's best for your subordinates and the organization. Usually, promoting subordinates to other departments is best all around, even for you. If you promote people out of your area on a regular basis, that will build your reputation as a desirable manager to work for. Good people will want to join your group. You'll be the boss who selects good people, develops them, and finds opportunities for them. The other kind of manager who rarely lets go of anyone is a zoo keeper—people go in, but never get out.

Have you ever given anything away because it was in the best interest of the organization to do so? Maybe not, because you probably get rewarded for building bigger and better empires. But the truth is, you may not need all the people you have, you may supervise a function that is outmoded and useless, you may operate a facility that is only used to partial capacity, or have a function that logically belongs somewhere else. If you can, without wiping yourself out, reduce it, close it down, give it away. Do it voluntarily and let everyone up the line know you are doing it for the good of the organization. Your peers will think you are playing with a warped racket, but your boss and your boss's boss will be so startled that they will:

Recognize that you have a sound "corporate" attitude.

Be impressed. They'll never forget what you've done because so few are doing it.

Think you are nuts too. Maybe. But they will admire your courage, self-assurance, and the broad view you've taken.

Obviously, this is not something you can do every week, but you should look closely at your staffing and responsibilities:

Now, if you haven't considered it before.

Every time you go into a new job or take over a new area.

Every time there is a major change in the organization's overall direction.

Every five years, at least.

That leads directly to another thinking-up area.

SMALL IS BEAUTIFUL

You've noticed that America's long obsession with bigness is starting to wane. Big business, big universities, big government, big houses, big cars—all are being pared down. America can no longer afford such bigness, and institutions of all kinds as well as individuals are struggling to find ways to do more with less. Many businesses are cutting expenses and staff to protect profit margins; universities, hard pressed for money, are trimming administrative costs and even reducing faculty; government, the biggest of all bigs, has stopped growing.

On a more personal level, people are building smaller houses (big ones are too expensive to maintain), buying smaller cars (for the same reason), and even having smaller families.

Where is your organization headed? Is there a strong emphasis on expense and staff control? Are you trying to fight it? If so, you may not be thinking "corporate" and not showing the success-related qualities you should be. On any question of size or scale, as it applies to your area, ask yourself, "What would my attitude be if I owned this organization?"

If your answer is, "I would not increase that budget," or "I would cut back on people," or worse yet, "I would eliminate the whole function," your next question is, "How do I deal with that?"

Obviously, you're not going to commit employment hara-kiri and fall on your letter opener as you disband your whole department. You are still going to fight for your share of the budget pie and to justify the people you have. But you might try these four approaches to adapting to the new trend toward smallness:

1. When you have fought the battle, but lost, and your budget and staff have been cut, accept it like a good sport—after all, at that point there's nothing you can do about it. Remember, you're not the only one who's hurting. Make do the best you can with what you've got, rev up the positive attitude, and keep plugging for the good old organization.
2. If there is a part of your operation that is really unnecessary, or not being used to capacity, as we discussed above, suggest to your boss or higher management that you shut it down. They'll be impressed.
3. Do some creative problem solving (see Chapter 4) to find ways to make your operation leaner while still getting high-quality work done.
4. Learn to ask yourself questions like these about your work:
    - Could I do this less expensively? What's a cheaper yet effective way to do it?

- Do all these people have to be involved or could fewer handle this as well?
- Is this function or project really contributing something or could it be disbanded? What would be the effect on the organization if it weren't around?
- Do we need to take all this time? How can we do this more quickly?
- Are we taking the most direct path toward getting this work done? What's a shorter route that will involve less time, money, equipment, and people?
- Is this too fancy? How could it be pared down and made smaller and still be effective?
- Is this the best way to spend the organization's resources? What would be better?

A close cousin to keeping it small is keeping it simple. People joke about the KISS method (Keep It Simple, Stupid), but the fact is that many don't follow it. In an attempt to do the best job they can, they tend to make things too complex: reports too long and detailed; systems too obscure and complex; procedures too abundant, tangled, and hard to follow; forms too cumbersome and difficult to fill out; and programs too mammoth and time-consuming to use.

In the past, as things got more and more complex, more staff was needed to make sense of it all, and many organizations grew—just to keep up with themselves.

Today, of course, it's a different story, because most can't afford to grow much. Help your organization stay lean. Next time you are about to put together a program, procedure, form, report, or program, ask yourself:

"Is it needed?" Go ask the people who'll use it. And, since you've gone to the trouble of asking, *listen* to what they tell you. Maybe you'll hear that it isn't needed.

"How will it be used?" Again, ask the users and listen. What you learn may change the way you design your project.

"Is it the simplest way?" Be sure you cut out everything that isn't needed. Don't allow an extra word, instruction, line, paragraph, or step to creep in. Also, make sure your explanations are crystal clear. (See Chapter 5 on writing.)

"Will it work?" When you have it together in rough form and before you print eight million copies, try it out on someone. If it's a report, let someone whose judgment you respect critique it. If it's a program, get it out to some users to test. Almost nothing works perfectly the first time. Use what they tell you to do some fine tuning.

Keep it small. Keep it simple. Two valuable skills for you to master and use.

USING A PROBLEM-SOLVING APPROACH

You'll take giant steps toward "thinking up" and developing a positive attitude if you begin using a problem-solving approach. Look at every conflict, every discussion, every negotiation, and every decision, not with the old "How much can I skin the other person out of?" approach, but with the thought in mind, "How can we all come out of this better than we went in?"

Whenever two or more people work together, there are differences of opinion, territorial disputes, overlaps of responsibility . . . almost unlimited opportunity for disagreement. That is compounded by the fact that people whose work doesn't involve picks and shovels often find themselves lost in ambiguity, wrestling with situations that do not have clear-cut answers. Often, in those situations, they quickly become committed to answers, answers that seem to benefit them the most.

You do that too. Why not? You're going to try for what's best for you. You're not going to be some kind of idiot and just give everything away to the other person, right? Let's think about that.

Chapter 8, on negotiating techniques, describes a problem-solving approach for dealing with conflict. In essence, it is a way of not solidifying early into self-serving positions, but rather of taking time to look for options and alternatives to see if there aren't some to benefit everyone. Often, there are, even though they aren't apparent at first. You have to dig them out.

Let's look at an example. First, a sticky situation without problem solving:

Ed: John, how is the Acme order coming along?

John: Okay, we'll ship August first.

Ed: August first? What the hell good is that? I promised Acme July fifteenth.

John: You never asked me, Ed, and you know it takes at least a month to get out an order that size.

Ed: You guys take forever. Why don't you get those people off their duffs and get them going. I need that order July fifteenth or we'll lose the Acme account.

John: Can't do it, Ed. You should have talked to me before giving them a date.

Ed: Look, John, when you get an order you grab it.

John: Nobody could produce that order in two weeks, Ed.

Ed: Look, this is serious. I don't need excuses. I need that order. I'm sick of fooling around with you guys. Either get it out or I'm going to the V.P. and tell him I think we need a new production manager.

Whew!

Well, what was happening there? Two people who had cemented their positions early and were busy defending them (and blaming each other) instead of trying to find solutions. Lost energy, no movement toward getting out of the mess, only worse and worse relations between Ed and John that will make it tougher for them to solve this or to get anything done next time.

Here's another way:

Ed: John, how is the Acme order coming along?

John: Okay, we'll ship August first.

Ed: August first. What the hell good is that? I promised Acme July fifteenth.

John: July fifteenth? We've got a problem. I didn't know you wanted it the fifteenth and I can't get it out by then. Let's figure out what we can do.

Ed: Do? Produce it, that's what to do. Get it out by the fifteenth.

John: Now, wait, Ed. I told you that's not possible. Now calm down and let's see what options we have.

Ed: Options? What options? What have you got in mind?

John: Well, we could work overtime and pass along the extra cost to Acme.

Ed: They won't like that.

John: We could charge it to your budget.

Ed: I won't like that. Why don't you absorb it?

John: How about if we got half of it out by July fifteenth and the other half of it out by the first?

Ed: That might work. They wouldn't be thrilled, but I could talk to Acme about that. But wait a minute, that makes me think. What if we delayed the Blue Star order and shipped their product to Acme?

John: Hey, now you're talking. We could start shipping today if Blue Star wouldn't mind the delay.

Ed: I don't think the Blue Star people are in a hurry for the stuff. Let me call them right now and get back to you. Thanks, John.

Well.

Sometimes you can surprise yourself by finding options you never knew existed and also amaze yourself and others at how, by doing it, you can get out of tough situations without destroying working relationships, without having one party getting the pie and the other just crumbs; and, in the bargain, come out with good, workable solutions.

The key? Delay settling on your own no-give course of action. Take time to think of options and alternatives. (See Chapter 4 for ways to develop new ideas.)

Build the problem-solving approach into your work style. You owe it to yourself, the people you work with, and to your organization. It will make you better at what you do and get you seen by others as a brilliant strategist when it comes to getting out of tight spots.

WELCOMING CHANGE

If change bugs you, don't worry. It bugs everyone. But if it bothers you to the point you're constantly fighting it, you're probably wasting time, energy, and emotional reserves. It's silly to battle change, because change is inevitable. If you've been working a while, look back five years ago at your organization, your department, your job. Try to remember the people you worked with. There are lots of new ones now, aren't there? Think of what the important projects were, the hot buttons—they're different now, aren't they? Change happens.

When change comes and you are tempted to fight it, ask yourself:

1. Can I really do anything about this? Some change you just can't stop and you'll make a donkey of yourself trying.
2. Is it worth the time, effort, and possible damage to stop it? Sometimes you can stop a change, or slow it down, but you'll have wrecked yourself and your image in the process. You'll have done more harm to yourself than the change would have.

3. Is this change really all that bad, or would it actually, in the long run, be good for me? Instead of instinctively fighting every change, stop and think what the change would actually do to you—and *for* you.

Successful people accept change, even welcome it. They're confident enough to handle whatever comes and turn it to their advantage. They know how to make change work for them. How can you do that?

Anticipate change. What changes are likely to affect you in the next few months, years? Okay, you're no fortune-teller, but some change you can bet on. Technology, for instance, is changing everyone's life. What's on the horizon where you work? Jot down possible changes and how they will affect you.

Prepare for change. Once you have some idea about what's coming, prepare for it. Is part of your job going to be automated, so you have to use a CRT or personal computer regularly? Why not get the jump on the rest of the gang in the office and take a computer literacy course? Or get a book and read up on it. Or ask someone who has a CRT or PC to show you how to use it.

Make change work for you. Once you've identified a change and prepared, you can start plotting how you can make the change work for you. Are there parts of your job you can put on your personal computer, for instance? What else can that PC do for you? Make a list, begin thinking how to do it.

Once your peers and your management see that you welcome change, they will begin to see you as a very flexible, broad-visioned, future-thinking person. Once you see yourself as all those, and actually begin to become them, your own self-image will improve, and you will become more confident and better able to play a stronger leadership role.

For more on change, see Chapter 17 on stress.

REBOUNDING

Successful people come back quickly from setbacks. They learn from failure and use what they've learned to do better in the future. If it seems odd to be talking about success and setbacks and failures in the same sentence, remember, everyone, even the most successful people, have failures. The fact that you make mistakes sometimes and say and do things you wish you could buy back and do over is important, mostly because they are learning experiences. And you should view them that way. If you dwell on failures rather than successes, thinking you're the only one who ever screwed up, you're being too tough on yourself. And the choice is yours. You can tell yourself, "Oh my God, I goofed again. It's all over. I'm a loser. I'll never be much good" and act accordingly.

Or—your choice—you can say, "I messed up. I shouldn't have. I know better. But everyone does sometimes. Let's see what I can learn from all this and how I can do better in the future."

Remember, the only way to avoid getting burned is to go home, lock the door, and stay there. Do nothing.

When you do make a mistake, help yourself rebound:

Admit your obvious mistakes. This can be very disarming—people expect you to be defensive.

Tell people what you learned from the mistakes.

Carry on like nothing happened.

Don't make the same mistake twice.

LONG-TERM VS. SHORT-TERM THINKING

Put a nickel in any business journalist and he or she will sing the same song: The big trouble with organizations today is that they concentrate too much on the short range: Beat the quota for the week, beat last month's sales, keep the quarterly earnings up—while forgetting about what's needed to build the organization over the next five years. Sometimes, what's best for the short run might not be best for the future health of the organization.

Like everyone else, you're under pressure to produce right now. You're rewarded for current results. Your boss wants to look good today and leans on you to help. Senior management wants to give glowing reports to stockholders, the public, Wall Street, the employees, and anyone else who will listen, and gears the whole organization toward focusing on day-to-day results. No one wants to take lumps right now, even if it would mean building a better tomorrow.

Don't get me wrong. There's nothing wrong with the short term. It needs attention and has to be tended. And I'm not suggesting you suddenly forget all about what needs to be done before the week is up and sit around philosophizing about what might happen ten years from now. What I am suggesting is that you pay attention to *both* the short and long term.

Here's how:

- Every time you are faced with a decision of any importance, weigh it against your *vision* of how things should be (see above). Will what you plan to do help you move toward your ideal? If not, should you be doing it at all? Or, what better action can you take?
- Keep your department's and organization's major goals in mind. If there are five-year or strategic plans around, get ahold of them and study them. As with your personal vision, your short-term decisions and plans should support them.
- Practice taking a longer view. Ask yourself:

  What will this decision mean next year and the year after as well as tomorrow? What will it solve? What problems might it cause?

  How quickly will this be obsolete? Then what? Will you have to start over? Is there something else that will last longer?

  How will the situation that prompted the decision change in the next few years? What will those changes mean in regard to the type of decision you make?

  How much grief can you put up with now to do what's right for the future?

  What should you be doing now to build for the future? What kind of investment should you be making in terms of money, people, equipment, time?

  What will the pay-back on that investment be a year from now, two years, five years?

- Always show yourself as a long-range as well as short-range thinker, concerned about the future as well as the present. Get others you work with to think "future" by asking questions about the long-range implications of decisions and plans. Let your boss see how you think: "Boss, I'd like to do this because it would solve our problem, but I've been thinking about it and if I do this today, aren't we going to be in a bind a year or two out? We've got to find a better way."
- Think two decisions ahead. In a personnel move—promotion or transfer—for instance, think not only of that move but of the next one. Where is that person likely to be then, and is today's move going to prepare him or her for that next one? In reorganizing your department or redistributing work, think of what the next change is likely to be and whether this is the best way to support that. In buying equipment, changing office layout, adding to staff, think of the present change and the one after that. And ask yourself, is this present change taking us in the right direction to prepare for the next?

Your attitude. Build your confidence and your image by going for the most positive attitude you can. To do that, try your best to have a vision, think "corporate," accept smallness, use a problem-solving approach, welcome change, rebound from failure, and combine short-term with long-term thinking. Each of them will help you be seen as an upbeat, self-assured person and have others saying, "He's really sure of himself. You get the feeling he can do anything" or "She really sees the big picture. Asks the right questions and gets you thinking in broad perspective" or "He thinks like a top executive." Since you do have a choice and can select any attitude you want, choose the one that will help you get out ahead most quickly.

4. **It'll Never Work:** How to Be More Creative

When somebody comes to me with a new idea, I try hard to keep an open mind. I listen carefully and look for all the possibilities in it. Then I say, "For God's sake, we can't do that."

Frank Adams, Production Manager
Peoria Polyester Co.

Think of five creative people and list them in the spaces below. They can be living or dead, it doesn't matter . . . just write down the first five names that come to your mind.

Creative People

1. ____________________
2. ____________________
3. ____________________
4. ____________________
5. ____________________

Now look at your list. In what fields were your people creative? Are most of them in the arts? Maybe an inventor or two thrown in? Probably.

In the dozens of times I have done this little exercise in seminars and workshops, I have found that people in the arts are listed far and away most often: Mozart, da Vinci, Hemingway, Michelangelo, and Beethoven head the list. Then come scientists and inventors: Edison, Galileo, and Einstein, followed by a few legendary statesmen, usually Jefferson and Franklin (who could also be classified as inventors). I seldom get names of modern-day politicians or military leaders; and only once in a great while, if I push it, names of business leaders (Ford and Bell pop up most often).

No one has ever listed his or her own name. Did you? How long a list would you have to make before you came to yourself? Ten names? A hundred? A thousand?

It seems we think of two worlds, the creative one where all the artists and inventors live, and the other, where the rest of us plod along.

But certainly there are many creative things that happen in fields outside the arts. For example, we are surrounded by ingenious products and devices that have been developed by business and industry. Video games, freeze-dried coffee, latex paint, jet engines, pocket calculators, cassette players, and color TV—you could think of dozens more without really trying.

But because many of us don't think of ourselves as creative, and organizations often don't encourage creativity, many original ideas take longer to hatch than they should, and millions of others die off every day and are never put to use. But why should creativity be the province of the arts? It doesn't have to be. The rest of us have just as much right to original thinking as composers and painters do.

"Yeah," you say, "but I don't have the talent that Beethoven had." That's true. You don't. Few people have the genius to write scores for a hundred-piece orchestra. And fewer still can do that while they are stone-deaf, as Beethoven was, and can't hear a note of music.

But I'm not talking about such extraordinary feats as that. What I have in mind is tapping the creative potential that you and other normal people have and seldom use. To do that you must set a climate within which original thinking can survive and new approaches will be allowed to grow and blossom.

That doesn't take a special talent. It does mean changing your whole attitude toward ideas and developing new ways of treating them . . . your own as well as others'. You can learn to do that, and you can learn it fairly easily because chances are you have a lot more creativity inside you waiting to get out than you think you do. And once you learn to let it out, you'll find yourself using creative thinking to help improve other *Upward Bound* skills and in hundreds of other ways in your work and personal life.

What is creativity? Webster defines it as the "ability to create" which doesn't help much, but then defines "create" as "to bring into existence, to bring about through imaginative skill."

Another definition might be: "Creativity is the ability to free yourself from imaginary boundaries, to see new relationships and patterns and in that way accomplish new things of value (not necessarily monetary value)."

Neither of these definitions, Webster's or mine, rules out people outside the arts who do not have artistic talent or don't do artistic work. In fact, no less an authority than Peter Drucker tells us creativity and original thinking *have* to exist in business because they are critical to the very survival of organizations in the years to come.

> We must learn how to make existing companies, and particularly large companies, capable of innovation . . . It will no longer be sufficient to extend existing technologies to broaden them, modify them or attempt to adapt them. From now on the need will be to innovate in the true sense of the word, to create truly new wealth-producing capacity . . .*

If creativity is so important and if we all have it lurking inside, why is it so elusive?

Maybe working on a problem will help answer that question.

Using four straight lines, connect all nine dots below. Don't retrace or lift your pencil off the paper.

If you know the answer, try it with three lines. If you know that, too, think back to the first time you tried to solve this problem and how you went about it. The important thing is to experience trying to get a solution.

• • •

• • •

• • •

When you have given it a good try, check the end of the chapter for the answer.

I like this exercise because it illustrates many of the problems with creativity in everyday life. Did you have trouble finding the solution? If so, you probably encountered one or more of these common barriers:

Making wrong assumptions. Did you start out thinking you couldn't go outside the box? Nobody said you couldn't and yet almost everybody begins with that wrong and unnecessary assumption, and it causes many false starts.

* Drucker, Peter F., *Managing in Turbulent Times.* New York: Harper & Row, 1980, pp. 59–60.

In the case of the three-line solution, did you assume you had to go through the center of the dots? Again, that wasn't in the rules.

The most common wrong assumption is not about rules, but thinking because things are a certain way they always have to be. That shuts off a whole range of new possibilities before they are even considered and assures that any ideas you come up with are nothing more than fine tuning of what you have done before: broadening, modifying or adapting of existing technologies, as Peter Drucker said. Not very original.

Astronomers watched Uranus for years before they recognized it as a planet. Why? Because since the beginning of astronomy, it was assumed that the solar system extended only to Saturn and not beyond. Even after they saw its motion, astronomers refused to believe. "It's a comet," they said. Not until a scientist named William Herschel challenged the assumption and speculated that the solar system could possibly extend beyond Saturn was Uranus accepted as a planet. But that was back in the 1700s and we would be more receptive today. Wouldn't we?

Who says the solar system has to end with Saturn? Who says you can't go outside the box when connecting the dots?

Wrong assumptions set up imaginary boundaries and restrictions that suppress innovating thinking.

The First Rule of Creativity is: Don't let assumptions stifle your creativity. Throw every one of them out.

Going for a fast solution. We're under a lot of pressure today to come up with answers. "You've got a problem? Here's what to do." In your haste, you may overlook a whole bunch of alternative solutions, or ideas that could lead to solutions. And once you're committed to a course of action, you probably won't want to listen to other suggestions even if they might lead to better solutions. I've watched hundreds of people working on the nine-dot problem. Most grab their pencils and start drawing lines. Only a handful pause to think about the problem and consider alternate ways of solving it.

Fast solutions don't leave time to explore new relationships that are essential to creativity.

The Second Rule of Creativity is: Discipline yourself to take time to look for alternatives. Stay open and generate as many as you can think of before deciding on one.

Not wanting to make mistakes. You know what happens if you're wrong. When you were a kid you got spanked or hollered at. Or kept after school. It hurts to make mistakes. You learned that early in life and probably have tried to avoid them from then on. And because that's so important, your first impulse may be to reject any idea that has a chance of being wrong.

Did you reject ideas when you were solving the dot problem? Even though no one was watching you or scoring your work? Most people do and some of the ideas they reject, like going outside of the box, can lead to solutions.

But if you don't allow new ideas to hang around, if you don't summon up the courage to try them out, you probably aren't going to get many original answers. Creativity and originality are based on new ideas, new perceptions, new relationships. They demand that you get beyond the world of the known into the unknown, the uncertain. Exploring those vaporous areas always leads to mistakes, wrong turns, blind alleys, revising, starting over. To get the one you have to accept the other. One of the many barriers to creativity on the job every day is unwillingness to tolerate or be patient with anything other than acceptable ideas. Most people are too inhibited, too constrained on the job to let true creativity come out.

Let me give you an example from a common situation at work. Let's say you are asked to a meeting on expense control. "We all know costs are up," your department head says, "and there's a good chance several of our sections will be over budget this year. What can we do to get all our people to watch expenses?"

An idea flashes into your head. "Any section that stays within budget gets a free dinner party at the Ritz la Ritz Hotel."

Do you jump to your feet and tell the world about your inspiration? Probably not. Because you evaluate it first. And you find all kinds of things wrong with it: It would cost even more money and put everyone over budget; it probably is a frivolous answer to a serious problem and so on.

So what happens with that idea? Probably nothing. You'll never say it out loud with all those flaws in it. After all, you don't want to seem like an aardvark right there in front of your boss and everybody else.

That's too bad because your idea could lead to something usable. It has an element of reward in it that is intriguing, that could, if worked on, turn into a good, new solution.

Instead you search around for a more conventional, more acceptable solution. "I think," you could say, "we need a letter from the president to all section managers stressing the importance of expense control." That's a safe idea, but not too original. The president writes four hundred letters a year stressing the importance of everything and nobody pays any attention to any of them.

On the other hand, let's say you are drunk or courageous that day and decide to come right out with your original idea. "Let's buy them dinner at the Ritz la Ritz," you say. Silence. Some polite nodding, not agreeing, just recognizing that you have said something. Then someone, let's call him Ed, says very politely, "That's a good idea, but dinner for all those people would be damned expensive. I don't think we could afford to do anything like that." Everybody nods in agreement. What Ed is really saying is, "That's a stupid idea and just shows that you aren't very practical. I've just established, on the other hand, that I am a realistic, hard-nosed businessman, looking for down-to-earth solutions."

Now what happens? Well, most people don't enjoy having their ideas stomped on and you probably don't either. So you may just think, "The heck with it, see if I help you any more," and just drop out of the meeting, sitting quietly, glancing at your watch, until it is over. Or, you may lurk in the bushes, waiting for Ed to come down the path. "What I think," he says at last, "is a letter from the president to all section managers stressing the importance of expense control." You know what to do. Go ahead and stomp him.

I know you recognize the situation. We've all been to meetings where those things have happened. When did you last have a way-out idea at work? What happened to it? Did you tell the boss about it? Or, more likely, did you think about it, change it, and water it down until it was as safe and comfortable as your living-room couch?

Starting with way-out ideas, letting them flourish is the best way to get original solutions. Ideas that start out as acceptable are okay, too, and we have a need for them, but they probably are not going to lead to anything very new and different . . . and will not produce any dramatic leap forward.

Because of our attitudes toward anything out of the ordinary we probably work at thirty to fifty percent of our creative potential.

> *The Third Rule for Creativity* is: To get solutions, you must create an atmosphere where you and others are comfortable expressing new ideas (even if you make mistakes by coming out with bad ideas), an atmosphere where ideas are not immediately evaluated and attacked.

Using only your left brain. One way to understand creativity better is to take a peek at the right brain/left brain theory. A number of studies have been done in recent years with people who have had brain injuries or brain surgery. Scientists have found that the two halves of the brain control specific types of behavior.

The left side of the brain is the cautious, orderly side, favoring analytical, logical behavior. The left side keeps you on time, helps you count, and remembers words and names. It helps you be organized and do procedural work.

The right side of the brain, on the other hand, is a maverick. It is the "let's try it" side: creative, emotional, and sensitive. The right side is fun-loving and tends to take risks. It is conceptual, seeing the big picture, shapes and forms rather than words.

Our culture tends to encourage and reward left-brain thinking and discourage right-brain. Our school systems provide precise lessons requiring exact answers. Schools offer few courses in creativity or imagination where thoughts can wander outside given limits. Since business is money oriented, most people in business tend to be dominated by numbers, and ability to work with numbers (left) is more highly prized than that of original thinking (right).

Numbers are fine, but there has to be a balance to a business to grow. There has to be new thinking, original thinking, to move an organization ahead. When you tried to solve the nine-dot puzzle, did you try only rational, logical reasoning? Did you try letting yourself go and coming up with some wild ideas? Probably not. Most people don't.

> *The Fourth Rule of Creativity* is: To open up true creativity, you have to shed inhibitions and move from left-brain toward right-brain thinking.

That doesn't mean *total* right-brain thinking because both halves of the brain have an important role in creativity.

Even people in the arts need both types of thinking. Painters need to have the ability to see shapes and forms (right) while at the same time mixing colors in precise combinations (left). A pianist must have expression and feeling (right) but also must be able to hit the notes in the correct order (left). A writer must come up with new ideas (right), but also must organize masses of material in a logical way (left).

Here are nine steps to increasing your personal creativity, and helping those around you to increase theirs.

Step 1. Tell Yourself You're Creative

If you want to be creative, it's more likely you will be if you start out by saying, "Boy, am I creative." That sounds too obvious to even bother with, but it bears saying because you probably don't go into too many situations with that mental set. How often have you said, "I'm creative and I'm not going to settle for anything less than a creative solution to this problem"? Probably not often. Start doing it.

Step 2. Pick a Project and Explore It

If you want to be creative, you have to have something in mind to be creative about. A vague feeling that you want to be more innovative isn't going to do much for you. So decide on a project to tackle in a new and innovative way. Pick a task, old or new, but one that doesn't seem to have a clear focus. If you can, single out one that has a lot of visibility in your organization . . . that could make you a hero if you come up with a new solution.

Then ask yourself these questions about the project:

Why do I want to work on this?

What will happen if I come up with an innovative solution? What will I get out of it?

What is the apparent problem?

What is the *real* problem?

What has been tried before?

To what extent was that successful? Not successful? Why?

Why explore the problem? Because as you explore a problem, it may change. Or your perspective on it may change.

NASA scientists worked a long time trying to find a metal alloy for manned space flight that wouldn't burn up in the incredible heat of space-capsule reentry. The problem? "Metal burning up on reentry."

That slowed them down for a long time until someone stepped back to explore the problem and saw that the *real* problem was not metal burning up, but protecting the astronauts.

That led to the development of the ablative heat shield that burned on reentry, but slowly enough to keep the astronauts from roasting.

Step 3. Set Modest Goals

Don't expect to become a wizard overnight. After all, you are only human and you have years of conditioning behind you that has built strong inhibitions. Tell yourself you are going to try like crazy to be innovative. But if you fall short of your expectations, don't worry about it. Being creative takes practice. Pick up and try again.

Step 4. Be Prepared to Work Hard

If being creative takes practice, it also takes hard work. That isn't easy for most of us.

Thomas Edison said, "Invention is 1 percent inspiration, 99 percent perspiration." Plan your work. Think through what you want to accomplish. Get a mental picture of a good finished product. Set aside time.

Creative solutions take longer to find than conventional ones. Be prepared to revise, redo, tear up, and start over.

People who come up with creative ideas don't just sit around and wait for them to pop out. Even ideas that come in flashes of inspiration are usually preceded by hours, weeks, and even years of thinking about the problem.

Step 5. Try to Keep Your Left Brain Quiet

Tell yourself that you don't have to go for a perfect solution right off, that it's okay to entertain thoughts that may not be acceptable in their present form.

Think of many approaches and ideas. Ask others for ideas and write them all down, even ones that are offered jokingly. Linus Pauling once said, "The best way to have a good idea is to have lots of ideas."

Take any ideas or thoughts that come along, even if they don't seem to apply to the problem. Don't evaluate anything.

Make yourself laugh purposely. Think of outrageous approaches: illegal, immoral, surprising. Think of something that would get you fired if you did it.

Don't worry about the present order of things. Experiment. If something has always been a certain way, that's good reason to think of the opposite way.

Expect some uncertainty, anxiety. As I said before, if you're going for new approaches, you are traveling out of the world you know, away from what exists. That means you'll run up blind alleys, make mistakes, and feel some frustration. You'll worry the hell out of your left brain. The alternative is to stay with the conventional, safe thinking your left brain loves.

Push your inhibitions into a closet and shut the door. Take some risks, have fun with unusual ideas. Don't worry about it. Nothing will happen. You are just looking for ideas and if they are off the wall, so what? You don't have to do anything with them.

Step 6. Play with Thoughts and Ideas

Write down any and all ideas you get, otherwise they'll evaporate.

Look over your list of ideas now and then and pick out some to play with. Change them, modify them, build on them. If looking at your list triggers other ideas in your mind, add them to your list.

Use analogies. Analogies can be very helpful in creating new ideas. Drilling deep oil wells posed a problem because walls of the shaft tended to cave in, until a driller in Pennsylvania made a connection between his stovepipe hat and the oil-shaft problem. "My hat is like something that could be slid down an oil-well shaft," he thought. That led to the invention of casings. Two unrelated items that had lots in common. Sometimes purposefully forcing two unrelated things together will produce ideas.

"How can we build sales of our new soft drink? What's *un*related to soft drinks? How about a tree? What can we learn from a tree? A tree has leaves and branches and sap flows through it. Suppose people's houses were like leaves . . . and our soft drink the sap. Maybe we could pipe it into homes like city gas or water. Better yet (building on that idea), how about home delivery if you buy it by the case. Maybe we could have a subscription and delivery service like newspapers. Sign up for a year and get a case a month automatically delivered to your door."

Look at your project or problem from many viewpoints. Can it be made larger? Smaller? Turned upside down? Reversed? Made a different color? Shape? Raised? Lowered? Speeded up? Slowed down? Can you get inside it and look at it from the inside out? Can it be combined? Eliminated? Used for something else? Can the symptom be made the solution? (Example: Ice cream tends to melt. Why not make a cone with a lip on it so you could drink the melted ice cream rather than having it drip all over your shirt? Then market "sippin" cones.)

Look for clues everywhere. When your mind is busily working on getting ideas, even when you are not actively thinking about the problem, clues can jump out from everywhere if you are alert for them. Recently, at a cocktail party four friends of mine who had just formed a consulting firm were talking about the struggle they were having to find a name. They wanted a name that indicated there was a group of them and that they were very forward-looking. Many names were suggested during the party (some of them illegal or immoral) but none that anyone took seriously . . . until a bunch of us were saying good-bye at the door and one fellow asked the hostess for a pencil and paper. And he drew

4SIGHT

"Wow!" everyone said. "That's a great logo. What made you think of that?" He pointed to the house number on the door: "44." Clues are everywhere.

Borrow wherever and whenever you can. Genius is knowing what to steal. Most creations are not begun from scratch, but are combinations, modifications, or new interpretations of work that has been done before. Find out what others have done on problems and projects like yours and borrow. Look at nature . . . take an object like a tree, as I did above in the soda anecdote, and make it somehow solve your problem.

Relax and have fun. Playing with ideas, once you get used to it, can be a joyful experience. The more fun you are having, the more likely you will be to move toward right-brain thinking, i.e., come up with a dandy new approach.

Step 7. Take a Vacation

Sometimes when you get away from a problem for a while, you can come up with new and fresh approaches. You've probably experienced the common phenomenon of puzzling over a tough problem at bedtime, then waking up the next morning with a way to solve it. Sometimes it helps to get away. Take a coffee break. Work on something else for a while. Walk around the block. Get stoned. Whatever you like, but get away.

The best vacation you can take for getting new ideas is one that puts you in a rich environment. Read a good novel. Go to a posh restaurant or to a concert. Go to the beach or to a ballgame . . . anywhere there are many sensations. Some may provide great clues for you that will trigger ideas.

Step 8. Evaluate What You Have Done

Only after you have really turned yourself loose and given yourself free rein to develop a list of ideas and approaches, and only after you have stretched to get more ideas when you've run dry, should you go back over your list to see which ideas you can use. Pick the ones you feel are best and plan how to try them out . . . when, with whom, how to introduce them. If they work fairly well, use them again, making improvements each time.

Take others that you like but aren't quite usable and work on them. Go back, work through steps 5, 6, and 7 again.

In the course of generating ideas, you may think of many that are good ideas but don't apply to the specific project you're working on. Start an idea file. Put those ideas and others that pop into your mind from time to time into your file. Ideas are elusive. If you don't write them down and put them somewhere, you'll lose them. Go through your idea file once in a while. It will help you remember how creative you really are.

Step 9. Reward Yourself

Take yourself to a movie, go play tennis or whatever you like to do, even when you make small progress, even when you come up with ideas that are only a little more original than usual. Tell yourself, "See, I knew you could do it, you rascal. You're getting more creative all the time. Let's go have a chocolate sundae."

Below is a Guide to Personal Creativity which summarizes the nine steps in checklist form. You may want to copy this to keep in your desk.

Now that I've given you some guidelines for opening up your creativity, I should give you some cautions:

First of all, even though organizations are fond of talking about innovation and creative new approaches, they tend to be hesitant about adopting

Guide to Personal Creativity

1. Use self-talk, "I am Creative."

Expect to get creative products

2. Explore your project. Ask yourself

Why do I want to do this?

What will happen if I'm successful? What will I get out of it?

What (how hard) have I tried before?

To what extent did I succeed? Fail? Why?

3. Set modest goals

Accept human limitations

Don't expect your work to be in a museum overnight

4. Be prepared to work hard

Remember Edison: "Invention is 1% inspiration, 99% perspiration."

Take lessons, get advice, criticism

Plan. Think through what you want to do. Get a mental picture of a good finished product.

Revise, redo

5. Keep your left brain quiet

Don't start out going for perfect solutions

Think of many approaches, and ideas that relate to your project. Go for quantity. As many as possible.

Let all thoughts come out no matter how absurd. Don't evaluate. Don't be afraid to be wrong.

Make yourself laugh. Think of illegal, implausible, immoral, or surprising ideas.

Don't worry about the present order of things. Experiment. Try things you know you're not "supposed" to.

Expect uncertainty, anxiety. Using your right brain takes courage.

6. Play with thoughts and ideas

   Build on ideas to get new ideas.

   Use analogies and unrelated objects or situations.

   Look at your project from many viewpoints. Can it be made larger, smaller? Turned upside down, inside out? Eliminated, combined, reversed, altered?

   Look for clues everywhere. Even in unrelated areas. Borrow from wherever you can.

   Relax and have fun.

7. Take vacations often

   Put your work aside and do something unrelated

   Immerse yourself in a rich environment

8. After you've given yourself free rein, evaluate what you've done. Pick the best things. Try them and if they work fairly well, use them again and build on them.

9. Reward yourself. Even for small progress.

   "See I knew I could do it."

The gift of fantasy has meant more to me than my talent for absorbing positive knowledge

Albert Einstein

them. Generally, the older and larger an organization is, the more difficult it is to bring about change from the traditional. Creativity itself can be somewhat suspect.

A friend of mine was in a meeting recently with his top management. He made the comment that one of his peers, who was at the meeting, was a very creative guy. He thought it was a compliment. The peer didn't. He rushed up to him after the meeting and said, "Thanks, but let's keep the creativity stuff out of sight. I don't think you win any points in this department for being creative."

You should be aware that you may get some sideways glances as you start using your creativity techniques at work. But you will be amazed how quickly people will support you once they see the results.

Second, as you move toward more creative ways of looking at your job and your organization and its problems, you may encounter more frustration because you will see so many opportunities. Because of this you may even make more work for yourself.

Third, you may find you have to become a better salesperson. Since new ideas are not easily accepted, you may have to become better at selling them.

But you will also have the excitement of exploring new ways, venturing into the unknown, and building new and better approaches.

Have fun, and happy creating.

Below is a Personal Creativity Plan that will help you get started. Fill out the plan and take off into a world of new ideas.

PERSONAL CREATIVITY PLAN

Date: ____________

1. I expect to be successful at being creative because I've been creative before. Creative things I've done include:
   ____
   ____
   ____
   ____

2. What do I want to do more creatively? ______________________________
   ____
   ____
   ____
   ____

   I want to do this because: ______________________________
   ____
   ____
   ____
   ____

   If I'm successful, this will happen: ______________________________
   ____
   ____
   ____

What (and how hard) have I tried before? ______________________

To what extent did I succeed or fail? Why? ______________________

3. What modest goals will indicate I'm beginning to be successful? ______

4. Knowing I have to discipline myself and work hard, when will I do this? How much time will I need?

What help (advice) will I get? From whom? ______________________

What fantasy finished product do I envision?

5. What "way-out" uncensored thoughts do I have about this project? ____

6. What other ideas do they trigger in my mind?

7. What will I do to get away from this and stimulate new thoughts?

8. Looking at questions 5 and 6, what are the best ideas I've had so far? How and when will I try them out? How will I modify them so they will be usable?

____

____

____

____

9. How will I reward myself for modest successes?

____

____

____

____

Answers to the Nine Dot Problem:

4 Lines

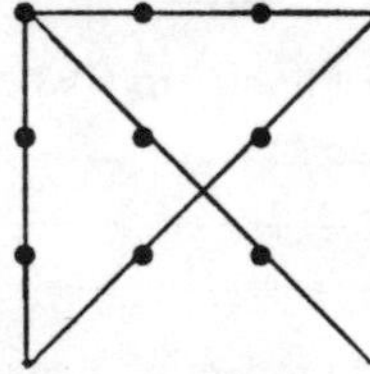

3 Lines

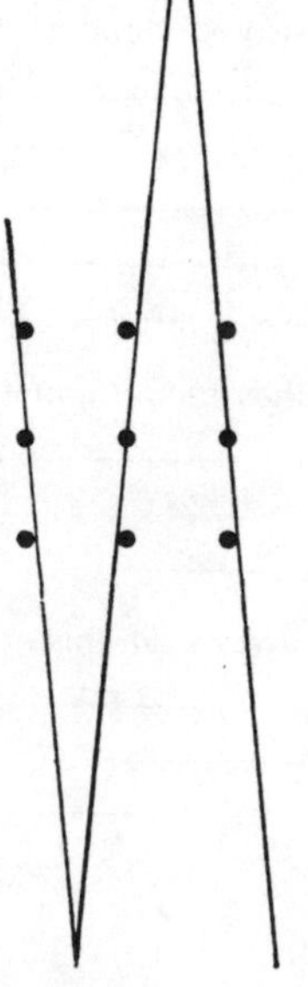

Communicating

5. What Did He Say? How to Write Well

Multitudinous skills interact to contribute to executive effectiveness; however, I can aver with maximal certitude that trenchant writing lies near the pinnacle of the tabularization.

Beginning of an article, titled, "Communications, Key to Success," by Henry Blacksmith, President, International Interface

Lots of people have trouble writing, even top executives. That's not surprising, because writing is an awkward thing to do. It is the most difficult form of communication we have. It is not like talking, because it doesn't allow us to use "ums" and "ahs," incomplete sentences and changes of direction. It is not like thinking because it can't capture streams of images and thoughts the way the mind sees them.

Writing is more formal than talking or thinking. When you write you have to search out words—the right words—to describe what you mean, then put them down on paper for all the world to see, in proper order so they make sense to others, and don't embarrass you when you read them later on.

Writing is a relatively new skill. From the beginning of the human race, people had thoughts or made sounds to communicate, but only recently did they begin to write.

As soon as you become a writer instead of a talker or thinker, you can get attacked by writer's bugaboos. Bugaboos are self-doubts and negative feelings that come around the minute you pull out a pen and a blank sheet of paper. When you're sitting around talking or thinking, bugaboos are usually on vacation.

Here are some bugaboos writers have to deal with:

I can't seem to get started.

Writing takes too much time.

Writing is easier for others than it is for me. I wasn't born with that talent.

I don't have the vocabulary. I can't think of those five-dollar words like some people can.

I get all tangled up in words and sentences.

I get off on too many sidetracks.

Sometimes what I write is hard to understand.

I never get it right the first time.

There's too much material to organize.

I don't know if my writing will accomplish anything.

I can't write.

Even professional writers get the bugaboos. Me, for instance. People who have read my books or articles say to me, "Boy, you can really write." But when I'm alone, working on a manuscript, sometimes I think, "I can't write. Words get in the way. There are too many thoughts to bring together and, besides, there are lots of people who could do it better." AARGH, the bugaboos!

Red Smith, the great sports writer, once said, "Writing is easy. All you have to do is sit down at the typewriter and open a vein."

With so much working against good writing, it's no wonder we have problems with it. Even people who fancy themselves good business writers don't write very well . . . much of what passes for business writing is too long, too boring, and too hard to follow.

But most of us, with some determination and work, can become better writers. Good writers—great writers—don't start out that way. Every one of them had to learn the craft. Writing does not come naturally. But it is worth learning. It is highly visible, and good writing is impressive. It will help you get out ahead of the pack and stay there.

HOW TO WRITE WELL

Here are eight rules for good writing. They apply whether you are writing a memo, a letter, or a report:

1. Write with the reader in mind.
2. Decide what your purpose is.
3. Say exactly what you mean.
4. Keep it as short as possible.
5. Make your point in the first paragraph.
6. Use a format that guides the reader.
7. Write quickly: Build your writing speed.
8. Arouse the reader's interest.

Note that there are no rules here on grammar or sentence structure. I'm assuming you know most of the basics and need help putting it all together. If you do need help with the basics, get *Elements of Style* by Strunk and White. It is in paperback and, unlike the grammar books you remember from grade school, it's easy and fun to read.

Now, let's look at each rule. Watch out, bugaboos!

1. Write with the Reader in Mind

For many people, reading is hard work. Make reading what you write easy for your readers. Put yourself in the reader's place. If you don't like to wade through long wordy reports, you can bet your reader doesn't either. If you don't like to read stuff that's hard to understand, your reader won't either. If you feel frustrated when you have to dig all through something to find the conclusion, your reader will feel that same way.

What about special types of readers? If you are writing a memo to the folks in the accounting department, should you give them paragraphs of philosophy? Is that what turns them on? Heck, no. Give them numbers. That's what they like to see.

Take a minute before you start writing and ask yourself, "Who are my readers?" and "How can I write so they'll relate to it?"

2. Decide What Your Purpose Is

Anything you write at work should have some purpose, usually to make something happen. You are not writing short stories to entertain your reader—you are writing, most of the time, to get your reader to do something.

Before you put one word on paper, decide what you want to accomplish by writing. Stop and jot down the ending to this sentence: "I hope, as a result of reading this (memo) (letter) (report), my reader will ____."

If you can't figure out what you want the reader to do, maybe you shouldn't bother writing.

If you do write, be sure every sentence and every paragraph helps accomplish this purpose, getting your reader to do what you want him or her to. Any that doesn't help is excess baggage and should be deleted.

3. Say Exactly What You Mean

Your reader is much more likely to do what you want if he or she understands what you are saying in the first place. That sounds like a dumb thing to say, but it bears mentioning because there is a lot of runaway writing floating around today—almost designed, it seems, to confuse the reader. Don't you write that way. You won't if you follow these rules.

Use small, simple words. The smaller and simpler the better. Many people at work seem to think good writing has to include lots of big words. It doesn't.

Ernest Hemingway is a writer who did very well using little words:

> He started to pull the fish in to have him alongside so that he could pass a line through his gills and out his mouth and make his head fast alongside the bow. I want to see him, he thought, and to touch and to feel him. He is my future, he thought. But that is not why I wish to feel him. I think I felt his heart, he thought. When I pushed on the harpoon shaft the second time. Bring him in now and make him fast and get the noose around his tail and then around his middle to bind him to the skiff.*

Find any big words there? No. Hemingway wrote in a straightforward, powerful style that got his message across. You can learn a lot about clear writing just by looking at how he used words.

Try using simple words. Leave polysyllabic words like "polysyllabic" to college professors. Quit trying to impress people with big words. Chances are they'll be more confused than impressed.

Always look for the simplest, most direct way to say what you have to say.

* Ernest Hemingway, *The Old Man and the Sea.* New York: Charles Scribner's Sons, 1952, p. 95.

> Waste materials should be deposited in the proper receptacle.
>
> Throw trash in the basket.

Winston Churchill said, "Short words are best, and short words when they are old words are best of all."

Use short, simple sentences. Oh, you may want to throw a longer one in once in a while for variety, but normally short is better. Look at the Hemingway quote again. Most people at work write sentences that are twice as long as they should be. Limit yourself to fifteen to twenty words. It's great discipline and will make your writing much easier to understand.

Stick to one idea in each sentence.

> The meeting will be held on Thursday, August 5, with the express purpose of deliberating a course of action for the Conner project so that implementation of the second phase can be activated by September 1.

Why allow all that underbrush to grow in your writing? Look what happens when you clear it out:

> We'll meet on August 5 to discuss the Conner project and decide what to do. I'd like to start phase 2 by September 1.

If you get bogged down in the middle of a sentence, it's probably because you're trying to stuff too many ideas into it. Try breaking it into two sentences and everything will fall into place.

Stay away from the passive voice.

> It has been decided that all employees will use the rear parking lot.

Who decided? Someone in the faceless bureaucracy. Maybe Mr. Barrett, the president. Or maybe Mr. Phelps, the janitor. Since you don't know, do you care? Where are you going to park?

> Mr. Barrett decided that all employees will use the rear parking lot.

A lot punchier, isn't it? Excuse me a minute while I move my car.

When you are writing instructions and procedures, use "you" to involve the reader, and to indicate exactly who should do what.

> The report should be submitted by the first of each month.
>
> You should send in the report by the first of each month.

The next time you read something and are a little confused as to who is doing what to whom, look to see if it is written in the passive—it probably is, and shouldn't be.

Use "I" when you mean "I." Some folks think using "the writer" instead of "I" makes everything more formal and dignified. I think it makes everything awkward and clumsy. If you're talking about yourself, say "I."

Sometimes, to be modest, or to show good team spirit, people will say "we" when they mean "I."

> We have read your letter and we would like to meet with you to discuss it further.

Sounds like a roomful, doesn't it? Won't the reader be surprised when he or she goes to the meeting and there is only one other person there. "I" would be clearer.

Try a conversational style. Who says business writing has to be as stiff as a eulogy? People are still people, even after they go to work, and they still respond in very human ways to humor and friendliness.

> Dear Mr. Jones:
>
> We have reviewed your letter of July 17, regarding the Jenkins matter, and we appreciate your taking the time to contact us.

If you walked into Mr. Jones's office, you wouldn't say, "we have reviewed" or "Jenkins matter" or "contact us." You'd say, "Thanks for the letter." Why not say that in writing too?

> Dear Mr. Jones:
>
> Thanks for the letter.

He knows that his letter was about Jenkins. He wrote it, and you don't have to explain that to him, unless he sent several letters on several different subjects.

There's nothing wrong with writing the way you talk, unless you curse a lot. If you're stuck, try reading what you've written out loud. If it sounds stilted and forced, say what you're trying to say out loud, as though you were talking to a friend, then write that way.

Here are some other things you can do to sharpen your writing:

- Be consistent. If you capitalize a term in one sentence, do it in all sentences. If you begin a list with action verbs, use action verbs all the way through. If you underline some headings, underline all that are of equal value.
- Use bullets to set up points in a list as I have here.
- Use headings in reports or long memos to tell the reader where the breaks are and what's coming.
- Use charts and graphs wherever you can in the text to make things clearer.
- Stay away from jargon and technical words (unless your readers are all technical people). Avoid acronyms (unless you are sure everyone understands them).

  Oh, I know, the Manager of Jargon, Technical Words, and Acronyms in your company is making up great new ones every day to keep everyone confused, and it's tempting to use them to show how with it you are, but restrain yourself. Your reader may not know what they mean and won't know what you're talking about.

4. Keep It As Short As Possible

This is closely related to saying exactly what you mean. The shorter your message, the more likely it is that people will understand it—provided, of course, you've covered all the necessary points. Also, it's more likely

WORDS TO WATCH OUT FOR

Common in business writing, they are often used incorrectly or they tend to clutter up writing.

Irregardless. There is no such word. Use regardless.

Remuneration. Often misspelled renumeration. Better to use *pay.*

Re: Often used to precede the title of a memo. Just use the title; everyone will know if it's at the top of the page and underlined that it is what the report is about.

Interesting. A vague, weak, and overused word. Show why it was "interesting" rather than just saying it.

Utilize, optimize, prioritize, any "ize." If you mean use, or make best use of, or put in priority order, say that. *Finalize* belongs with this group too.

Implement. We implement everything these days. Try "carry out" or "get started."

Interface, Interact, Interpersonal. These words take simple concepts and make them seem formidable. Use "meet," "work with," and "people" instead.

Bottom Line. May sound very financial and businesslike, but this is overused today. Try "result" instead.

Very Slightly, Awfully, Basically. Vague modifiers that don't add any information. "Prospects for the quarter look awfully bad." How bad is that? "We may lose 2.5 million this quarter." Oh.

Hopefully. This is a frame of mind. Don't use it to mean "I hope."

Unique. Means without equal, one of a kind. Therefore, something can't be "the most unique" or "very unique."

Orientate. This word is in the dictionary, but it is clumsy and hard to say or read. Use "orient."

Affect vs. Effect. Hardly anyone understands the difference. Why we need both of these words in our language is beyond me. If you want to use them correctly, follow this advice from the *American Heritage Dictionary, Second College Edition: Affect* is most commonly used in the sense of "to influence" (how smoking affects health). *Effect* means to bring about or execute: layoffs designed to effect savings.

Etc. Shows you're lazy. Either complete the list or end it. "Etc." implies there is more, but you haven't gone to the trouble to find out what.

they will read it. Writing at work is not like writing for your English professor. It is not valued by the pound. In fact, the opposite is true, especially when every day sees a new blizzard of paper. Mark Twain admonished writers to take out one word in three to make their writing clearer and more vigorous.

Your best hope of getting people to understand and commit to a course of action is to say exactly what you mean *and* keep it as short as possible. The figure below shows how these two work together to influence your reader.

CLEAR

Most likely to get reader to act	Concise and to the point (Headline, road sign)	Long, but exact (Encyclopedia)	
SHORT			**LONG**
	Concise, but vague (Riddle)	Long and vague (College term papers, articles written by psychologists)	Least likely to get reader to act

MURKY

Three more points on being short:

Take out as many *that*'s and *which*'s as you can.

> As you know, public speaking is a task that most people find hard to do.

What good does the word *that* do? None. In a long report, you might have twenty or thirty unnecessary *that*'s and *which*'s. Take them out.

> As you know, public speaking is a task most people find hard to do.

Get rid of other fillers and wasted words. Take another look at the little gem on public speaking above. "Is a task" doesn't add much so you can take that out. "Most people" is unnecessary—who else, Airedales? "To do"—Who needs it?

Why not just say . . .

> As you know, public speaking is hard.

And how about that old favorite, "as you know"? If the reader knows, why remind him? Why not just say:

> Public speaking is hard.

FILLERS, REPEATS, AND OTHER PHRASES TO AVOID

True fact. A fact, by definition, is true.

Advance plan. Just say "plan."

In depth. Overused. We do everything in depth now. Or pretend we do. Do it, but don't say it.

At the present time. That means "now."

In regard to.
With reference to. Use "about."

On an annual basis. A long way to say "yearly."

In the majority of cases. Try "mostly."

Current status. Status is good enough. It implies current.

One of the most, the fact that, in any case, as you know, it should be noted that, thanking you in advance. All are vague, meaningless, and can be left out altogether.

Take action. A hard way to say "act."

Ballpark, back to the drawing board, in view of the above, state of the art, hands-on, feedback, meaningful, viable, optimum, please don't hesitate to call, enclosed please find, I'm in receipt of your letter of November 11, will you kindly inform me, parameter, input, factor. All clichés that will bore your reader to death. Avoid if you can.

In fact, if the reader already knows, why write the sentence at all? Leave it out.

Stop here and dig out something you have written. Some memos, a report or two. Read through them with these two questions in mind: How could I say it more clearly? How could I say it shorter? When you look at your writing that way, you'll be amazed at how many vague words and unneeded words and phrases you've used.

When you have said what you want to say, stop. Period.

5. Make Your Point in the First Paragraph

Or, if you are writing a report, in an executive summary at the beginning.

You should do that because (a) you are not writing a mystery novel, and there's no point holding out till the end, and (b) your readers get a ton of stuff to go through every day, just like you do. A lot of it they skim. Sometimes they may not get past the first paragraph. If you want to be sure they get your point, that's the place to put it. Some writers feel they have to ease readers into their material and write two or three tone-setting paragraphs. Do that, if you feel you have to, then go back and cross out everything up to the place you make your main point. Make that the start of your report or letter. Say what you have to say clearly, concisely, and EARLY.

Pick up a newspaper and look at some articles. You'll see most of them tell you who, what, where, when, and why in the first paragraph. That's because people read newspapers the same way they read the stuff you send them, and often don't get past the first few sentences.

Once you're sure you've gotten your message across, use the rest of your memo, letter, or report to support your conclusions.

6. Use a Format That Guides the Reader

When you're writing a long report, break it into pieces, and label them to help the reader through. This allows the reader to read as much or as little of the report as he or she wants to—and still get your message.

Here's a format you can use:

TITLE: Your title should indicate clearly what the report is about. Obvious? Watch for titles of reports that come across your desk. How many tell you what's inside? Don't try for drama or aesthetics. Leave out technical words, jargon, and acronyms.

SUMMARY: This should include the subject of the report, the conclusions or findings, and the recommendations. It should be less than a page in length.

INTRODUCTION: The purpose of the report, why it was done, and what benefits you hope will come out of it. Keep this to one page or less too.

CONCLUSION: What you found out: one page or less.

BODY OF THE REPORT: How the report was compiled, who was involved, when it was done, and detailed results.

APPENDICES: These should include statistical information, charts, lists, and tables that are too long to include in the body of the report. Any supporting information that can be included in the report should be, so the reader doesn't have to flip back and forth.

Give each section of the report a heading, and if the report is long, use tabs to separate sections. If the report is very long, shorten it. Ask yourself, "Have I told the reader everything he or she needs to know? Have I told my reader other stuff that he or she doesn't really have to know?"

Don't write your report in the order you put it together. First write the body and put all your statistical information in order. Out of that you can write your conclusion and introduction. Last of all, after everything else is done, write your summary.

7. Write Quickly . . . Build Your Writing Speed

One reason people don't like writing is that it takes too much time. You might be surprised to learn you can cut your writing time by following two points discussed above:

- Decide the purpose of your writing before you begin: What you want to accomplish and what you want the reader to do. This will help you stay on the subject and not go down a lot of time-consuming blind alleys.
- Use small words and simple sentences. Thinking of all those big words and building complex sentences takes time and slows you down.

If you keep those firmly in mind every time you write and practice them until they become second nature to you, you will find yourself writing much faster.

Here are other things you can do to save writing time:

- Use a dictating machine for memos and letters instead of writing them longhand.
- If you write many similar letters, write a bunch of standard paragraphs to cover most situations and number them. Then, instead of handwritten pages or a dictation belt, you'll give your secretary something that looks like this:

  Dear Mr. Edwards:

  Paragraphs 6–13–2–18

  Sincerely

- Better yet, put the whole thing on a word processor and let the computer worry about it.

8. Arouse the Reader's Interest

Your writing can be clear and concise, but if it doesn't interest the reader, it might not get read, or, even if it does, it might not move the reader to do anything.

Include thoughts and images that will capture your readers' attention and get them involved in what you have to say. Again, think in terms of who your readers are and what turns them on.

For example, offer your readers hope that you will make their job easier or life better. Everyone is interested in those. If that's what your memo or report is going to do, tell the reader early, right up front with your main point or conclusion. Stress anything that will benefit the reader. Maybe you've discovered some dramatic statistic or trend. That can also be a grabber. Put it in the opening paragraph.

While the reader is going through your memo or report, chances are he or she is thinking of objections to what you've said. Anticipate these, and throw some in—along with ways to overcome them. That will help to sustain interest and show you are pretty smart.

If you are going to discuss the report with your reader, hold out one or two objections and wait for them to come up in the meeting. Then show your brilliance by dealing with them deftly, even though you are hearing them (it seems) for the first time.

If you are stumped as to what would interest the reader, try creative thinking (see Chapter 4).

THE MECHANICS OF WRITING

Getting Started

Before you put a word on paper, think about your reasons for writing (see above) and what you want your readers to do. Using three by five cards, write down the points you want to make (one per card)—points that will get your reader moving in the right direction. Don't worry about the order or the wording. Get your thoughts down as quickly as possible.

When you've done that, collect any information you will need to flesh out your points. Go out and talk to people who know. Study reports, operating figures, computer analyses, and whatever you need. Add notes to your three by five cards. As you do your research, you may discover new points. Write new cards for them. Be sure everything in your cards supports your overall purpose and no extraneous items sneak in.

Then, go back and number them in the order you'll want to use them, keeping in mind what I've said about conclusions and interest getting coming first. Now, arrange the cards in the order you've numbered them. This is your outline.

Writing Your First Draft

Many folks beginning a project will spend too much time trying to think of a perfect way to start. My advice: Whip out some paper and write down whatever comes to you. Just get some words down to get yourself into it. It doesn't matter what they are at this point. The very act of writing helps you to think of what and how to write, so it's important to be doing it. Start with a nursery rhyme if you have to, but write something. A false start is almost a necessary part of the writing process. Once you have gotten into it and have built up some momentum, ideas will begin to flow and your writing will come easier. You can always go back and do the beginning last.

Don't worry too much about how beautiful your writing is at this point—you'll be revising it anyhow. Write your first draft knowing you will throw it out.

Revising

When you have written all the way through your first draft, go back and revise it. It helps if you leave it alone for a day or two, if you have time, to get new perspective on it.

It may look awful when you read it, but that's how first drafts are supposed to look, so don't let that turn into another bugaboo.

Using scissors, tape, and a colored pen, go through and edit like a maniac. Use all the techniques for clarifying and shortening discussed above.

Cross out and write over. Start over where necessary. Cut out any paragraphs that are pretty good and tape them into your revision. One option most forget when revising: If a sentence or a paragraph does not revise easily and you are having a hard time making it fit, take it out altogether. Maybe it just doesn't belong.

Another consideration, when you are revising, is this. If something you have written bothers you somehow, makes you feel a little uncomfortable, it will probably bother your reader too. Take it out or change it.

Write instructions (and apologies) to your secretary in the margin of your draft and give it to her to type (on a word processor, if possible, so changes can be made easily), double-spaced, with wide margins on the left for notes and more revisions. When the typed copy comes back, go through it again making a final revision. If you expect there will be several revisions, ask your secretary to number and date them. Use the proofreading symbols below to communicate changes to the first typed copy to your secretary.

If this seems like a lot of revising, it is, but nobody writes anything that's perfect the first time—nobody—and if it's important, it's worth doing well. Besides, each revision is less and less work so they go progressively faster (unless you get an inspiration along the way and decide to take a whole new approach).

Finishing Touches

Ask your secretary to type the final copy with plenty of white space, headings capitalized and/or underlined, pages numbered (so you can refer to them in discussions), and, for reports, a nice cover sheet with the title, your name and/or department, and the date. You may want to put it in a binder to dress it up.

If what you are writing is super important or you are not sure the final copy is right, give it to some people to read: people who work with you, peers, or, if it will help get their involvement and support, people above you in the organization.

If your message is to someone above your boss, *always* include your boss in the review process. It will get his or her commitment and help establish a good feeling of communication between you. Also, you may be amazed at what good ideas and insight your boss has!

Edit to cut down size, take out unnecessary words and phrases, making your writing simple and clear, be sure it's accurate, rearrange and improve the order and flow. And finally, look at what you've written from the reader's point of view.

PROOFREADING SYMBOLS

Here are some symbols you will find helpful. Your secretary probably already knows them, but you might want to ask, to make sure.

Symbol	What It Means
(line through)	Take out letter or word(s)
¶	Start a new paragraph here
≡	Make this a capital letter
/	Make this a small letter
∽	Transpose these words or letters
∧	Insert
STET	Disregard this correction; let it stand as it was

Here's an example of the use of these symbols.

~~As you can see by now~~, proofreading symbols give you a simple way to let your secretary know what changes you want to make. ¶ If you were a professional Editor, you would use many other symbols. But these should allow (eight symbols) you to take care of ~~most~~ (STET) buisness writing situations.

Here are some final thoughts on writing.

- Sometimes, you just don't have it. If you have made an honest try and nothing worthwhile is coming out, put your writing aside. Come back to it later in the day, or, if it can wait, the next day.
- It's always good to warm up. If you're about to start a big report, knock out a couple short memos first, just to get going.
- Pay attention to your thoughts when you are writing. Often your best ideas will come when you are actually writing.

- Set deadlines for yourself, especially if no real deadlines exist. Plan to have so much writing done by a certain time, and stay with your schedule. Deadlines help you get writing done and also put pressure on you to do the best you can in the shortest time.
- Write all you can. Take on extra writing assignments if you have to. As Samuel Johnson said, way back in the 1700s, "You learn to write by writing." Sam knew what he was talking about.
- Once you start to develop your skills, you will find that writing becomes more and more fun. It is a giant video game, with all those words out there floating around, infinite ways to put them together—and you at the controls.
- Spell names right. Take an extra few minutes to find out correct spellings. The same goes for titles—get them right. Why alienate your reader right from the start by getting his name or title messed up?
- Writing is one of the few ways people have to judge you. They can see how you look and dress, how you speak, how you handle your job, and how you write. How you write has a strong influence on how you are viewed in the organization. Learning to write well is worth every minute of time and effort you put into it. Writing well is an *Upward Bound* communication skill that will be noticed and admired throughout your organization. It will help you stand out from the crowd because you will be one of the few who can do it.

6. I Hope the Earth Will Swallow Me Up: How to Speak Effectively

"Unaccustomed as I am to schmublic peeking. . . ."

Opening of a sales-convention talk
by Arthur Davidson, V. P. Marketing,
Amalgamated Tea Bag Corp.

Psychologists have found the ability to speak well . . . whether to one or one hundred . . . is closely related to success. Yet, many people have trouble expressing themselves, especially in front of groups. It seems as though a large percentage of managers and professionals view public speaking as:

- A formal, stiff process used to get information from one place to another in the dullest possible way.
- A painful experience, something to get over with as quickly as possible.

And because of this, each day thousands of working people miss opportunities to impress the devil out of their co-workers and bosses by showing off speaking skills few others have.

If you have trouble speaking to groups, if you are nervous, hesitant, and stumble through; if, when it's all over, you have a feeling you were ordinary and uninspiring, you have a great chance to make dramatic improvements in your image at work. Speaking is one of the most visible of *Upward Bound* skills, and your ability to give a professional talk in front of a group will gain respect for you far beyond the importance of the points you make in your speech. Somehow, people assume anyone good in front of an audience must automatically be competent in many other areas.

There is no law that says just because everyone else at work is a boring speaker, you need to be too. Think about it. Any time you are lucky enough to be able to be up in front of an audience, you have a roomful of people with little else to do but focus on you. That's not something to avoid, or rush through; it's an *opportunity* to do something special.

This chapter will help you take advantage of that opportunity. While it may not turn you into a candidate for anchorman on network news, it will help you learn methods the pros use when they speak in front of groups: six steps that will enable you to master this imposing *Upward Bound* skill.

By the end of this chapter, you will know how to:

1. Prepare a presentation.
2. Practice it.
3. Deliver it with confidence.
4. Use anxiety constructively.
5. Use high impact visual aids.
6. Evaluate your performance and learn from it.

Let's look at each.

A Note on Preparing and Practicing

Never give a presentation, no matter how short or seemingly insignificant, without preparing and practicing. Remember, your time in front of a group is your showcase. Use every opportunity you get—even five-minute presentations in meetings—to enhance yourself in everyone's eyes.

As a rule of thumb, you should prepare and practice in a 10 to 1 ratio to the length of the talk. If your presentation is to take thirty minutes, you should spend five hours preparing and practicing. (If your presentation is an hour, it is too long and you should shorten it.) Ten to one is an average, a benchmark. For very complex or very important presentations, you will want to spend even more time getting ready.

1. HOW TO PREPARE

1. *Analyze your audience.* Put yourself in the audience's shoes. Imagine you are the audience hearing your talk: How much background do you need? How much detail? What turns you on? What will get you interested in listening to this subject? What do you want to get out of it? Once you know what your audience wants, you can figure out how to "sell" the benefits of your topic to them.
2. *Be sure you have an objective.* Decide what it is you want to happen as a result of your presentation. Do you want the audience to do something? Decide something? Or just absorb information? Let them know what you want them to do near the beginning of the talk and again at the end.
3. *Do your homework.* Research your topic so you know enough about it to make every point in your talk clear and believable. Don't try to skim over points with just half knowledge. Anticipate questions, and make sure you have the facts to answer them.
4. *Plan your format.* When you are sure you know your audience, your objectives, and your subject matter, begin thinking about the best way to "stage" your presentation. *How* you give your talk can be more important than what you say. Here are some options. Note that good presentations are seldom just talking from the front of the room, but usually involve the use of visuals, handouts, questions and answers, discussion, and sometimes even practice. (See page 88.)
5. *Plan your delivery.* For that part of your presentation that does involve talking from the front of the room, you'll have to decide if you want to use a script, notes or outline, key words or a memory aid.

   Script: For important speeches, and especially if copies of your talk are to be distributed, you will want to use a script. You should also use a script if you are nervous about the talk and want a security blanket. Here are some thoughts on preparing scripts:

   - Have your script typed on the right two-thirds of the page, leaving a wide margin on the left you can use to write instructions to yourself.
   - Use that margin to indicate when to change slides, when to pass out materials, when to refer to charts, or when to show a film or video tape. If you have an assistant running the slides for you, he or she should have a copy of the script too.
   - Have the script typed double-spaced. Triple space is unfamiliar and hard to read. Also, have it typed in upper and lower case, not all capital letters. You are not used to reading all caps, and they make

If Your Objective Is This . . .	Try This . . .
To update the audience, give information.	Give a short front-of-the-room (or head-of-the-table) presentation with slides, handouts. Allow time for questions and answers.
To get approval of a project. To get support, commitment.	Review the project, with emphasis on its benefits. Use charts and graphs to clarify points. Use handouts to summarize. Get the group involved. Lead a discussion on what the project will do for them and how it could be improved or strengthened.
To get the audience to implement a program.	Cover how the program works and give examples, if possible, of how it worked well in the past (or worked in other organizations). Use slides, flip charts, or overheads to summarize facts, statistics, or financial figures. Use handouts for details. Ask for questions. If the group is small enough, lead a discussion on how to best put the program into action. Cover obstacles first, then how to overcome them.
To produce a change in attitude or behavior.	Describe the new attitude or behavior, and how it will benefit the members of the audience. Show the desired attitude or behavior (film or video is good for this). If the group is small enough, lead a discussion on the new attitude or behavior and then have members of the group practice using it.
To teach the audience a new skill or technique.	Describe the new skill or technique and how it will make the work of the audience easier and more professional. Show the skill on video or film or live. Have members of the audience try using the skill.
To entertain.	This is tricky, because what you think is hilarious may make great stone faces out of your audience. You can use any or all of the techniques above, or a film or video tape. If you aren't sure, get some outside professional help with this one, or stay away from it altogether.

it harder for you to pick up complete words and phrases from your script.

- Never carry a sentence or key thought from one page to another. Finish them on the page on which they began so there is not an unnatural pause while you change pages.
- Include facts that you may need, but will not use in your talk, at the end of your script for questions and answers.

Notes or Outline. Use notes or outline if you know the subject well, and/or if you are a seasoned, confident speaker. Notes or outlines will guide you through the talk and will help you look up and talk more to the audience. They will not, however, give you exact words to use or every thought you may want to get across, so make sure you are comfortable using notes.

Key Words. Key words also free you up to concentrate on the audience. Key words can be written on a piece of paper, three by five cards held in your hand, or can be on slides or charts. If you use charts, pencil in lightly (on the side of the chart where you will stand) supporting notes on comments you want to make about the chart. If you use overhead transparencies, write your notes on the cardboard frames.

Memory Aids. For information on memory aids, see Chapter 14. Certain aids can help you remember major points in your talk and can lead you through from start to finish—as though you had your key word three by five cards in your mind. Using them well can make you look like a magician. ("Janet gave that whole talk without one note. I don't know how she did it!") But they are not foolproof. Make sure you are secure in your ability to use them before you rely on them to get you through a major presentation.

6. *Keep your audience's attention.* Here are seven factors that are sure to reduce your audience's attention span:

- Lack of interest in the material.
- No clear reason why it's important.
- High level of anxiety about the topic.
- One-way presentation. No participation by the audience.
- Time of day. Right after lunch; late in the afternoon.
- Distractions. Phones ringing, people coming in and out.
- Lack of preparation or skill on your part as the presenter.

Remember, people become catatonic very quickly when someone else is talking. The chart below says it all.

Attention Span by Type of Presentation

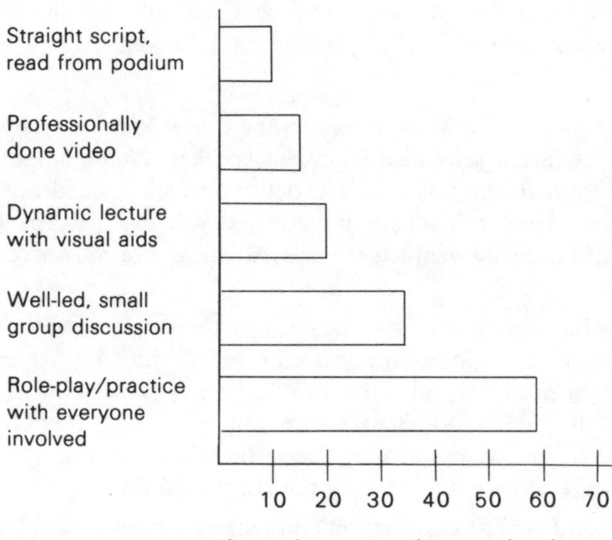

Don't expect to read from a script for half an hour, with no visuals, and have everyone's attention. You won't. Some will begin drifting after five minutes and you will lose everyone after a quarter hour. Even when they are paying attention, people tend to remember little of what's given in lectures. Attendees at a psychological-society meeting in England were asked, two weeks after the meeting, to write down what they recalled. Of the points actually covered in the speeches, attendees remembered an average of only 8.4 percent! And 42 percent of what they said they remembered was incorrect . . . much of it was not even in the meeting.

7. *Plan the parts of your talk.* Here's how it should flow:

Opening Grabber. Use an attention getter right at the beginning to get the audience on your side and to convince them that listening to you is going to be worthwhile.

Attention getters include:

- Tension breakers. Sometimes, in a formal, stuffy setting, just a "hello" and a big smile are enough to get everyone relaxed.

- Questions to stimulate interest, like "How would you like to increase productivity by twenty percent?" or "What would happen to sales if we introduced a typewriter that could think?"
- Friendly comments stating the problem and indicating you and the audience are in it together.
- Startling facts or statistics. "We could have led the industry in widget sales last year except for one thing."
- Stories about things that happened to you that are pertinent to the subject (audiences love personal stories if they are well told and have some meaning).
- Opinions or statements by experts on the subject.
- Comments on how others have solved the problem and benefited from it.

Don't open with:

- A joke. Unless you are a master storyteller (most of us are not) and the joke is pertinent to what you will be talking about. (It's often hard to find a match.)
- "It's an honor to be here," which is trite, or "It's a pleasure to be here," which is overdone and also funny when the expression on your face tells everyone you'd rather be shoveling camel dung in the Gobi desert.
- "Mr. Chairman, Mr. President, members of the council, and distinguished guests." Everyone will be asleep before you are through with that opening including the chairman, president, members of the council, and the distinguished guests.
- Anything negative or apologetic. If you begin by saying, "There are lots of people more qualified to talk on this than I," or "I'm not very good at talking in front of groups," everyone will believe you and you may as well throw the rest of your presentation in the basket and do a half hour of birdcalls. Few will be inspired to listen to you, and those that do won't be swayed much by what you say.

I once heard a speaker say to a group that had paid good money to hear him, "Good morning. This will be a little rough, because I really didn't start to prepare it until last night." Expressions of disgust were evident everywhere, and several people got up and walked out. Everyone should have, not only because they were getting ripped off, but because that was a lousy opening.

Your Objective. Tell your audience what you hope will happen as a result of your talk. "When we're done here this afternoon, you'll understand the WACKOFAX program and want to begin using it in your department. You'll be anxious to get the same improvement in work flow that many others have had."

This is the first part of the old speech-writing chestnut "Tell 'em what you're going to tell 'em, tell 'em, tell 'em what you've told them."

When you're putting together your statement of purpose, stay away from "I" statements. Bring in your audience with "you" and "we" statements. Use rhetorical questions, speak to your audience's concerns, and remind them of benefits.

Content. This is the part of your presentation where you spell out the specifics of your proposal, project, or program, the "tell 'em" part.

You should:

- Be brief. Remember that attention spans are short.
- Use simple language and a conversational tone. Listen to newscasters on TV. They use clear, precise words and sentences, not pedantic language. You should do the same to get your points across.
- Use visuals or words as road signs to help the audience keep track of where you are:
  "I will discuss three methods:
  The first method is . . .
  The second method is . . .
  The third method is. . . ."
- When you've planned what you will say, go back and take out everything that doesn't help you meet your objective, and anything that obscures your main points. See Chapter 5 on how to write simply. See if you can take out the first paragraph or two and find the real beginning of this part of your talk.
- Use as much variety as you can to sustain interest. Use lecture, visuals, questions and answers, and discussion.
- Avoid the use of jargon, acronyms, and clichés.

Closing. Here's where you get the payoff for all of your efforts. Parts of the closing include:

- A summary ("tell 'em what you told 'em").
- A statement that you've accomplished your objective (or hope you did).
- A reminder of the benefits to the audience.
- An outline of the action you want taken.

The closing should be brief, positive, and hopeful that the audience will do what you want. It should also be supportive: "I will help you in any way I can—just ask."

8. *Plan your materials and equipment.* As a final step in your preparation, go through your script and list each and every thing you will need at the live presentation: copies of the script, slides, overheads, handouts, awards, videotapes, films, charts, felt-tip markers, tape, slide projector, overhead projector, screen, VCR, extension cords, adaptor plug, podium, lights, microphone, speakers, and, if you are speaking to an outside group, business cards.

2. HOW TO PRACTICE

No professional in any field performs without practicing. You shouldn't either. Never try to give a presentation without practicing. Even if you feel your written script is dynamic, you will want to change it when you say it out loud. Spoken words are not the same as written words.

Here's how to practice. (This concentrates on a scripted presentation, but the basics are the same for notes, outlines, key words, and memory-supported presentations.)

1. The first time you read the script aloud, do it in any quiet, private place. Don't invite critics. You'll only be embarrassed. Read it all the way through. Critique it yourself. Then grab your pencil and begin revising.
2. Change words that don't sound right, find new words or phrases for those you stumble over, eliminate parts that are not relevant (even though you love them), take out unnecessary words or phrases (where you can get the message across just as well without them), and eliminate repetitions—unless it's to drive home a point. Put in bridges and transitions from one train of thought to another.

   Revise or take out anything that gnaws at you, even a little. It probably won't sound right to the audience either.

   Don't hesitate to chop up your first draft. In fact, if you don't chop it up, something is wrong. Nobody ever wrote a speech the first time. Legend has it that Abraham Lincoln wrote his famous address on the way to Gettysburg on the back of an envelope. Could be, but I will bet he was knee-deep in envelopes before he got it right.
3. Have your script typed, then take the typed copy and mark it up. Underline those words in each sentence you want to stress and use a

slash where you want to pause. Highlight key words in each paragraph with a yellow marker so that when you get to know your script, you will be able to glance down at the key word, then say the rest of the paragraph while looking at the audience. After each key point, put an arrow pointing upward ↑ . That will remind you to pause and keep looking at the audience after you say that sentence instead of dropping your eyes back to the script. Doing that will help emphasize the point and indicate to your listeners that you have just said something important.

Put a mark like this ⁄ after some of your sentence ending words so you will remember not to end every sentence with your voice dropping. Up endings ⌒ do not sound like questions, but they are a higher tone than the usual down ending. This adds variety and interest. Listen to any news announcer on TV tonight and count the up endings versus down endings. You will be surprised at how many you hear.

Other marks you can make in the margin include "Look Up" or "Smile" to remind yourself to do those (especially at the start of your talk); and "Slow" or "Speed Up" to remind you to vary your pace and add interest.

Never go into a presentation with a clean script. Your script should look worked over and lived with. It should be covered with underlines, slashes, arrows, pencil corrections, and notes to yourself. It should be as familiar as an old friend.

4. Read your script out loud into a tape recorder following all your marks. Notice how professional you sound. Try speaking to a mirror so you can practice looking up, maintaining eye contact, smiling, and otherwise making your facial expressions match the tone of the script (worried, pleased, amazed, confident—anything but scared, nauseous, or sweaty). Use videotape if it's available.

5. Practice your speech using all the slides, charts, and other aids you will be using in the live presentation. Practice the slide changes. Put in blank slides where there are long sections between slides. You may find, as you do this, that you have to change your visuals or your script to make them fit.

6. If your speech is important, practice once on a live audience. Invite your boss—to make him or her a partner and show him or her how terrific you are. Invite others who will give you candid opinions. If there is discussion built into your presentation, practice that with the audience also. Discussions almost always take unexpected turns, and practicing with a live group will help you anticipate possible responses your real audience might give.

7. When you are not practicing, daydream a little about your presentation. Think about how fabulous you will be and how you will captivate your audience. Great speakers visualize everything that will happen in a successful presentation, including the applause at the end—it helps prepare them to go out and make it happen.
8. And then, just before your presentation . . .
   - Check your material list to see that you have your script, and all the slides, handouts, and other items that go with it.
   - Check the room setup to see that it is the way you want it.
   - Make sure all screens, projectors, and other equipment you need are there and are working.
   - Check the location of the light switches.
   - Run through your slides quickly to make sure they are in order and are in the tray correctly. Slides have a habit of jumping around in the tray. Cue up films or videotapes so they begin immediately when you turn them on. Don't make your audience sit through sixty seconds of color bars; it will seem like a year.
   - Think of the opportunity you have to show how good you are. Make up your mind to go for it and to have a good time.
   - Warm up. Find a private place to say the first few paragraphs aloud before you go on.

3. HOW TO DELIVER YOUR SPEECH WITH CONFIDENCE

Okay. The moment of truth has arrived. You're on. Here's how to handle it like a real pro.

1. By this time you should be so comfortable and familiar with your script, notes, visuals, that actually giving the talk seems anticlimactic.
2. Before you even say anything, look up and smile. That will show your audience (and you) that you are confident and happy to be there (even if you're about to sprint for the "exit" door). The audience wants to feel that you are warm, friendly, and secure and will be relieved if you look that way. They don't want to suffer through a stiff, impersonal lecture, punctuated only with nervous hemmings and hawings. It is important to establish an "up" mood right off. How you appear to the audience at this point is much more important in winning them over than anything you say to them. Let your warmth

come through at the start and they will be more inclined to listen to you.

3. When you look at your audience, you may see a lot of grouchy expressions. Don't worry about it. Those somber looks don't mean they hate you (usually, anyhow). They mean people are concentrating, listening hard to follow you into the talk. It's normal, so expect it and live with it.
4. As you begin talking, use as much eye contact as you can. Look up from your script often. Start out by looking at someone you know will be supportive. Look at that person for four to five seconds until you get a nod or a smile. That will make you feel better. Glance back at your script and look up at someone else in another part of the room. In a large group fix on someone three-quarters of the way to the left side, toward the back. Then switch to someone in the same spot to the right side. Many people in your sight path will think you are looking at them too.
5. When you look down at your script, move your eyes, not your head. Keep your head up, ready to focus out on the audience.
6. If you are working from a script, slide the pages, don't turn them. Don't have your script stapled, paperclipped, bound, or put in a three-ring notebook. Turning pages can be distracting and very noisy, especially if you are working in front of a microphone.
7. Trust your visuals. Look at your audience. Don't keep looking around to see which slide is on the screen.
8. Stay with what you have rehearsed successfully. Ideas may come to you during the presentation, but let them slide by, unless you are a seasoned presenter, because they may lead you into blind alleys that are difficult to get out of.

   There is one exception to this, and that is if you are getting negative vibes from your audience—then you don't have much to lose by editing on the spot.

   But first, be sure you are really getting bad signals from a large number of the audience. To do that you must . . .
9. Learn to read your audience. Listen to what your audience is telling you:

Good signs:

Nods, smiles	Note taking
Leaning forward	Applause
Eye contact (watching you or your visuals)	Laughter (only if you have said something funny)

Neutral signs:

Frowns or sober expressions. As discussed above, these often signal concentration, not disapproval.

Bad signs:

Yawning	Looking at watches
Staring out windows	Side discussions
Idly thumbing through handouts or other materials	Fidgeting
Falling asleep	Heading for the door

To adjust for bad signs, you may want to speed up your delivery, leave out some sections of secondary importance, give the audience a one-minute stand-up break at the end of a section, or quickly summarize, close, and get off.

10. Keep your paws off the podium. In fact, don't even use a podium if you can avoid it. But if you do, don't lean on it, hold on to it, drum your fingers on it, pound on it, or even touch it. Stand back from it and use your hands, not for holding on but for gesturing to help bring your speech alive. Nothing looks sloppier than a speaker hunched over the podium, holding on to the sides like he or she was whistling down White Face Mountain on a bobsled.

Build parts into your talk that will take you out from behind the podium. Come out to discuss charts, slides, or handouts that are self-cueing. Come out for questions and answers and discussions. When you are out, stay out for a while; don't keep darting back and forth.

11. Speak in a normal voice when using a microphone. It's designed to do the amplification, so don't yell into it. Don't even speak directly into it—speak across it—otherwise it will pop and hiss. Keep the mike between you and the audience. If you want to look toward the right side of the audience, move your body to the left, don't just turn your head or you will be talking into space and the mike won't pick you up. Better yet, use a lavaliere microphone. It will always be in the right place and will give you freedom to come out from behind the podium and move around. Tuck the cord under the back of your belt so you won't trip over it.

12. Use your hands. Gesture. Gesturing helps punctuate your talk and keeps you from standing like a wooden Indian or from rattling change in your pockets. Keep your hands about chest high and turn your palms outward slightly (you'll tend to use your hands more if you do this). Try these simple gestures—build them into your next speech.

Message You Want to Convey	Gesture to Use
Welcome, we're in this together	Hands forward, palms up.
Numbers: first point, second point, etc.	Hold up appropriate number of fingers.
Big	Spread hands wide (keep elbows in so you don't flap your clothing).
Small	Hold hands up almost together in front of your face.
Thinking	Point to your head.
You, the audience	Point to them.
Me, the speaker	Point to yourself.
We won! We can do it!	Make a fist and punch the air over your head or clasp your hands over your head.

Remember, facial expressions are gestures too. Be sure yours fit the tone of what you are talking about. Don't smile, for instance, if you are giving a eulogy for your dear, departed boss, even if you are stepping into his job.

Watch standup comics, announcers, actors and actresses (including those in commercials), and politicians (most of whom are trained speakers). See how they use their hands and facial gestures. You may not have even noticed it much before, but think how flat their presentations would be without gestures.

13. Don't use nonwords or meaningless expressions such as "ah," "oh," "you know," and "like." They are annoying and distracting. Don't feel as though there has to be constant sound coming from you—there doesn't. In fact, a pause can help add variety and give the audience time to think about what you just said. If you lose your place momentarily, don't worry about it. Just be quiet till you gather your thoughts, then go on.

14. Exaggerate words as you say them. Make your gestures broader than you think they should be. When you do, they will seem just right to the audience. If you don't, you will seem dull. Guilty of the management monotone. Many people read their scripts without varying their tone, pace, loudness, or emphasis, and without using gestures because they are afraid of looking like a nut. What they look like is statues. It's okay to exaggerate a little, ham it up. It will add life to your presentation. Slow down, speed up, pause for emphasis, draw out key words, reduce your voice almost to a whisper for very serious points, use facial expressions and gestures to animate the points you are making.

15. If you open the session to questions, follow these guidelines:
    - Be sure you have anticipated questions and researched the answers. Have co-workers think up possible questions, then make sure you have the answers.
    - Listen carefully to questions from the audience. Be sure you understand the question so you don't answer something that wasn't asked. (You'll be amazed, if you listen for it, how many times you'll hear this happen.) If you don't understand the question, ask for clarification.
    - In a large group, repeat the question for the audience. Say it in words as close as possible to those used by the questioner.
    - Acknowledge questions from many people. Don't let one or two monopolize if there are other hands in the air. Say, "Let's see, who hasn't had a chance yet?" and select someone who hasn't.
    - If you don't know the answer, say no. Don't try to bluff it. Keep in mind Mark Twain's comment: "I was gratified to be able to answer promptly and I did. I said I didn't know."
    - Don't let people box you in with leading questions. If someone asks, "In the situation you described, would it be better to fire the employee right away or wait thirty days?" You don't have to choose. Maybe you don't like either alternative. The right answer for you could be: "I wouldn't fire the employee at all. Here's what I'd do . . ." If so, that's what you should say.
16. If you plan to lead a discussion as part of your presentation, see Chapter 7 for guidance on how to handle groups.
17. When the session is over, don't rush off. (Especially if you have a lavaliere microphone pinned to your lapel. You'll pull the cord out by the roots.) Stand still and look around. Savor the moment. It's over and you made it. Thank the audience, collect your papers, smile, and then step down.

4. HOW TO HANDLE NERVOUSNESS, MAKE ANXIETY WORK FOR YOU

Have you heard people say they would rather die than speak in front of a group? That's not so farfetched as you might think, because surveys have shown that public speaking leads the list of people's worst fears by quite a bit. Twice as many mention speaking as their top fear as list death.

It is normal to be nervous about speaking to groups. Even some professional actors who spend their lives in front of the camera don't like to speak live before groups. George C. Scott said in a *Playboy* interview, "I cannot speak in public extemporaneously. I'm a nervous wreck. I shake all over like a dog shaking water off." But anxiety and the adrenaline it produces can actually help you if you channel it correctly.

Think about what makes you nervous. It's fear of not doing well, of embarrassing yourself in front of everybody, isn't it?

The best way to reduce that kind of stress is to *work hard enough preparing your talk that you know it is dynamite,* and to *practice it long enough that you are comfortable and confident* with it.

Here are other tactics to use.

1. Don't get to your speaking location too far ahead of time. You'll only sit around and sweat. If you can't help getting there early, keep busy. Set up, practice, do some unrelated work, or find someone to talk with.
2. Warm up. This will give you something to do and loosen up the old vocal cords so you won't sound like you've been breathing helium when you first begin.
3. If there are others speaking, too, and if you have a choice, try to go on first. Then you won't have to sit and worry about how good the others are, and how calm they are (they actually aren't but nervousness usually isn't very noticeable to others).
4. As noted above, don't let those somber faces out in the audience throw you. Expect it. They love you—they're just concentrating.
5. Pretend you are giving your talk to one friend in the audience. If you don't have a friend in the audience, visualize one there.
6. Tell yourself, "This will be over pretty soon. Nothing is going to jump up and bite me, so it won't hurt. I might as well enjoy it. Besides, I've been through worse things than this and done them successfully."
7. Remember, the audience is with you. They want you to succeed. No one wants to sit through a dull, amateurish speech given by someone who is insecure and scared to death. They want you to be confident, animated, interesting, and enjoyable. So be that way.
8. The best outlet for your nervous energy is your hands. If you use them right (see gestures above), you can add lots to your talk, while discharging giant blue sparks of high voltage inside you. Any movement helps. However, don't:

    - Pace. Moving about is okay and adds to interest. Methodical pacing is distracting.
    - Rock from side to side.

- Rattle change.
- Fidget.
- Scratch.

To avoid any of these, plant your feet in a comfortable stance, get your hands up and use them to gesture.

For more on handling stress, see Chapter 17.

5. HOW TO DESIGN AND USE HIGH-IMPACT VISUAL AIDS

Visual aids—slides, overhead transparencies, flip charts, films, and videotapes—will help your audience keep track of where you are in your talk, will make it more lively and interesting for them, and, best of all, will help them remember what you said. We've already seen that visual aids can more than double the attention span. They can also boost retention by as much as six times.

Designing Visual Aids

Include only one idea per visual.

Use only key words or symbols, don't try to capture long quotes, text, or complex forms. Use headlines and show only as much detail as you need to get your point across. Eliminate every word or line that isn't necessary.

Use five to six lines per visual at the most.

Design visuals to follow your talk exactly. Don't have one set of words, or sequence of words, on the visual and another in your script.

Use two simple visuals rather than one complex one.

Charts are better than words.

If you want to show	Use a
A trend	Graph
Comparisons	Bar chart
Relationship to whole	Pie chart

Pictures are better than words. Color is better than black and white. But don't make every word or line a different color. That may be pretty, but it will be hard to read. Use one or two dominant colors per visual.

Always use words that are familiar to your audience.

Using Visual Aids

Plan your room arrangement so everybody can see your visuals. Theater style, U-shaped, or V-shaped arrangements are best. Stay away from round tables, or very long tables.

Make sure you have indicated in your script or notes where your visuals should appear.

Types of Visuals	Advantages	Disadvantages
Slides	colorful can show scenes as well as words easily changed, stored	need photography skills need special equipment for closeup can get out of sequence have to show with lights out
Films, Videotape	action, interest-getters	can't revise; they get outdated quickly expensive to make or buy need equipment and expertise to produce can't be done quickly
Overheads	easy to make simple to show can put notes on borders can show with lights on can write on	professional quality involves some expertise can be boring and colorless
Flip charts	easy to make flexible can pin on wall and keep in front of group can prepare ahead, or use to record information on the spot don't need projector	tend to get worn and tattered can't use with large groups bulky to carry and store

Don't read your visuals to the audience. Let them follow along watching the visuals as you give your talk. If you use charts or graphs, you may have to explain them.

Be careful not to stand in front of your visuals. Stand to one side so everyone can see.

Sometimes, use visuals for humor or to break up your talk. Throw in a surprise now and then.

Don't use slides, films, or any visuals that require a dark room for meetings right after lunch. Everyone will fall asleep.

Use flip charts for recording key discussion points.

The chart on page 102 shows common types of visual aids and their advantages and disadvantages.

6. HOW TO EVALUATE PRESENTATIONS AND LEARN FROM THEM

Obviously, you won't become a spellbinder the first time out. Giving great presentations takes practice and experience.

A good way to build your skill is to pay close attention to presentation techniques. Use the Presentation Analysis form, following, to:

- Evaluate your own performance (objectively, of course) after you've given a presentation.
- Have others evaluate your performance.
- Evaluate others as they give presentations. You should become critically aware of how every presenter you see handles his or her speech. This is true of live talks as well as the constant parade of presentations you see on TV.

Good luck with your presentations. I hope they become a joy rather than a burden, and your new skills will quickly help you stand out from the pack.

PRESENTATION ANALYSIS

PRESENTER: ____________________ TOPIC: ____________________

REVIEWED BY: ____________________ DATE: ____________________

Content	Very Good	Okay	Needs Work	How to Improve
Opening (use of "grabber")				
Purpose clearly stated				
Main points easy to follow				
Flow logical				
Topic right for audience				
Benefits to audience stated				
Interest level				
Content				
Length				
Closing				
Other ____________				
Delivery				
Animation				
Personal warmth				
Enthusiasm, confidence				
Use of podium				
Use of microphone				
Control of nervousness				
Eye contact				
Gestures				

Variation of pace,
tone, loudness,
emphasis

Use of visuals

The Best Part of the Presentation Was:

____

____

____

Areas that Could Be Improved Are:

____

____

____

7. There Goes the Afternoon: How to Run Meetings That Get Results

We'd better get started. I'm sure Joe will get here, but we can't wait any longer. We're fifteen minutes late already. Well, I had to look all over for topics for our monthly meeting but I found some. Let's see . . . oh, I want to read a report by the systems people on their plans for the next five years. That will interest some of you. Then, let's see . . . we have to decide on the consultant's recommendation and I want your honest opinions on that. I have some pretty strong feelings about it, as you know, but I'd really like to hear how you feel . . .

Beginning of a meeting led by Allen Martinson, Continental Quiche Corp.

A friend of mine who works for an insurance company has two rules about meetings:

1. Never call a meeting.
2. Never go to one.

He makes exceptions, of course, but that's exactly the point. Instead of thinking of meetings as the normal everyday way of doing business, he thinks of them as the unusual, something to do only after all else has failed.

I know other people who will do almost anything to get out of meetings. They will lie, cheat, make up lame excuses, call in sick, or plead burn-out. Meetings have a bad reputation and deserve every bit of it.

WHAT'S WRONG WITH MEETINGS?

Several thousands of years ago, Og, a caveman, called the first meeting. He was hungry and wanted some tiger stroganoff, but knew he couldn't hunt tiger all by himself. So he got his friends together to get their help. He hardly got started when Roc interrupted with a story of a great gal he'd just clubbed. Klu wanted to get back to a nap he'd been taking and wasn't listening to either of them. He kept yawning and checking the position of the sun. Ek had built a fire on the first try that morning and wanted to talk about that.

After an hour Og knew he wasn't getting anywhere. They hadn't really talked much about tiger hunting and they'd decided nothing. So he thanked them and went back to his cave. Have you ever been to a meeting like that? Meetings haven't changed much, have they?

Meetings are a lousy way of getting things done, and yet the average manager spends thirty-five to fifty-five percent of his or her time on meetings. Even the top brass can't escape. A recent survey showed that senior managers spend just short of half their time in meetings. And I'll bet a third of all that meeting time is wasted.

Why? Well, here are a few reasons . . . you may be able to add to this list from your own experience.

- People don't know what the meeting is for.
- No one is clear about what's to be accomplished.
- There's no agenda or timetable.
- Meetings run too long.
- They are boring.
- Discussion wanders and is unfocused.
- People tell "war stories."
- There are too many items to be covered.
- No one wants to talk about the real problem.
- Some participants aren't interested, shouldn't be there.
- There are too many distractions, interruptions.
- Visuals and handouts are nonexistent or poorly done.

- People are uncooperative.
- The boss has already decided on a course of action. The meeting is a rubber stamp.
- People attack each other's ideas.
- Meetings are used when other methods would be better.

Peter Drucker tells us, "There are a number of common symptoms of poor organization . . . first, the symptom of too many meetings attended by too many people . . . The human dynamics of meetings are so complex as to make them very poor tools for getting any work done."*

Does that mean all is hopeless? That you have to go on wasting your time in meetings or lying to get out of them? No. There are things you can do to make meetings useful and effective . . . to make them very powerful tools for getting work done. Meetings can be important personal opportunities for you. They are ready-made vehicles for your personal P.R., where you can show off your knowledge, judgment, and leadership skills. Meetings, believe it or not, can help you move out ahead of the pack. Let's look at the four keys to dynamite meetings: planning, informing, conducting, and following up.

PLANNING. If you were to ask most people what a meeting is, they'd say, "A bunch of people sitting around a table discussing things." That's the image that comes to mind. And, unfortunately, that's where most of us start out with meetings . . . in the actual meeting itself, skipping a very vital step—planning.

Meeting planning is not some academic exercise, but a critical step if you want to put together a meeting that gets results. It works. It makes your meeting work.

Planning does not have to be a lengthy time-consuming affair. For simple meetings you can do it on the train on the way to work or in a few minutes at your desk.

Planning is a matter of thinking things through: what (is the meeting for)? who (should be there)? and how (should the meeting be run)?

At first glance, you might say, "Heck, I know those things without thinking about them," but chances are you don't. Let's find out. Pick a meeting you will be running in the near future, and we'll work our way through the Meeting Planning Guide below.

* Drucker, Peter. *Management: Tasks, Responsibilities, Practices.* New York: Harper & Row, 1974, p. 548.

MEETING PLANNING GUIDE

Date of Meeting ______________ Time ________ Place ______________

- WHAT is the purpose of the meeting? ______________________________

What do you want to happen as a result of the meeting?

Could that result be accomplished another way? ☐ YES ☐ NO

If yes, how?
- ☐ telephone call
- ☐ memo or report
- ☐ teleconference
- ☐ stand-up meeting
- ☐ other ______________________________

- WHO will attend?

Attendees	Possible Problems (feelings about the issue, levels, cliques, etc.)

How to overcome problems: ______________________________

Is the list right? Should others be invited? Some scratched from list?

Invite	Scratch

- HOW will the meeting be held?

  What room layout will you use? (sketch below)

  What's the best format?

  - ☐ presentation
  - ☐ discussion
  - ☐ creative problem solving
  - ☐ small groups
  - ☐ combination
  - ☐ other

  What materials/equipment do you need?

TYPE	SPECIFIC LIST
Audiovisual	
Handouts	
Flip charts, chalkboards, etc.	
Other	

____

How will you open the meeting? ______________________________

____

____

____

Start with "What." Describe the purpose of the meeting. Is it to get a go-ahead on a project, solve a problem, share information, or follow up? Or is it to get budget approval, build ownership by involving people, test the waters, get feedback, or what? Decide what the purpose of your meeting is and write it in the space provided.

If you have trouble doing that, you may want to scrap your meeting. If there is no clear purpose for a meeting, don't have one. If your meeting is a WAHI (we've always had it), cancel it. Stop having weekly or monthly staff meetings if there is no real agenda. Call meetings when you absolutely have to have them, not just because they're on the calendar.

Now fill in your "Wanted Outcome" . . . what you hope will happen as a result of the meeting. If you can't think of an outcome, or don't think that the meeting will lead to a worthwhile outcome, don't have a meeting.

Before you decide to hold a meeting, think about other ways to get your work done. Check them off on your planning guide: telephone calls, memos, teleconferences, five-minute stand-up meetings.

Don't hold a meeting:

- If you can't describe what it's for or its outcome.
- If there is an alternative.
- When you have no time to plan or prepare.
- When key participants aren't available (you'll have to hold *another* meeting for them).
- When cost (time) outweighs the benefits. (Think of your last meeting and who was there. Take a guess at the hourly pay for each, multiply by the number of hours the meeting lasted and add it all up. Was it worth it?)

If you are comfortable with the purpose and outcome you described, then go ahead with your plan. Arrange the date and place of the meeting and fill them in at the top of the page.

Then decide *WHO* will attend. Write down the names of all those you think should be at your meeting. Opposite each, note potential problems. How does each feel about the issue to be discussed? What are their levels . . . will one tend to dominate because of his or her position in the organization? What does each know about the issue . . . how much can they contribute? How can each influence the possible outcome you have in mind?

If there appear to be possible problems, think through how you can overcome them and note that in the space provided. For instance, if one person will easily sway the whole group with his or her opinion, should you meet separately with that key influencer ahead of time to make sure you get support?

Look at your list. Are these the people you need to get the outcome you want? Do you need *all* of them? Remember what Peter Drucker said about too many people at meetings. Are there others who should be there and aren't on your list? Make your adjustments.

Now it's time to think about *HOW*. This includes:

When to have the meeting. Here are some thoughts. Avoid holding a meeting right after lunch . . . people go to sleep. If your meeting is long, schedule it before lunch or before quitting time. It's amazing how fast people come to agreement when they're hungry or have to catch a bus. Pick a time and enter it at the top of the guide.

Where to have it. Consider the best layout. (See Exhibit 1, Meeting Room Layouts.)

What's the best format? These are some choices:

Presentation from the front of the room followed by questions and answers is best for straight information giving. See Chapter 6 on how to give presentations.

Discussion is best when you want agreement on an issue and you want people to feel ownership in that agreement.

Creative Problem Solving is best when you want lots of new ideas or original solutions. See Chapter 4 for information on creativity.

Small Groups are good when there are several topics to be discussed (each group can take one or two and then report back) and when you want very active participation (people tend to jump in more in smaller groups than in large ones).

A Combination of two or more can be good if you have several purposes for your meeting. You might want to start with a presentation, for example, to convey some background information, then break into small groups to get people actively discussing issues.

What handouts, visuals, and equipment you will need. Decide in advance and list them on the guide. Check them prior to the meeting. If you are using slides, for instance, run through them quickly right before the meeting. For ideas on the use of audiovisual equipment, see Chapter 6.

How to open the meeting. Try to find a "grabber" to start the meeting. Use humor if you are comfortable with that approach; otherwise, use an interesting fact, a surprise, or a short movie on the topic. People expect the worst from meetings and are easily delighted. Once you have their attention, hit them with a hoped-for outcome they all like: "Just think, if by the end of this meeting we could . . ." That will get them all working hard to help you make it happen.

INFORMING. One problem with meetings is that participants often don't know what the meeting is about and aren't sure why they have been asked to be there. That prevents them from preparing for the meeting ahead of time and may lead to some hostility. How often do you go to meetings without knowing much more than what's marked on your calendar? How do you feel about that?

Prepare and send out an agenda ahead of time, using the Meeting Agenda Format. When putting your agenda together, involve key people who will be at the meeting. Ask them if they feel your purpose is on target, and what result they hope for. They will feel ownership and will help you during the meeting.

Also, to gain even greater commitment, ask key people to prepare and lead parts of the meeting.

When you have completed your agenda, make notes on your copy and use it as a guide for leading the meeting.

Attach background materials you want participants to read before the meeting (keep readings short—you can't expect people to wade through volumes to prepare for your meeting). Don't cover anything in a meeting

MEETING AGENDA FORMAT

Date of Meeting __________ Time __________ Time __________

Meeting Arranged by: ____________________ Phone __________

Attending: ______________ ______________

______________ ______________

______________ ______________

______________ ______________

Purpose: ______________________________

Desired Result: ______________________________

____

____

AGENDA

Time	Topic*	Led by

* Put urgent/difficult topics first. Add a descriptive word or phrase to indicate what will be done with each (discuss, decide, etc.).

that can be read ahead of time. If, when you get to the meeting, you suspect some haven't read the materials, just go ahead as if they had. They will next time.

Depending on the topics you are covering, it may not be necessary for every participant to be there for the entire meeting. If that is so, let participants know that although they are welcome to stay for the whole thing, if they're pressed for time, they can stop in for a portion of it.

CONDUCTING. When you call a meeting and take up others' time, you incur some heavy responsibilities to them and to yourself. Here are some very important Dos and Don'ts:

DO

- Try to get the most done in the least possible time.
- Start on time. Don't wait for stragglers (except the big boss—you might run a tight meeting, but you're not nuts). Waiting for latecomers punishes the people who got there on time.
- Restate the purpose of the meeting and the wanted outcome. Write it on a flip chart or chalkboard so everyone can see it. Ask the participants to add to it or modify it. Cover the agenda.
- Follow your agenda, keeping within the time allotted. As planned in your agenda, do the tough items first. People usually are more creative at the beginning of a meeting.
- At the start of each topic, remind the group of the time allotted. "We've set aside only fifteen minutes to talk about the Denver trip. Let's see how much we can cover in that time." When people know there's a time limit they'll work harder.
- If you are giving a presentation, make sure it is attention-getting and crystal clear, one that will motivate people to act. See Chapter 6 on how to give presentations.
- Manage the discussion:

  Keep everyone on the subject.

  Help everyone participate. You can do this by the skillful use of questions (See Exhibit 2, Questions).

  Control individual personalities (See Exhibit 3, Handling Individual Personalities in Meetings).

Protect ideas. Don't evaluate ideas and don't let others do it either. Ideas will flow much more freely if participants know their ideas are not going to be attacked.

Listen (See Chapter 11 on how to listen).

Ask for facts or explanations if statements are unclear.

Summarize periodically.

- Decide a course of action and get agreement on who does what and when.
- End the meeting on time.

DON'T

- Hog the meeting if the meeting is to get others' opinions.
- Wing it. (You'll waste everyone's time, including your own, if you don't plan and prepare.)
- Lose control and let the meeting wander.
- Kill ideas or let others criticize ideas.
- Schedule a meeting for longer than an hour, if you can possibly avoid it.
- Try to write things in a meeting. Group authorship is tedious and painful. Instead, write a draft, send it to everyone, and ask them to pencil in comments and send it back.
- Call a meeting to decide if the decision has already been made. Save everyone a lot of grief and just tell them what the decision is.
- Try to manipulate the group. You'll never get away with it. Don't use leading questions. Don't write down your interpretation of comments and opinions. Write down what was said. If you aren't clear on the meaning of what was said, ask.

FOLLOWING UP. Even if the people leave a meeting all juiced up, once they get back to their jobs, their regular work takes over, and end-of-meeting feelings fade quickly. What seems important when leaving the meeting room may be hard for most people to remember a week later.

Try to get a clear-cut statement of what the group wants to have happen as a result of the meeting—do this near the end of the meeting itself. You may want to write it on a flip chart or ask someone to take notes.

Then, soon after the meeting, send each participant a summary of what happened in the meeting and an action plan. Send copies to everyone else who has an interest in seeing those things happen. This will help keep memories fresh—and, besides, putting things in writing somehow makes them more official and harder to ignore.

In your summary of the meeting, include a copy of the agenda, a list of decisions that were made, an action plan, and the date of the next meeting, if there is one. Use the Meeting Follow-up Guide.

MEETING FOLLOW-UP GUIDE

MINUTES

Purpose of meeting ______________________________
When held ______________________________
Who attended ______________________________

____

____

Agenda (attached)
Summary of the issues ______________________________

____

____

What was decided: ______________________________

____

____

Next meeting: __________ Date: __________ Place: __________

ACTION PLAN:

WHAT WILL BE DONE   WHO WILL DO IT   BY WHEN

MEETING EVALUATION GUIDE

DATE: ______________ LEADER: ______________________________

PURPOSE OF MEETING: ______________________________________

	Yes	No	Opportunities for Improvement
1. Planning			
Was meeting well planned?			
Was meeting the best vehicle?			
Were right people there?			
2. Informing			
Was purpose clearly communicated?			
Was agenda complete (topics, timing, logical flow)?			

	Well Done	OK	Needs Work	Opportunities for Improvement
3. Conducting				
How well did leader keep to				

How good was presentation?				
confident delivery				
won over the group				
points clearly made				
use of visuals				
supporting assertions				
restated main points				
controlled anxiety				
How well was discussion managed?				
set climate for new ideas				
stayed on subject				
handled individual personalities				
use of questions to draw out/control group				
listened				
protected ideas				
encouraged group to build on ideas				
4. Action Plan and Follow-Up				
How clear was follow-up?				
action plan developed?				
How good were minutes?				

- Summarize just what was in the meeting. Keep your summary brief so people will read it—outline form is good.
- If there was disagreement, include opinions from both sides.
- Don't edit or interpret. Use people's comments and ideas as they were originally expressed.
- Try to make the summary interesting to read.
- Get it out as soon as possible after the meeting.

If you are really intent on improving your meetings, you should evaluate them. You can use the Meeting Evaluation Guide. Fill it out yourself, or have others fill it out and discuss it with you. It will help you take a hard look at how your meeting went and how you can improve in the future. You may also want to use this to train others in holding better meetings. As they begin thinking about the ways your meetings can be spruced up, they will also begin thinking about *their* meetings.

If you meet with a group on a regular basis, be sure to get them involved, using the Meeting Evaluation Guide. They will become more cooperative and understanding participants.

How to be a meeting participant. So far we have looked at skills of the meeting leader. It also takes skill to be an effective participant in meetings. Meetings can be a showcase for you, even as a participant. They give you a chance to show several others at once how astute you are and how well you operate in a group situation. Here are some thoughts that will help you, as a participant, take advantage of the special exposure meetings give you.

1. Always do your homework. Never go into meetings unprepared. If a meeting shows up on your calendar and you don't know anything more about it than the time and place, contact the leader, find out what he or she hopes will come out of the meeting and who else will be there. Ask if you can have handouts or reading material in advance. Research the topics. Get opinions of other people. Form your own opinions and back up arguments.
2. During the meeting express your thoughts, supported wherever possible with facts and figures. To talk in meetings, you may have to interrupt and jump in. Usually, you will have to carve out your own space; no one will call on you.
3. Keep on the subject. Don't introduce other agendas. Keep your comments brief, but long enough to establish your points.
4. Help the leader. When others get off on outside issues or begin telling

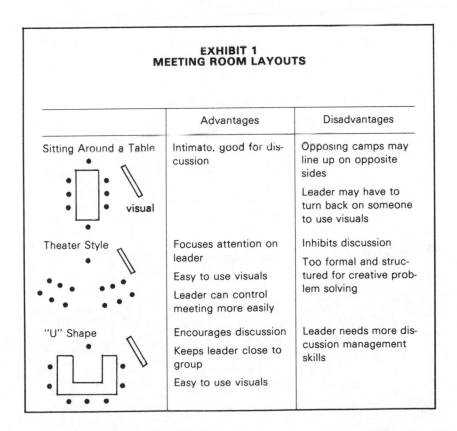

war stories, interrupt gently and say, "We're getting a little off the subject here, maybe we should get back to our topic." If someone tries to hog the floor, jump in and ask, "How do the rest of you feel?" Use all the tricks outlined in Exhibit 3, Handling Individual Personalities to help the leader. The leader may not know them.

If the leader doesn't give you a clear statement of what you are supposed to do after the meeting, try to get one from the group.

5. Protect ideas. Help the leader set an atmosphere where people will feel comfortable expressing ideas even if they aren't perfect. When someone begins attacking another's idea, say, "That idea probably has faults, Fred, most ideas do. Let's just let ideas come out for now and evaluate them later."
6. Mind your manners. Remember the meeting is your showcase. Don't attack others in public or embarrass them. That wouldn't build your image as a team player or one who has great interpersonal skills.

EXHIBIT 1
MEETING ROOM LAYOUTS

	Advantages	Disadvantages
Sitting Around a Table 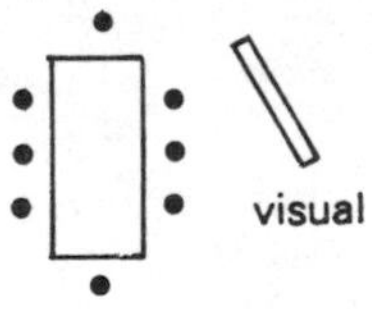	Intimate, good for discussion	Opposing camps may line up on opposite sides Leader may have to turn back on someone to use visuals
Theater Style 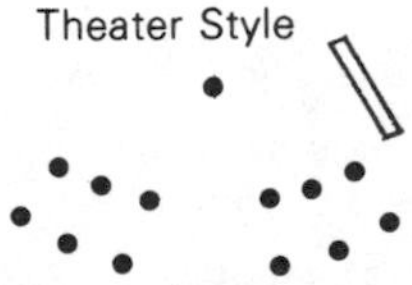	Focuses attention on leader Easy to use visuals Leader can control meeting more easily	Inhibits discussion Too formal and structured for creative problem solving
"U" Shape 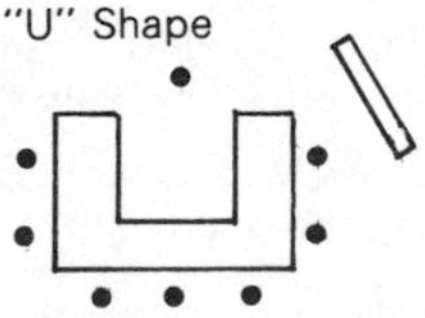	Encourages discussion Keeps leader close to group Easy to use visuals	Leader needs more discussion management skills

That's about it for meetings. All that may seem a lot to go through for something as simple as a meeting. The fact is, though, meetings aren't simple. They are very complex and to get them to work effectively takes time and effort. And practice. As you try out the techniques described here and get to know them better, they will take less and less time and after a while will become second nature to you.

Good use of meetings can help make you a hero in your organization. It is an *Upward Bound* skill you can't afford to be without.

EXHIBIT 2
QUESTIONS

Questions are important tools for the meeting leader. The best leaders use questions to stimulate discussion and to control the meeting. Study your meeting plan before the meeting. Think about who is attending and how they are likely to act. Plan questions beforehand that will help you get the right involvement by the participants and move the meeting in the direction you want it to go.

Questions That Influence How People Will Respond

Type of Question	Use To	Examples
OPEN (Often begin with WHY, WHAT, or HOW)	Get participant(s) to talk, expand on a point, and to stimulate discussion.	"What do you feel should be done?" "How does this proposal affect your operation?"
CLOSED (can be answered "Yes" or "No" or with single word)	Get specific information.	"Are you on schedule?" "Do you have anything to add to this?" "What date will the project be completed?"
OVERHEAD	Allow anyone to respond Get discussion going Generate ideas	"What thoughts do any of you have on that?" "Folks, what's our number one priority?"

Questions That Influence Who Will Respond

Type of Question	Use To	Examples
DIRECT	Get response from specific person Move discussion away from "takeover artist" Probe	"Sam, give us some background on this, will you?" "Sally, can you explain what the new problem involves?" "Mary, what's your opinion?"
RETURN	Pass on a participant's question to someone else To avoid answering the question yourself To get involvement of others To find out more about the question or what's behind it	"Fred, how do you feel about Jack's question? How do you see us handling that?" "I understand your question, Sue. I'd like to know how *you* feel about it." "Ed, since you brought it up, why don't you talk about it a bit?"

EXHIBIT 3
HANDLING INDIVIDUAL PERSONALITIES IN MEETINGS

Type	Characteristics	What to Do
SKEPTIC	runs down the group runs down purpose of meeting runs down values of others runs down task jokes aggressively	Get others to comment on his remarks. Let them handle it Build up confidence of group so his effect is lessened

EXHIBIT 3 (*Continued*)
HANDLING INDIVIDUAL PERSONALITIES IN MEETINGS

Type	Characteristics	What to Do
GLOOMY GUS	acts negatively resists kills ideas shows why it won't work holds onto ideas group has abandoned	Confront with "Let's get new ideas out and evaluate them later." "There are problems with all ideas but . . ." Ask what he likes about idea
TAKEOVER ARTIST	wants to lead has hidden agenda calls attention to self talks too much has answer for everything	Don't direct questions to him Direct questions to others Ask him to wait
SIDE-DISCUSSION SIDNEY	starts up own discussion with those sitting nearby	Interrupt him and say, "Sid, I don't want to miss anything. Do you have some thoughts for the group?"
WANDERER	tells war stories gets on other topics confuses discussion with extraneous issues	Say, "That's a good topic (story) but we're here today to talk about ______. Let's get back on topic." Direct topic-related question to him
BURT REYNOLDS	has "who cares" attitude makes a point of noninvolvement horseplays jokes	Ask direct topic-related questions Ask for advice Praise something he has said or done
SHY CY	quiet, nonparticipative unsure of self	Brief beforehand Ask direct question and help Praise ideas that he gives or use as example

Getting What You Want

8. **How Much?** How to Negotiate So Everyone Comes Out Ahead

"Boss, I really deserve a raise."

"Son, this country deserves an honest politician, but we aren't getting any."

Conversation overheard at
International Anamoly, Inc.

Negotiation is not just something labor and management do at contract time. People negotiate every day for all kinds of things. Every time you try to make a change, get someone to act, or make things better for yourself, you negotiate. You negotiate with your boss, co-workers, subordinates, spouse, friends, salespeople, and customers. You negotiate to change a meeting date or to get a discount, faster service, a better restaurant table, or more budget money. You negotiate housework, vacations, what to have for dinner, and who will take the dog out. You haggle with all kinds of people, in all kinds of situations, all the time. Anytime you want to make something happen that involves other people, you end up negotiating. You negotiate so often you may not even realize you're doing it. Because negotiating is so vital to your success in your work and in the world, it has to be included in our list of *Upward Bound* skills.

Think back on the last few weeks. Using the Negotiation Chart below,

NEGOTIATION CHART

(1) WHAT I WANTED	(2) FROM WHOM	(3) WHAT I TRIED (My Approaches)	(4) WHAT HAPPENED	(5) WHAT I SHOULD HAVE DONE

describe three negotiations you initiated. Try to pick three in which you didn't do too well.

In column 1, indicate what it was you wanted; in column 2, who you wanted it from; in column 3, how you tried to get it; and in column 4, what happened. Leave column 5 blank for now, and we will come back to it later.

How did you feel about negotiating when you were doing it? Was it fun, or was it a stressful experience? Afterward, did you feel satisfied and proud, or frustrated and angry? Negotiating can and should be fun and rewarding. But it is only if you know how to do it. That's what we'll look at in this chapter.

TYPES OF NEGOTIATION

Either you get what you want or you don't, and, if you get what you want, somebody else has to give it up. You gain a yard, the other guy loses a yard. That's negotiation, right?

That is one type of negotiation, all right, and many people who are naïve about negotiating or just plain sadistic use it, but there is another type, more effective, where both parties come out better off. I call it problem-solving negotiation.

Here's an example. You and Sam have just been promoted to jobs of equal level. Between you, you will be running a branch office. You have sales and marketing and Sam has administration. In the space your facility occupies, there is a corner office. You both want it.

You: Sam, I ought to have that office. I've got customers coming in and we have to make a good impression on them.

Sam: Yeah, I know, but you're on the road half the time. Why let that space sit empty? Anyhow, I've been with the company longer and should have first choice.

You: Well, it looks like we'll have to work out of our cars until we find some way to settle this.

Looks bleak, doesn't it? After all, there's only one corner office. But wait. Let's use a problem-solving approach: What is it that you and Sam want? The corner office, sure. But beyond that. The view? Status? Central location? Comfort? What is it about the corner office that turns you on? Is that the same as what Sam likes about it? It might not be and you had better find out, because that could help lead to a solution. Let's say you ask Sam:

You: Sam, why do you want the corner office?

Sam: I don't care about the view. But I do want the people here—after all, most of the staff report to me—to know I'm not a second-class executive. Besides, I can watch the people, see everything that's going on, from there.

Once you know what both parties really want, what their needs are, you can begin to do some creative thinking about a solution.

Your needs	Sam's needs
to impress customers	to be thought of as your equal
	to be able to see what's going on in the office

Now, what kinds of ideas could we come up with?

- Build yourself a Taj Mahal near the reception area and give the corner office to Sam.
- Build Sam an office near to and the same size as the corner office, with windows looking out over the entire area.
- Split the corner office in half, extend each half to neighboring offices (A).
- Share the office. You get it when you're in town. Sam other times.
- Move to another facility with two corner offices.
- Do away with offices altogether and use open landscaping.
- Turn the corner office into a conference room and you and Sam take the offices alongside of it.
- Have a drawing with all employees present to see who gets the office, so everyone knows it was assigned by chance, not rank.

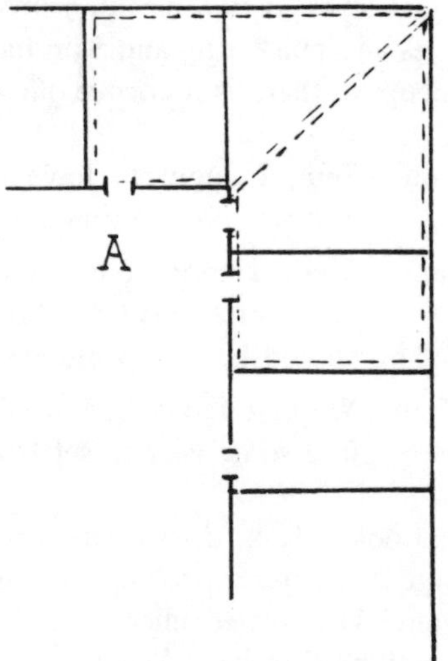

DEFINITION OF NEGOTIATION

Surprise! Negotiation is not—or should not be—all screaming and threats. It is not table pounding, power plays, and manipulation. It is not a hypertensive experience guaranteed to send your stress-o-meter past 1000. Effective negotiation should be a process in which two or more parties use a problem-solving approach to build something better for all.

That doesn't mean you are not going to drive a hard bargain to get what you want, or won't be willing to take any concessions you are offered. It does mean you will go into your negotiation using tough, effective techniques that will enable you to control the process and lead it toward the outcome you want, but you'll do it with problem-solving methods that will help you bargain more like a diplomat than a tank commander.

TEN PRINCIPLES OF NEGOTIATION

1. In most cases there is a solution that can benefit everyone. Always go into a negotiation using a problem-solving approach, looking for ways both sides can be better off. Don't think in terms of you and your opponent. Think of you and the other problem solver (OPS).
2. Anything can be negotiated. Don't just accept the established order: "That's the rule," or "That's the way we've always done it." Rules are made by people; people can change them. A sign on the wall, a printed policy, a price tag, instructions from the president, budgets, salaries—none of these are inviolate. They all can be changed if you want to take the time and energy to do it. Anything and everything is up for grabs.
3. To get anyone to sit still for a serious discussion, you first have to get his or her attention. You do that by letting that person know you can help or hurt him or her in some way or another. Since our focus here is on something better for everyone, you will emphasize how you can help. Then you will not only get attention, but receptive, positive attention.
4. Needs are seldom what they first seem to be. What the OPS says he or she wants may not be what he or she really wants.
5. It's always better to negotiate for someone else rather than for yourself. Or, it's always better to have someone negotiate for you. That way the decision maker is removed from the actual discussion. You can always say, "Charlie would never go for that," which is easier than saying, "I don't go for that," and besides, Charlie is not there so no one can work on changing his mind. Or you can use Charlie as a delaying tactic—"Let me get back to you after I've talked with Charlie." On the other hand, *you* don't want to negotiate with a second party; you want to bargain with the person who can make the decision. Find out beforehand who that is and try to meet with that person, not his or her agent.

6. Always go into any negotiation with more than one option. If you have only one option, then you are apt to care too much, want it too badly, and give away too much to get it. "Ed, I really think I should go on that Denver trip." "I know you should, but you're spread pretty thin as it is. You've got that Wart Remover ad campaign to finish." "I know, but I really want that Denver trip. I'll work nights and weekends to get it done. I'll even cancel my vacation."

   "Well, I guess if you put that kind of extra time . . ."

   Cancel your vacation? Wanting to be part of the action in Denver is one thing—and pretty important to you. But was it important enough to cancel your vacation? Maybe that's giving up too much. Maybe other options would have been to:

   See if the whole Denver trip could be postponed.

   See if you could have accomplished the same thing by going to Denver after the Wart campaign was finished.

   Go to Cincinnati instead.

7. The amount of clout your OPS *thinks* you have can greatly influence the outcome of the negotiation. Clout comes not only from your position in the organization but also from other sources. You can establish clout (real or imagined) by showing that:

   Others like your idea and are on your side. It helps if they are high up in the company and/or experts in the field.

   You have the background and experience to be an expert yourself and therefore know what you're talking about.

   Company policy, traditions, and culture support you.

   Fairness dictates that you are right.

8. The more time you can get another party to invest in the discussion, the more he/she will want to get an agreement.
9. Agreements tend to be reached when you are running out of time. Try to schedule your discussions right before lunch, or last thing in the afternoon if you know the OPS has to catch a train (but watch it—if he or she doesn't, you may end up being there till nine o'clock).
10. The more you know about the OPS and his or her needs, hard as they may be to pin down, the better your chances of coming up with a great solution.

THE PROCESS OF NEGOTIATING

Although you may think of negotiating as nothing more than sitting down and discussing issues, there's more to it than that. There are five steps in the process:

1. Planning and preparing
2. Bidding
3. Discussing and compromising
4. Agreeing
5. Setting the stage for the future

Let's look at each.

Planning and Preparing

In your rush to get things done, you might be tempted to skip this step. Don't do it. Here's why. If you take the time to analyze where the OPS is coming from, and what his or her needs are, you can plan your "how can we help each other" approach much better.

Also, knowledge is power. The more you know about the issue to be discussed, the better chance you will have of overcoming the OPS's objections and showing how you can both benefit.

Be sure you know as much about the issue as the OPS does. That may mean asking him or her for information. If you can't find out what you want directly, go to others in the organization.

Always think in terms of the OPS and his or her point of view. What does the OPS really want? Don't forget psychological needs like ego and self-esteem. Think back on what the OPS has said or done in the past. Is there any history on this kind of issue? People are pretty predictable. Most are likely to do the same tomorrow as they did yesterday.

With all that in mind, fill out the Negotiation Plan before you go into your next negotiation.

The Negotiation Plan will help you put together a strategy for finding the kind of solutions that make everyone involved a winner. It will also help you understand and be more tolerant of the OPS's position. You'd better hope the OPS is filling out one too.

In column 1, write down what you want to accomplish. Try to dig for your real needs. You want the corner office—but think beyond that to *why* you want it. Underneath that, list other options you have if you don't get it.

In column 2, list the real goals of the OPS, as far as you can find them out or guess at them.

In column 3, enter the similarities between your goals and attitudes and those of the OPS.

Then, knowing your own goals and those of the OPS, and the similarities between them, go to column 4 and think of ways you can build on similarities and use a problem-solving approach to look for solutions that will benefit both of you.

Here are some thoughts on planning and preparing:

1. When planning your negotiation, arrange to hold it on your home ground, if possible. That will make you feel more secure and give you a little extra clout just because it's your turf.
2. Always negotiate face-to-face, not on the telephone. That's especially true if the OPS calls you and wants to bargain. You don't have time to prepare, but the OPS may be well prepared. Calls don't give you much time to think or do calculations. Phone calls seem to make it more urgent to make up your mind. If the OPS calls you, say you are tied up and will call back. Call back after you have done your preparation. On the other hand, phone negotiations can work in your favor if *you* prepare and *you* make the call. Just remember, before you use the phone, it's easier for the OPS to say no on the phone than in person.

   If you do call, follow up with a memo of what was discussed. Write it yourself so you can use your own interpretation.
3. Go into every negotiation with high goals. Assume it will be successful and you'll both come out better. Get into the problem-solving frame of mind early, during preparation, and stay there.
4. To the extent possible, start building the problem-solving relationship during the preparation, even before you sit down to talk, by sharing some information with the OPS and telling the OPS you need his or her help.

Bidding

When you first begin your discussion, state what it is that you want to accomplish. Tell the OPS you want to find a way both of you can benefit by your getting it. That's where the OPS's help is needed—ask for it.

Remember these things:

- Start high. A low opening position on your part will give the OPS the idea you don't want much and aren't really serious.

NEGOTIATION PLAN

(1)	(2)	(3)	(4)
What do I want? What other options do I have?	What does the OPS want? What are his/her real goals? What is OPS's attitude likely to be on this?	What similarities are there in our goals and attitudes?	Building on similarities and using a problem-solving approach, what sort of answers can we come up with that will be better for each of us?

- Once you have told the OPS what you want, he or she will probably give you an opinion on it—it could range all the way from "fine, go ahead," in which case there won't be any need for the negotiation, to "not over my dead body," which might indicate the OPS doesn't care for the idea. That sounds funny, but remember, his/her initial emotional reaction might be a misdirection to get you to change your proposal, delay it, or otherwise gain some advantage. The OPS may give you reasons for his or her position. Don't automatically assume they are true. If you believe that they are, you'll be boxed in by them. Whatever the reaction, you'll have to judge what it means in terms of the gap between your position and the OPS's and how much territory you'll have to cover.

  Try to understand the OPS's point of view. Ask questions to clarify; tell the OPS you understand and paraphrase what he or she has told you to prove it. At the same time . . .

- Don't give away anything about your position you don't have to. Don't ever say, "I'll be ruined without this and I need it at any cost," even if that's true. It's better to let the OPS think you have lots of other options.

  Don't tell the OPS what you will do if you don't get what you want. Let him or her wonder and worry a little.

- Always leave the OPS an out. Never get into a take-it-or-leave-it situation.

Discussing and Compromising

Once you have established your positions, you can get down to the hard work of trying to get each other to move and narrow the gap between you. Follow these suggestions:

- Discuss issues on which you're pretty sure you'll agree first. That will get them out of the way and establish an atmosphere of agreement. It will also get the OPS to invest some time in the discussion before getting to the tough part. Having made that investment, he or she will be less likely to say "the hell with it" and walk out.
- Generate as many alternative solutions as you can between you. Get the OPS involved in the problem-solving spirit early in your discussion. Use Chapter 4 to help you find creative new alternatives. When you have identified many options, you can begin to sort through them, find ones that seem to satisfy both you and the OPS, and start to work out ways to use one or more of them.

- Try not to make the first concession. Let the OPS do that. If you wait him or her out and the OPS makes the first move, you'll have a psychological advantage and also know how much the OPS is willing to move. If the OPS makes a big first concession, you'll know he or she will make others. If, in our example above, Sam had said, "I really want the corner office, but you've got a point about the customers. Why don't we agree you can use the office any day you've got a customer coming in, then let's talk about who has it the rest of the time," you would know right away that, under certain conditions, Sam would be willing to give up the office and that's important.
- When you do make concessions, make small ones.
- Use questions to direct the OPS and get him or her to go in the direction you want. See Chapter 7 for information on how to use questions. Ask lots of questions during the discussion to get information. You may get more than you thought you would. Even dumb questions can get the OPS to tell you a surprising amount.
- As you and the OPS are talking, watch out for verbal and nonverbal clues to his or her real feelings. "Oh, that reminds me," or another offhand comment may precede some very important thought. "To be honest about it," sometimes leads to a statement that is pure fantasy. Sitting forward can indicate real interest; staring out the window, none at all.
- As you go along, pause to summarize where you've been and point out what you've agreed on.
- Sometimes it helps to shut up. Silence can make the OPS nervous and may influence him or her to say something to fill the void—something he or she didn't especially want to tell you.
- Don't let your own needs get in your way. If you are feeling pressure about being late for another meeting and want to get agreement in a hurry, ask yourself if it is necessary to settle today or would tomorrow be just as good. If you have to settle today, can you miss that other meeting, postpone it, or get back with the OPS after the meeting is over? Be patient. Always ask yourself, "Should I hold off now and wait to get a greater gain later?"
- If you come to a point you can't agree on, pass it by and get onto more common ground. Say, "Let's sleep on that one and try it again tomorrow."
- As you are going through the give-and-take of the discussion, keep thinking, "How can I help the OPS save face if he or she makes a concession?" Sometimes the OPS won't give ground only because it

would harm his or her self-esteem. Keep searching for ways to protect his or her ego.

Agreeing

At some point in your discussions, you should come to an agreement. If you have used a good problem-solving approach, you and your OPS should both be better off than you were when you started.

Always paraphrase what you think you've agreed to and ask the OPS if that's his or her understanding.

Setting the Stage for the Future

If the issue is an important one, follow up with a memo thanking the OPS for his or her cooperation and restating your perception of what you agreed to.

No matter what has happened during the discussion, try to end on a positive note, so that your next discussion will be that much easier. That may be hard to do if fistfights have broken out, but try.

Then, the next time you come up against the OPS, you can say, "Hi, Sam, let's talk this out. We got into it pretty heavy last time, remember? But we came out well and I expect we will again."

So there you have it. Remember, go for the problem-solving approach and try to get the OPS to work with you to find a solution that will be good for both of you.

Now that you have looked at negotiating in some new ways, go back to the Negotiation Chart you worked on at the beginning of the chapter and complete column 5, "What I Should Have Done." By looking at how you could have done better in past situations, you will be able to make better plans for the future.

Also, try using the Negotiation Checklist that follows to remind yourself of key actions in the process next time you are ready to sit down with an OPS to work out something important.

NEGOTIATION CHECKLIST

PLANNING AND PREPARING

- ☐ Use the problem-solving approach.
- ☐ Do your homework. Know as much as the OPS does.
- ☐ Identify what the OPS wants, as far as possible.
- ☐ Use the Negotiation Plan chart to decide:
  What you want.
  What options you have.
  What the OPS wants. His or her goals and attitudes on the issue.
  What similarities in your positions you can build on.
  What mutually beneficial answers you can come up with.
- ☐ Schedule meetings on your home turf, face-to-face.
- ☐ Set high goals. Assume you'll be successful.
- ☐ Set the problem-solving atmosphere early, before discussions begin, by involving the OPS.

BIDDING

- ☐ Ask the OPS for help. Set problem-solving atmosphere.
- ☐ Start high.
- ☐ Don't give away your limitations or boundaries.
- ☐ Leave the OPS an out, not "take it or leave it."
- ☐ Consider the OPS's reaction and what it means.
- ☐ Try to understand his or her point of view.

DISCUSSING AND COMPROMISING

- ☐ Discuss easy issues first.
- ☐ Don't make the first concession.
- ☐ Make small concessions when you do.
- ☐ Use questions to find what the OPS wants.
- ☐ Watch for verbal and nonverbal clues.
- ☐ Summarize periodically.
- ☐ Keep quiet sometimes.
- ☐ Don't let your own needs get in your own way.
- ☐ Help the OPS save face.

AGREEING

- ☐ Restate the agreement and ask the OPS if that is his or her understanding.

SETTING THE CLIMATE FOR THE FUTURE

- ☐ Follow up with a letter restating the agreement and setting a positive tone.

Building a Team

9. Tell Me about Yourself: How to Select and Train People to Get the Job Done

Manager: You'd be good at this kind of work, don't you think?

Applicant: Yes, sir.

Manager: Good, good. Glad to hear it. I like people with confidence.

Portion of an interview observed at Orlando Overkill Inc.

HOW TO SELECT GOOD PEOPLE

Whenever you hire someone to work for you, you have an opportunity to do something nice for yourself, to move yourself ahead by getting another person to help you and your department do good work.

The trouble is, if you are like most of us, you will be tempted to pick people for reasons other than their ability to do good work.

What's important to you in people? What do you like in applicants? A firm handshake, good personality, sincere smile, shined shoes? Those are all fine, and you should look for any or all of them if you want to, but be sure you base your final selection decision on something that really matters: specific evidence of the candidate's ability to do the job.

Doesn't every interviewer do that? Maybe you're thinking, "I do plenty of hiring, and I always check up on ability." Maybe you do, but plenty of employers don't. Every day thousands of candidates are selected or rejected based on characteristics that have nothing to do with the work itself—but have a lot to do with the personal whims of the hiring manager.

Recently I asked a group of managers from various companies what they would look for in a job applicant. In less than fifteen minutes they came up with the list below.

What Do You Look For in a Candidate?

Appearance
Motivation/drive
Education
Work experience
Career goals
Interest in my work/organization
Record of accomplishment
Positive attitude
Good health
Intelligence
Common sense/judgment
Tenacity
Enthusiasm
Ability to learn
Ability to get along with people, empathize
Leadership
Problem-solving ability
Follow-through
Good communication skills
Listening
High energy level
Writing ability
Speaking ability
Good memory
Team player
Organization sense
Creativity
Courage
Maturity
Calmness and composure
Persuasiveness
High standards, goals
Able to relocate
Ambition
Cheerfulness
Willpower
Tact
Resilience
Honesty
Logical mind
Foresight
Confidence

I told the group I was impressed with the volume of things they would look for, but asked, "What about demonstrated ability to do the job?"

"Oh, yeah," they all said.

I admit I led them into a trap. When asked that question, any of us would list similar skills. And many of those skills and personal qualities are very important—to certain jobs. Your list has to be tailored to each type of job you are filling.

When you convince yourself of that, and begin looking carefully at what it takes to do the specific job you are trying to fill and begin selecting applicants who have those skills, you will have an *Upward Bound* edge on your peers because you will be hiring better people and your work area will be producing better results.

Here's how to select good people.

Analyze the Job

Many managers begin the hiring process by getting resumes of lots of candidates and comparing them. Because you want to get ahead of the pack, you will begin by first deciding what skills are necessary to do the job well.

That means, before you even begin to look for applicants, before you write an ad or contact an employment agency or start calling around within your organization to find prospects, before you look at one resume, you will think about the job you are trying to fill and what it takes to do it successfully.

Here's how to analyze a job. Start by taking a sheet of paper and drawing a line down the center. Label the left column, "Major Responsibilities" and the right column, "Skills Needed." Call this your Job Responsibility/Skills Chart (or JR/S Chart for short). Then go to it. List the major responsibilities and rank them in order of importance, number 1 being the most important. Then list all of the skills needed to handle that responsibility well. (Note: Think of "skill" in a very broad sense to include knowledge, attitude, and personal qualities.)

Here's an example. Norman H. Hipple, sales manager for International Interstice Corporation, filled this chart out recently for a sales rep. job.

JOB RESPONSIBILITY/SKILLS CHART

JOB: Sales Rep.

MAJOR RESPONSIBILITIES	SKILLS NEEDED
1. Make effective product presentations.	Good attitude. Good appearance. Confident manner. Good speaking and presentation style. Good knowledge of product.
4. Develop customer leads	Attention to detail. Initiative. Tenacity. Ability to handle rejection, stress.
2. Handling complaints	Good writing skills. Ability to deal with people. Problem-solving skills. Customer-service attitude.
3. Making the sale	Good use of negotiation techniques. Ability to overcome objections, close the sale.

Let's look at Norm's rankings. Getting leads is no problem so that's rated lowest (4). Competition makes classy product presentations, so he's ranked that highest (1). Handling complaints and making the sale fall in between, so he's numbered them (2) and (3), respectively.

The skills opposite "Make effective product presentations" are more important than those involved in any of the other responsibilities. So Norm will spend more time exploring product presentation abilities in the selection process, particularly in the interview, and certainly will spend more time thinking about how candidates stack up on those skills before deciding which to hire.

Go ahead and make a JR/S Chart for a job you want to fill.

Once you have made your JR/S Chart, you can begin searching for a candidate, and when you find one, compare the skills he or she has against your chart. You must obtain evidence the candidate has those skills. Ask an applicant if he or she can write well and the answer will be yes. Every time. Even if the applicant thinks of English as a foreign language. Evidence, if it's to mean anything, has to be in the form of specific examples of things that the candidate has done. Speculation on what he or she might do doesn't count.

Review the Candidate's Background

Study the resume, application, or, if in-house, the candidate's file. What has the candidate done in the past? What does he or she claim to have accomplished? What skills do you think were needed to do that? Are they similar skills to what you need, or are they skills of equal difficulty (indicating the candidate might be able to learn the new skills)?

What specific questions does your review of the resume or application trigger, questions that will prod the applicant to give you examples of how he or she used the skills successfully? For instance, if a candidate for Norm Hipple's sales rep. job listed on his resume that he increased sales thirty-five percent in his last job, Norm would want to ask, "Tell me exactly what you did to get those sales increases. What sales-promotion techniques did you use? Tell me what you did on a day-to-day basis."

Conduct the Interview

There isn't a manager around who'd bring anyone into his or her department without having an interview. No wonder—it's the best method we have for selecting people. It's the best, but it isn't very good. That's because:

1. Interviewers get tangled up trying to use complicated interviewing systems and never find out much about the candidates.

2. Interviewers hold friendly discussions and don't press candidates for details and examples, then end up basing their decisions on superficial impressions.
3. Candidates exaggerate (oh well, lie) during interviews.
4. It is hard to measure important attributes like motivation and initiative in interviews and many interviewers don't even try. Swift Eddie who comes on like a fire engine in the interview may turn out to be semicomatose on the job.
5. Interviewers tend to make fast judgments about candidates (in the first few seconds of the interview) and then can't and don't change them even if the evidence developed in the interview indicates they should.

Here are four steps that will help you overcome those interviewing problems.

Step 1: Prepare. A quick read of a resume just before the interview is not much preparation. It will help, but not much. It's better to take time to

- Go back over your JR/S Chart.
- Note areas on the resume you identified that might give you clues to how well the candidate has developed the skills on the JR/S Chart. If you're looking for someone good at problem solving, for instance, and an applicant's resume indicates he or she worked at an airlines ticket counter, you know you're on to something. Plenty of problems there. You'd want to ask that applicant for specific examples of how he or she solved problems that came up at the counter.
- Make up specific, digging questions that will help you find out about skills. For example, "What happened when a flight was really late or canceled?" "How did you handle all those angry customers?" "What did you do to help them? Could you give me a specific example of what you did?" "Could you tell me about a problem you solved especially well and exactly how you did it?" "Can you give me an example of a problem you couldn't solve and how you handled the customer in that circumstance?" Always tie questions back to your JR/S Chart. See Interviewing Techniques following for more on questions. Remember, you are trying to find evidence in the candidate's background that he or she has used a needed skill effectively.
- Once you have your questions firmly in mind (jot them down if you tend to forget, but use key words and glance at them; don't read them off a long list during the interview), you're ready to sit down with the candidate.

Step 2: Hold the interview. Here's a simple, effective way to hold an interview that will get you the information you need.

- Establish rapport. Interviewers place great stock in this part of the interview. Its purpose is to put the candidate (and you) at ease, so you can sit around and gossip like cousins at a family reunion, but some interviewers think of it only as talking about the weather, telling jokes, and complimenting the applicant's clothes. That's great for those who are comfortable with small talk and can do it easily. Some people can't but insist on trying anyhow because it's the thing to do. And then it comes off strained and phony.

  Meanwhile, the candidate is getting more nervous, not less, because he or she wants to talk about the job, not feel embarrassed by the groping around for trivia. Think about it. If you're not good at small talk, don't do it. But, on the other hand, don't club the candidate by opening the interview with your toughest question. Pick an area on the resume that is of common interest, or one you feel the candidate might like to talk about. Select something nonthreatening.

  "It looks to me like you got canned in that job. Ha, ha, I got fired once too," is not what I had in mind, even though it may be something you have in common. This is better:

  "Say, Joe, I was looking over your resume and I saw you like fixing up antique cars. That really caught my eye. How do you go about picking out a car to work on?"

  A question like that can start Joe out on safe and familiar ground, but can also start producing information for you on Joe's decision-making ability, attitude, and negotiating skill.

- Get information. Dig. Polite conversations are fine, but won't help you learn much about how well the applicant can do the job.

  Go ahead and hold your conversation, but dig too. Digging doesn't have to be an abrasive grilling. It can and should be an expression of sincere interest on your part in the candidate.

  Ask the digging questions you made up ahead of time when you reviewed the resume. Listen like a maniac. Catch the candidate's attitude toward work and people; his or her demonstrated initiative, problem-solving ability, selling skill, or whatever else is important to the job. Be sure you get specific, concrete examples of what he or she actually did, not what he or she would like to do. The question is always "Will you give me an example of what you did?" not "What would you do if . . ." If you don't pin them down, applicants will just tell you what you want to hear. They know what sells.

  Jot down key-word notes so you can remember what the applicant told you, but don't sit there writing pages of quotes and analyses. If you do, you'll miss half of what the candidate says, and make him or her feel you are more interested in writing than listening.

- Sell your organization and the job. The candidate wants some reassurance during the interview that you like what you're doing and have some pride in the organization. He or she wants to know something about the job and wants to feel it's important and exciting.

  Say something about the organization and the job even if the candidate is a grade-Z loser you wouldn't hire in a million years. It's expected and you would be rude not to.

  When you are describing the job, tell the candidate about the tough parts as well as the nice parts. Tell him or her about your management style and what you expect. Spell out your standards. Let the candidate know exactly what he or she is in for.

- Answer questions. Give the candidate plenty of time to ask anything he or she wants to. You can tell a lot about the candidate's views and motivations from questions. Here are some examples from recent interviews I've observed. Think about each and the impressions it gives you of the applicant.

Applicant Questions

1. I see your last quarter's earnings were up ten percent. Is that the kind of increase you want, and, if not, what are you doing to raise it?
2. How much vacation time do I get?
3. What's the career outlook in a job like this? If I do well, can I expect to move up? Where have others been promoted to?
4. What's your company do, anyway?
5. What are the company's growth objectives and how will my job contribute to them?
6. Is there a lot of evening and weekend work involved?
7. Are you looking at any new products or services; if so what kind?
8. I know you provide a car. Any chance I could get an Olds instead of a Chevy?
9. How much latitude will I have? What will my responsibilities/authority be?
10. Do I get a discount?

Probably the odd-numbered questions on the left, which are about careers, the work, and the organization, impressed you. Chances are the even-numbered ones, which are "what's in it for me" questions or show lack of preparation for the interview, didn't.

- Close: Try to end on a high note, if only to get yourself out of the interview quickly. If the candidate flunked, it's best not to discuss that in a face-to-face situation, because the candidate will think he or she has passed with flying colors and will want to argue about your decision. That can lead to nasty scenes in which your nose gets remodeled, so it's best to avoid the issue altogether.

  Say something like, "Sam, I've enjoyed talking with you and about your skills. I have other people to talk with about the job, but I should be able to let you know in about two weeks. Is that fair enough?"

  Stand up, move toward the door, and show the applicant out. Usually, that will be it. You haven't said yes, but you haven't said no either, so the candidate doesn't want to louse up his or her chances by arguing, especially since there's nothing to argue about.

Step 3: Decide. It's a good idea, as soon as the interview is over, to write down your thoughts on the candidate's ability to perform the skills necessary to do the job. Use the key-word notes you have taken to write out more complete descriptions of how the candidate answered your digging questions and what important skills or attitudes he or she demonstrated.

Then compare the information you have on the candidate with the skills you listed on the JR/S Chart to see how the applicant stacks up. Does he or she have most of the skills needed to do the job? Some? Only a few?

Using the JR/S Chart will help you decide based on the candidate's ability to do the job.

If you are interviewing several candidates for the same job, you will want to compare them. Decide which applicant has the highest "scores" in the most important skills—that's the one you should choose. If there are several who have high scores, you've got a nice problem. Pick anyone and you will be right.

One more thing. Selection is not one hundred percent JR/S. Ninety percent maybe, but not one hundred percent. You will see candidates that seem just right for a job who have high scores on the JR/S skills, but still give you the gut feeling something is wrong. Chances are, if you go ahead and select one anyhow, you will have trouble later. It happens too often to ignore. Unscientific as it may seem, you must pay some attention to your gut.

Step 4: Let the candidate know. Whatever you decide, contact the candidate with an answer within two weeks, if possible. If you need more time to see other candidates, write or call and explain.

Never let someone who has taken the time to come for an interview wait more than two weeks. Sound obvious? The truth is, a distressing number of employers let applicants wait for long periods of time, or forever. Imagine going for an interview and then never hearing. What punishment would you give for that if you could?

Interviewing Techniques

Now that we have covered the interviewing process, let's look at interviewing techniques. Here are some suggestions:

1. Don't get hung up on techniques. Study them, practice them, but don't let them dominate. A lot of pseudo-scientific stuff has been written about interviewing. You have probably read about encoders, filters, biases, patterns, interpersonal data reciprocation (talking), and enough other scary jargon to make you forget you're supposed to be interviewing a live person. Learn what you can from all that, but don't let it put you off and don't concentrate so hard on using one rigid interviewing approach or another that you forget about being human.

   You must be spontaneous, flexible enough to go with the flow to a reasonable degree, and you must let some of your natural, personal warmth show through. Following a system too closely will make you seem like a robot. And that won't exactly establish the kind of atmosphere where the candidate will let down his or her guard and be candid with you. Think of the interview not as a mechanized, programmed, superstructured questioning session, but as a planned and gently guided discussion, aimed at getting the best possible exchange of information between two people. Make it as relaxed and pleasant as you can, while at the same time using your digging questions. That way you will sell yourself and the job to the candidate and also get the information you want.

2. Use questions to guide the interview. Questions are the interviewer's best tool:

   Digging Questions: Follow-up questions, usually in a series, used to get more and more detailed and precise information. "Then what did you do?" "Can you tell me exactly how you did that?" "Could you explain what you did, step by step?"

   Open Questions: Questions that begin with who, what, where, why, how, to what extent, and require more than one-word answers. Use these to get the applicant to open his or her mouth—and talk. "What were you responsible for?" "How did you feel about that job?"

Closed Questions: Questions that begin with, for example, do you, how many, would you, that can be answered with one word, like yes or no. Use these only when you want a precise response. "When will you be available to start work?" "How much do you earn now?"

To illustrate what we've been talking about and show the flow of an interview, here are some typical interview questions and the purpose of each.

Question:	Purpose:
I noticed that you're a skier. I am too. Where have you skied lately?	Open question to begin the interview and establish rapport. To put the candidate at ease and give him or her some safe, easy ground to start off on.
Let's talk about those customers who are hard to sell. Think of one you know that was worth a lot in potential sales but turned you down flat. What did you do?	Digging, open question to find out candidate's ability to: overcome objections be tenacious handle people handle rejection and stress negotiate make presentations
What did you do the last time you got a complaint from a customer? How about one you thought was unfounded?	Digging, open question to find out candidate's: attitudes toward customer service ability to handle people ability to handle stress, to operate under pressure negotiating skills ability to be creative
Tell me about a time you had a strong disagreement with your fellow workers. What did you do about it?	Digging, open question to find out the candidate's ability to: work as a member of a team handle conflict use problem-solving approach
I see you introduced the new X450 line in your territory. How did you do that exactly?	Digging, open question to find out candidate's ability to: do sales promotion make presentations sell ideas be innovative and creative

Question:	Purpose:
What can I tell you about my organization?	Open question to: lead to the "selling of the company" part of the interview find out what's on the candidate's mind see how well the candidate prepared for the interview
I still have some others to talk with about this job, but I should be able to let you know in two weeks. Is that all right with you?	Semi-rhetorical, closed question to end the interview and get the candidate out the door with a minimum of discussion.

3. Listen. A good half of any interview is listening. During the digging questions, almost all your energy should go into listening. Listen for the real meaning of what the candidate says and for evidence of what he or she is capable of doing. Evaluate later. Listening is so essential to good interviewing, I would urge you to read Chapter 11 before your next interview to polish up your listening skills.
4. Be quiet sometimes. Silence is also a good interviewing tool. It can take the place of a digging question. Silences are awkward and nerve-wracking in a one-on-one situation, but be brave and use them. They give the applicant time to think, to expand on statements, and (sometimes) to give you more information than you thought you would get. Often the candidate will keep talking to fill the gap. Resist the temptation to add something yourself or change the subject. The comments an applicant makes after a few moments of silent thinking are often further beneath the surface than the ones that came before.
5. Keep control of the interview and guide it. Explore new avenues as they open up, give the candidate plenty of time to ask questions, but don't let him or her interview you. After all, you have the job opening and you have certain things to find out about the applicant's potential to do that job. When the applicant starts taking over, smile and say, "We'll get to that in a minute, but first I want to find out more about how you handled that situation you were just talking about."

Here are a few additional thoughts on interviews:

Watch out for first impressions. Discipline yourself to hold off making any judgment about the candidate at least until after you have asked your digging questions. Then you will have better information about what the applicant can do in addition to how he or she looks.

When you're upset because interviews are taking so much time away from your work, remember, selecting good people for your team is one of the most important things you can do as a manager. No good people, no good team, no good manager.

If an applicant has personality quirks that will hinder him or her from doing the best job or will hurt relations with you or your team, consider that carefully, even if he or she has all the right JR/S skills. You can coach the candidate and improve his or her dress and grooming, you can train to raise skill levels, but you can't change personality.

When you are evaluating candidates and trying to match people up with jobs, take a long view: Does this candidate have the skills to do this job? Could he or she learn them and how long would that take? (Don't turn down a potentially great person just because he or she doesn't have *every* skill you need. Good people learn fast and like to go into situations that demand they learn and grow.) Ask yourself what would the next step after this job be and does the applicant have potential for that?

And finally, remember, candidates are pretty sophisticated today. They take courses in interviewing and many applicants are well briefed. They know what you want to hear so you have to get beyond and underneath what they have rehearsed. Pleasantly, but persistently, dig, dig, dig until you start getting real answers.

HOW TO HELP YOUR PEOPLE GROW

Once you have selected your people, you will have to help them learn and grow. You will want to do that because:

You want them to do better and better work.

You want to be able to promote them to higher level jobs in your group and elsewhere in the organization, thereby giving your department a reputation as a fast-track place to work.

Learning and growing are motivators and people who broaden their horizons feel a sense of pride and satisfaction that reflects in their work.

Managers who supply good people for the organization are highly thought of. It's a good reputation to have.

Developing people is an important part of your management responsibility. Many managers have a vague sense that that is true and believe in training, but are a little puzzled about how to go about it.

If you are puzzled, these thoughts will help you:

You are responsible for setting the climate in which people can learn. The responsibility for getting the learning done is the individual's. Each person has to take the initiative to manage his or her own development. You may do some training and coaching of individuals who work for you, but overall, it's their job. To anyone who says, "I'm not being trained" or "I'm not learning anything," say, "What are you doing about it?"

To establish the climate, encourage your people to take advantage of every learning opportunity. Set the example by doing so yourself (after all, like everyone else, you're responsible for your own training). Get your people to read; ask questions; watch what's going on; develop networks; keep notes, diaries, and files; go to seminars; visit other companies . . . anything they can to learn as much as they can about their work, their department, and the organization. Challenge each of your people to look at every experience and ask, "What can I learn from this? How can I use it to do a better job?"

Be sure your climate setting is very clear. You may want your people to learn, but if you don't actively and openly encourage it, they may not be sure and will be reluctant to take time off from work for training.

Look for opportunities to encourage people to learn. When you spot a performance weakness in a person, think about ways he or she could learn to correct it. Discuss the problem with the person and suggest solutions. They might include attending a training program, getting help from a more experienced person, taking on extra work in an area, or reading a good book on the subject.

Consider the experience levels of your people. If some of them could benefit from broader exposure or new sets of skills, sit down with each person involved and figure out how he or she could get them.

Set "growth" standards. For example, tell your people, "I'd like every one of you to attend at least one workshop a year." Encourage people to select programs that will help them on the job. Ask them to consider company programs, if your organization has its own, and pursue outside programs given by universities and private groups.

Don't delegate training to personnel. Notice so far I haven't mentioned the personnel department. Personnel may run courses and workshops, and some of them may be dynamite, but training your people is not the personnel department's job. It's yours (setting the atmosphere) and your people's. Use personnel courses and workshops if they are good, but don't think that just because they are there, responsibility for training belongs to personnel.

Don't confuse training with "programs"—courses, seminars, workshops. It's much more than that. Workshops can help, but only to a limited degree. Ninety percent of all learning happens right on the job, not in a classroom. People learn the most from the work they do, so how you structure jobs and what projects and work assignments you give people are important. Giving people task-force and committee assignments, for instance, can really help them broaden their knowledge and skill.

People also learn a lot from their leaders. So, the more time you spend with your people, showing them how, discussing problems and difficulties with them, coaching and guiding them, the better. Be sure your people feel they can come to you and ask questions.

If you do send your people to courses, be sure you know what's in those courses. If you do, you will be more likely to understand why your people are trying out things on the job, and you'll be more supportive. If you don't know what a course is about, go to it yourself and find out.

Don't send everybody to everything. If you do send people to courses, look at your people as individuals. Think about each of them and their performance on the job. Where are their weaknesses? Where does each need help? Where is each of them going next? What skills and knowledge does each need to acquire to improve in the job, to get promoted?

Try to make your people better than you are. That may seem threatening, and it may sting if any of them get promoted to a higher job than you have, but that's desirable in the long run. Somebody is going to get promoted to those big jobs, and if it isn't you this time, it may as well be someone you helped develop. Remember, to have an image as a people developer is to be seen as a solid, corporate-thinking manager on the way up.

How Adults Learn

Before we leave developing people, we should spend a few minutes on how learning happens.

People have to want to learn. Learning is hard work and they won't normally do it unless they're motivated in some way to do it. The best motivation is seeing "what's in it for me?" If you can convince me that learning something will make me richer or happier, or head off being broke and miserable, I'll try to learn it. If you can't, I may not. It is up to you as a manager to explain the reasons for learning to each of your people.

The material to be learned has to be presented in an understandable way, and in a way that makes learning easy. A foot-thick procedure manual may be clear as a bell as a reference, but a devilish hard thing to learn from. One glance will cause people to remember all sorts of other important things they have to do. An hour-and-a-half lecture may be technically perfect, but not effective if most of the audience snores through it.

People learn best when they participate in the learning—in discussion sessions, filling out tests and questionnaires, practicing or role playing. Active involvement keeps people alert, interested, and helps them remember what was covered.

Learning disappears almost instantly if it is not used. As soon as someone learns something, he or she should have a chance to use it back on the job, and should continue to use it on a regular basis to retain the knowledge or skill.

Learning needs feedback. That's one reason teachers give marks in school. At work you don't hand out grades, but you can

1. Recognize a person is trying to use a newly learned skill and tell him or her that you recognize it and are pleased that he or she is trying.
2. Give that person feedback on how well he or she is using the skill. Give encouragement if the skill is being used well, coaching if it's not.
3. Reward the learner for using the new skill and for his or her overall desire to learn.

Sometimes, learning is changing old habits. Changing deeply ingrained and comfortable behaviors is a tougher job than learning a new skill. People with old habits will often say, "The new ways are terrific, we should have used them ten years ago!" then go right back to doing what they've always done. People who are trying to learn a new behavior and to change an old behavior must

1. Recognize the need to change and want to change. (The old "what's in it for me?" again.)
2. Understand the new behavior.
3. Consciously substitute the new way for the old at every opportunity.
4. Reward themselves for minor successes.
5. Receive reward and recognition from others.
6. Not worry about occasional backsliding or lapses. That happens to everyone and a slip now and then doesn't mean everything is ruined.

So there you have it. Selecting good people is a big step toward getting out ahead of the pack. Remember to look for specific evidence of ability to do the job. Helping your people learn and grow is also important and is very exciting. Keep in mind, it's your responsibility to set the climate for learning. Your people are responsible for most of their own training. Together, good selection and training will do wonders for the productivity of your department and your reputation as a manager.

10. Over the Top: How to Create a Climate for Motivation

At one time or another, at some point in your career, you will be responsible for leading people. It may be a team of people in your own department that reports directly to you, or it may be a bunch from various parts of the organization, brought together to perform a specific task under your guidance, if not direct supervision.

Whenever you think of your team, think about this. The team members are not there just to get the work out. They are also there to make you successful. And they will do that if they are motivated to perform at such a high level they will be noticed throughout the organization. That will raise your reputation as a manager: The better your team performs, the better you will look—and be.

People have to be handled in very special ways to assure they really produce. Members of a team must be individually motivated and also must be eager to work in cooperation with all other members. If they are, they will get results beyond anyone's expectations.

In this chapter, we'll look at how to keep each of your people motivated to do good work, and how to get them to work well with others to produce outstanding team results.

HOW TO MOTIVATE PEOPLE

Boss: Mary, you've really got great potential. I know you'll do a fabulous job at this. Why, just the other day I said to the V.P., "Mary could go right to the top." All you need to do is to take advantage of this terrific opportunity, really produce the way we know you can and you'll have yourself some future around here.

Mary: Thanks, boss. [Boy, is he full of it . . .]

Conversation (and thoughts) related to me by Mary Watson at the time of her promotion to Supervisor, Amalgamated Gerbil Works.

You cannot motivate people to do their best by bullying them, making all their decisions for them, treating them like children, or trying to intimidate them. Note I didn't say you couldn't get them to work with these methods, because you can. People might work, but they won't give you their best.

Most everyone who hasn't been fast asleep for the last ninety years has heard that. Yet there are managers who persist in managing like tyrants. Some may do it because they don't really believe it can be done any other way, and still hang on to some ill-directed notion of what good management is; others don't trust people; and still others are basically insecure and don't want their people to look too good in comparison to them.

Whatever the reason, the total top-down approach to management kills initiative, enthusiasm, productivity, and creativity. Don't use it. Be sure you are not looking at your people as goof-offs who won't work unless prodded or watched every minute, or as competitors who might steal your empire away. Most members of your team want to do well, want to be proud of their work, and can help you conquer empires far more important than the one you have now.

Here are nine "turn-ons" you can use to get your people excited and eager to go the extra mile for you.

1. Let them know what's expected.
2. Keep them informed.
3. Give them control.
4. Give them start-to-finish responsibility.
5. Make them champions.

6. Give them feedback.
7. Give them reward.
8. Help them learn and grow.
9. Be approachable.

Each of those has to do with INVOLVEMENT, which is the overall key to motivation. The closer people feel to the organization, the department, and the job itself, the more they feel part of those, and the more likely they will be to feel good about themselves and their work, and feel eager to produce.

You have a lot to say about how your team members feel about their work situation, because much of it is under your control. Make sure you do everything you can to keep them involved—so they will do all they can to keep you on the *Upward Bound* track.

Let's look at each of the nine "turn-ons":

1. Let Them Know What's Expected

Don't assume your people know what they're supposed to do. They may not. Many bosses send folks off to work without really telling them what's expected, and people, not wanting to seem stupid, don't ask. They fumble around with trial and error, false starts, backtracking, and crystal-balling, while the boss wonders why things aren't getting done.

If you were to ask your people—and you should—what they think their jobs are, what they are expected to do, and what the standards are, you might get some surprises. Don't let your people wander until they screw up. Keep in mind:

The Principle of Misdirected Expectations

The less time you spend discussing with your people what you expect them to accomplish, the more chance they will accomplish something else.

What we are really talking about here is setting goals and standards. Meet with each of your people to talk about what they should do and how it should be done. Get their opinions and get agreement as to what the job is really about. Then ask each to write down what's to be accomplished (goals) and how well it is to be done (standards), so you can see if what they heard out of the discussion is the same as what you heard.

Don't try to spell out jobs in minute detail so individuals don't have any room to use their own talents and creativity. But do be sure you have a basic agreement with each of your people as to what the goals and standards are.

You can discuss goals and standards and get agreement or you can dictate them. But most people like top-down direction about as well as snakebite, so avoid it as much as you can.

That's summed up in:

The Principle of Autocratic Inaction

The more you *tell* people what to do, the greater the chance they'll do it at the lowest acceptable productivity level.

2. Keep Them Informed

People like to know what's happening. Make sure your people know what's going on in the organization: sales, earnings, new ventures, projections, problems, whatever is hot, so that they will feel a part of—and identify with—a larger, total organization rather than just their own work area.

Knowing where the organization is going and how it is doing is of real interest to most people. Keep yours up-to-date.

Look at all the reports, memos, analyses, financial data, and publications you receive regularly. Unless you are specifically told, "No one else is to see this," most of those are not top secret and can be shared with your people. Take the time and trouble to do it.

You don't have to be fancy about it. A five-minute stand-up meeting when the sales figures come in, for example, will help keep them tuned in . . . and turned on.

In addition to general information about the organization, you should be sure each of your people has the information they need to do their own work. You can't expect anyone to do his or her best without it. Not having the facts, and not being updated when situations change, forces people down some weird paths, one of which is illustrated by:

The Principle of Information Invention

The fewer facts available, the more people will assume and the more they will be wrong.

Don't let your team members guess. There is more information available today than anyone can possibly use, so no one should be without. Make sure each of your people has access to all the information he or she needs to do the job.

3. Give Them Control

People respond in astounding ways when they are given control—even a little—over the work they do. Having some say over how they do the work is a great motivator. Think of your own job and how much better you feel about the parts you have discretion over versus those that are dictated by your boss.

Letting people run their own jobs makes sense from a motivational point of view and also in another very practical sense. No one knows more about the work than the people who are actually doing it. Your secretary, for instance, could easily come up with ten ways to improve work flow if you asked. People out in the shop know thirty reasons why quality rejects are so high. What's more, they know how to fix the problem. But chances are, while managers sit in endless meetings trying to figure out what's wrong, nobody ever asks them. Encourage all your people to find better ways to do their jobs. Have a contest to see who comes up with the most innovative and workable ideas.

To be absolutely certain everyone understands what part of the job he or she controls and which parts require your involvement, sit down with each of your people and

1. Make a list of responsibilities for the job.
2. Decide together which are theirs and which are shared.
3. Agree on which decisions they make and which ones you make.
4. Make a copy of the list so each of you has one.

This can be summed up in the:

Principle of Shared Ownership

The more you allow your employees control of their own areas, the more ownership and interest they will have and the harder they will try to do a good job.

4. Give Them Start-to-Finish Responsibility

Doing little pieces of work doesn't turn people on. We know that from industrial assembly lines, where people who are turning one screw all day become so bored and feel so little for what they are doing, they turn hostile and even sabotage the very products they are turning out.

Don't fragment responsibilities. Look at the separate, discrete tasks your team performs. Then look at who does them. Are tasks that could form one complete, interesting hunk of work spread all over the place?

For example, in dealing with customers, do some of your people process orders, others do billing, others adjustments, and others collections? If so, consider cross-training people and giving each of them responsibility for all those functions for a group of customers. It will give them more interesting and more complete jobs, since they'd handle their customers from start to finish. It will make better sense to the customers, too, because they'll have one place to go for everything.

Rearranging work, even a little, to give people more responsibility for the total job has a dramatic impact on their feelings about work, their interest level, and the quality of their performance.

When a person has start-to-finish responsibility, that person realizes whatever happens on the job is up to him or her alone—a specific reflection of skill and competence. If the job is done well, he or she can take credit; if it is not, there's no one else to blame.

That can be summed up in the:

Principle of Animating Completeness

The more complete a job is, the more the person doing it will hustle to see that it is done right.

5. Make Them Champions

The tone you set, your attitude toward your team and the work it does, has a big influence on how the team members see themselves. To make sure your team feels good about itself, you must show that you:

1. Believe the work is important.
2. Are excited about it.
3. Are confident they'll do a great job at it and then some.

You don't do that by sending out memos loaded with phony clichés or bulletin-board posters with cute sayings on them like "Let's all tug together." You do it by being visibly "up" in meetings and in one-on-one discussions, continually coming back to the idea that what your group is doing is vital to the organization.

You do it by letting your fire show through as you tell your people individually, and as a group, you think they are outstanding and have what it takes to be even greater. You have to do this in a confident, sincere manner, and you have to do it often enough, over a long enough period of time that people begin to believe you. If you find it hard to give compliments or lead cheers, you may want to practice beforehand so it becomes natural and sincere. Just remember you will be telling people what they want to hear, so they will be *predisposed* to believe you.

When you do all that, your team members will respond—sometimes in fantastic ways.

The Principle of Inspired Self-Perception

People who feel like champions, act like champions.

That's the long and the short of it. Treat your people like champions. Make your people feel as though they've really come through, and let them know you're confident they will again and again, and they'll feel good about themselves and their work. They'll see themselves as successful, and that in itself is a powerful motivator to try and become more successful.

When you set goals with your people, set them high enough so they have stretch, but low enough to be attainable by anyone who really wants to meet or beat them. That gives everybody a chance to win and be a champion. If you have forty salespeople on your staff and you have one "top salesperson of the year," that's fine for that person, but it means "I'm not the best" to the other thirty-nine. Better to have a "Goal Beaters" Club and let everyone who meets the quota you set be a member. That way, maybe thirty-five of them will win.

As people beat their goals, hold a parade for them. A dinner maybe. In Acapulco. Ask the president to be there and say something inspirational.

Let the "Goal Beaters" set their own goals for next year and review them with you. This will give them ownership, involvement, and control over their own work.

6. Give Them Feedback

Nothing is quite so awful as coming to work day after day, plugging away trying to do a good job, but not really knowing how you're thought of. Only slightly better is hearing just once a year at performance appraisal time.

Some managers find it hard to give praise or criticism, or comment in any way on an employee's performance. But people need feedback like they need oxygen. They want to know how they're doing. It helps them correct performance problems and motivates them to build on their strengths. Feedback is not all that difficult to dole out. Make sure you are doing it on a regular basis and you are taking advantage of the:

Principle of Energizing Feedback

The more you give constructive feedback to your people on how they are doing, the harder they will try to do better.

Here are some additional ideas on feedback:

Give feedback immediately. There is a school of thought that says, when you see good or bad performance, make a note of it and stick that note in a file so you will remember to talk about it at performance appraisal time. That's nuts. When you see good or bad performance, tell the performer about it right then. Don't wait a year to correct a problem or to give recognition for a job well done. Pounce on it. Let the person know—right now.

Give precise feedback that will help people learn. If you say, "Mary Ellen, that was a good job," that's better than saying nothing, but not so good as saying, "That was a good job and here are three things I particularly liked about it: First, the report was complete and I didn't have to ask you to dig deeper; second, it was a week ahead of schedule which may save us six thousand dollars, and, third, your presentation of it using the charts was easy to understand."

Similarly, if you are giving criticism, do it in specific terms with the emphasis on improvement. "Marty, I don't think that contract you negotiated is up to your usual standard. Let me show you what I mean, and let's see what we can learn from it . . ."

Give feedback on good performance publicly. Give feedback on bad performance privately, one on one.

Listen. Listening is half of giving feedback. Give your team members a chance to talk. Invite comments: "Is that how you see it?" "Am I being accurate with that?" "What is your feeling on this?" Always listen; you'll learn something. (See Chapter 11 for more on how to listen.)

When you give feedback, you're doing more than just letting people know how they are doing. Giving continuous feedback helps you keep channels open with your people. If they know you're anxious and willing to discuss performance with them, they'll be more likely to initiate discussions themselves. They will bring problems and questions to you, they will be more open about what's going on, and they'll keep you better informed so you will have fewer surprises.

Don't confuse giving feedback with mollycoddling your people. Feedback is a powerful tool for urging your people to peak performance. You can still be a tough manager, set challenging goals and high standards with your people, and at the same time let them know how they're doing. You want feedback from your boss, don't you? Your people are no different.

7. Give Them Reward

Money is an obvious and always welcome reward, and you should see that your people are paid as well as they can be within the limits of your organization's policies. For exceptional performance, you should recommend pay that exceeds policy.

If paying your people well means some of them make as much as or more than you do, so be it. Never hold your people back because you feel you should maintain distance between your salary and theirs. It is unfair to them and will not meet their needs. And besides, having people that good and that highly paid is an indication of your ability to pick good people and train and motivate them, and can be a good argument for having your boss do something spectacular with your salary.

Make salary increases a special occasion. Don't tell people about them in a matter-of-fact way that sounds like it's coming out of the same computer that prints their paycheck, or worse yet, forget to say anything until after the increase has shown up in their pay. Hold a celebration. Take them out to lunch, buy a drink, at the very least sit down and talk with them about all the good things they've done to deserve more money.

Money, as important as it is, is not the only form of reward. There are many others, some of which don't cost anything, but can make people feel as good (almost) as getting a fat, juicy salary increase. Here are a few:

Give credit. People love to be recognized individually for doing good work. Often, particularly in large organizations, it is difficult to pinpoint an individual's contribution because each person is working as part of the team to make the department or the entire organization successful. That's fine, but it doesn't have the kick that being singled out as a champion does. Whenever you can, name names. Identify who did what. Give individual praise in meetings, on bulletin boards, in memos and reports and in person. Walk in, shake a hand, and say, "You did it. Good job."

Give awards. When your "Goal Beaters" get back from Acapulco, get everyone in the office together, especially the ones that didn't go. Have the GB's stand up and accept awards. Give them junk like pins and plaques. People love those things. Give them special letterheads and business cards with Goal Beater logos (whatever you make up) on them.

Give responsibility and status. Whenever anyone does something especially well, ask him or her to do something like it again. Make people resident "experts." Give your champions extra responsibility. Ask them for advice and then let everyone know you use it.

Give your people the best-sounding titles that your organization will allow. If you can call them all vice presidents, fine. Do it. They'll love it and feel proud. Get them the best office space and the best furniture you can. If it's possible, let them pick their own.

8. Help Them Learn and Grow

People like to learn and discover. They enjoy seeing old things in new ways, acquiring new skills and being able to look back and say, "That's the person I was back then, and this is the person I am now. I've really come a long way." People will put up with a lot that isn't so great in a job and still be inspired if the opportunity to improve themselves is there. Expanding horizons is a great motivator.

You are responsible for seeing that everyone who works for you is trained in his or her job. You are not responsible, however, for force-feeding "development" to everyone all of the time. You are a catalyst, one who sets the atmosphere that will encourage people to develop themselves. See Chapter 9 for more on developing your people.

9. Be Approachable

Lots of managers say, "I have an open-door policy." They say it, but nobody believes it. People right down the hall will tell you, "Wild horses couldn't drag me in there." That leads us to:

The Principle of Believable Openness

Showing you are approachable is much more effective than saying it.

Here are some approachability points to remember:

- Having someone to talk with—especially if that someone is the boss—is a great motivator for people.
- To be sure people are comfortable coming to you with their problems or questions, always treat what they say—whatever it is—with respect. You can keep a person out of your office forever by:

  Making him or her feel a little stupid for not knowing the answer and having to come to you for it.

  Giving the impression you don't have time to waste on such trivial stuff and want to get the discussion over with as fast as possible.

  Giving careless, vague answers and off-the-cuff advice.

  Don't do it.

- Actively invite questions. Drop in to see people in their own offices to find out how they are doing and if there's anything they need help with. Show you are happy when they ask.
- When someone does ask you for help, always follow up to see they get it—or let them know why not. Never let any request drop out of sight without some sort of response from you.
- Being approachable doesn't mean you are a pushover or that you have

to be best friends with your team members. It does mean you try to be understanding and feel empathy for others' predicaments and are willing to lend a hand when you can.

So that's motivation. Maybe you're thinking, "It takes a lot of work to keep people motivated." Yes, it does. But, if you are a manager, isn't your primary job to see that the people you oversee produce to their potential? What else could you do that would be more important? For your organization? For yourself?

Inherent in motivation is letting your people know what's expected, keeping them informed, giving them control, giving start-to-finish responsibility, making them champions, giving them feedback, giving them reward, helping them learn and grow, and being approachable. Powerful actions you can use to set an environment that is stimulating to your people.

Use the checklist that follows to be sure you are doing all you can to see that your people are motivated. Make copies of this checklist and fill one out at the end of each month to be sure you are doing your part to set a motivational climate.

MOTIVATION CHECKLIST

MOTIVATOR	CHECK IF USED LAST MONTH	IF SO, WHAT DID YOU DO?	WHAT WILL YOU DO NEXT MONTH?
Let them know what's expected.	☐		
Keep them informed.	☐		
Give them control.	☐		
Give them start-to-finish responsibility.	☐		
Make them champions.	☐		
Give feedback.	☐		
Give reward and recognition.	☐		
Help them learn and grow.	☐		
Be approachable.	☐		

HOW TO GET PEOPLE TO WORK TOGETHER

Coach: All right, men. Who knows what teamwork is?

Dudley: Teamwork is when all of us is like one happy clam, all our brains and muscles is extrapolating together, and there ain't nobody worried about hisself and we move together like we're supposed to without no hitches, so we can confound the other team and ourselves.

Coach: Thank you, Dudley.

Once you're sure you are doing everything you can to motivate individuals in your group, you can start thinking about how they work together as a team. That's important because

1. Much work is done by teams today: committees, task forces, project teams, and similar groupings are everywhere.
2. Teams are hard to motivate and control . . . many do not work well.
3. If you can put together winning teams, you will be looked on with respect throughout your organization because *good* teams can produce far more than the sum of what the members could produce working individually . . . one more feather in your cap.

Executives love to talk about teams and teamwork. It helps them conjure up images of behemoths struggling through sweat, mud, and compound fractures to win the Superbowl. People who sit around in immaculate, air-conditioned offices all day fantasize about being out there, head of a team where every player is putting victory ahead of everything else.

After Wingfoot Wilson rushes for sixteen thousand yards in one game against the Paduca Catatonics, breaking a forty-year-old record, he tells the TV audience, "I wasn't thinking about records. I was just doing my job. The important thing is that the team won the game. That's all that matters."

Wingfoot may or may not mean that. We'll see next year at contract time how much he asks for and whether he brings up the sixteen thousand yards.

Whether he does or not, Wingfoot certainly did produce and then said the right thing afterward. Anyone who manages people would like to have plenty of Wingfoots in his or her department. But it takes special handling to get people to "buy in" to being part of a team.

At work, the benefits of being on a team are usually much less clear than those of working alone, and, of course, the fact that people just naturally don't get along too well together doesn't make teamwork any easier either.

But the main reason teams don't work as well as they should is that they don't talk among themselves enough. They launch into their work (or what they think their work is) and don't bother to step back and look at what they are doing and how they are doing it.

Disciplining a team to take time to look at itself is the key to high-powered team productivity. Here's how you should do that and get the most out of your team.

1. Don't assume the team knows what it's doing. There can be a lot of confusion and disagreement in teams. If the team's mission is not discussed openly and consensus is not reached, there's not much hope for the team. That's true even for old, well-established teams. Members will tell you, "We know what we're supposed to do, we don't need to discuss it." But when you ask, "What is it you're supposed to do?" you'll get a different answer from each member.

   Block out some time. Get your group together and ask them to help you develop a mission statement for the team, the team's reason for being. Write their thoughts on a flip chart or blackboard so they all can see. Revise and modify as you go along. Eventually you may get a statement that everyone is happy with, but you probably won't get it in the first meeting. Maybe in the second, if you are lucky.

2. When the team has agreed on its mission, have it worked out what it is specifically responsible for, and what others outside the group have to do. Draw a chart similar to the Team Responsibility Chart below on a giant sheet of paper. Put it up on the wall and have the group discuss how to fill it in.

   First, write the mission statement at the top. Then have them break their mission down into tasks that have to be done to accomplish it. List those in the left-hand column.

   You may want to use more columns or other headings, such as advising, researching, reviewing, but the basic idea is the same. In the example shown, one task in accomplishing the mission is to develop the spring advertising campaign. That sounds fairly clear-cut, but what is the beginning and the end of that task for the team? Should the team actually produce the ads and put them in the paper? Or are others involved? In this example, the team felt there were others involved and that the team had planning and follow-up roles. If the team had not worked out this chart, however, there could have been much confusion and ongoing disagreement about what its role was. Taking a few minutes to fill out the chart helps everyone understand better.

TEAM RESPONSIBILITY CHART

MISSION: To promote sales of the XU-PU7 product line so that it will generate $7,000,000 in volume next year.

SUBTASKS TO ACCOMPLISH MISSION:	**WHO IS RESPONSIBLE FOR:**				
	PLANNING	**DEVELOPING**	**APPROVING**	**IMPLEMENTING**	**FOLLOW-UP**
1. Develop spring advertising campaign	Team	Ad agency	R. Edward	Individual Branches	Team
2.					
3.					
4.					

When the chart is complete, have it typed and send copies to everyone on the team and to anyone else whose name appears on it. If it's probable that outsiders will be listed on the chart, ask them to sit in with your team as they are filling out the chart. That way you will get ownership and commitment.

3. Make sure individual team members know what's expected of them to support the team. Have the team discuss and list responsibilities of all members (like coming to all meetings) and specific responsibilities of individual members (such as: Andy—take notes at meetings, have typed and distributed. Joan—arrange room for next meeting. Barbara—contact data processing for updates between meetings).
4. If some of the members of the team do not report to you, make sure their bosses know what's happening and agree with it. They may want to be included in your Team Responsibility Chart discussions too.
5. Have the team discuss how often it will meet, where, and for how long. Have the members discuss how they will communicate between meetings and how they will follow up to see if the team is accomplishing its mission. Also have the team discuss how it will be creative, solve problems and make decisions, handle new ideas, and handle conflict.
6. Every six months or so, have the team take time to look at how it operates. Find out if the members think the mission or responsibilities have changed, and, if so, how. Have the group rate itself using the following Team Rating Questionnaire. Have each member fill out a copy (anonymously if they want), then make a summary.

   When the questionnaire has been summarized, present the results to the group. Discuss those areas where the group has rated itself low and get ideas for doing better in the future. Get the team's ideas on how to capitalize on its strengths and overcome its weaknesses.
7. Note the question on conflict does not ask, "How well do we avoid conflict?" Conflict is necessary and healthy. A group that functions without disagreement and differences of opinion is a dead group. It is going nowhere. It is a victim of its own warm feelings about itself or of the lack of courage of its members to express their true feelings. You should encourage conflict—as long as it is constructive, does not kill off all new ideas, and is not built around personal attack. "Does anybody have any other ideas on the subject? . . . Come on, I know everybody can't agree one hundred percent. What are your thoughts?" A question like that can give permission to disagree and stimulate some good discussion.

   Alfred Sloan of General Motors used to get upset when people agreed too quickly on a course of action and would tell everyone to go away and come back when they had some differences of opinion.

TEAM RATING QUESTIONNAIRE

As a Team, How Well Do We:	Very Well 5	4	Pretty Well 3	2	Not Well 1
Run our meetings?					
Listen to each other?					
Do creative work?					
Solve problems and make decisions?					
Accept new ideas?					
Handle conflict?					
Carry out our mission?					

What is our greatest strength:

____

____

____

What is our greatest opportunity for improvement?

____

____

____

If conflict gets out of hand and becomes destructive, when it goes beyond temporary disagreement on an issue and becomes a more or less permanent part of your meetings, it needs to be dealt with. If one person is causing the problem, get him or her aside and urge backing off some, explaining how that would help the group.

If two or more members are involved, use a problem-solving approach. Have those members meet one-on-one and exchange views on how to channel their energies in useful directions. Have them discuss these areas with each other:

> Here are things you do that help me and here's why. I wish you'd continue to do them.
>
> Here are things you don't do and I wish you would, because they'd help me.

Here are things you do that hinder me and here's why. I wish you'd do less of them.

8. Finally, many times people are assigned to teams but are not appraised, recognized, or rewarded for the teamwork they do. The team, then, remains a distant second in importance to their own individual jobs. Be sure each person's contribution (or lack of it) to the team is recognized at appraisal time and more often in less formal discussions. Be sure good contributors are rewarded and know why they are rewarded.

Building a good team starts with individuals. When they are selected for their ability to perform and when they are motivated individually, they have the basics for being good team members.

But that's not enough. Just putting capable, motivated people together doesn't build a team. Members must sit down and agree on what they're supposed to do and how they will do it. That cannot be a one-time discussion. It has to happen again and again at regular intervals. When it does, a strong team will begin to emerge and your reputation as manager will start to skyrocket.

11. Huh? How to Listen and Understand

"Boss, we just lost the Userfriendly Computer account."
"Huh? Oh, good. Say, find out what's happening with the Userfriendly Computer account, will you?"

Recent conversation at
Danbury Downtime Corp.

Listening, at least listening with understanding, is more than just sitting back and letting words flow into your ears. It is an active skill, at least as hard as talking—maybe harder. There is no real communication unless the listener understands, accepts, and will do something based on what was said. So the listener has to take at least fifty percent of the responsibility for good communication.

Since listening is a communications skill, I could have easily included it with the chapters on writing, speaking, and running meetings. But it is so important to motivation and team building (poor listening is often the reason that people and teams get into trouble) that I have put it here.

A good listener has a real head start getting people fired up and eager to work together as a team. A poor listener does not. It's as simple as that.

Most of us are lousy listeners. We spend a third of each day in situations where we should be listening, but experts say we don't hear a quarter of what we should. There are some good reasons for that.

- We think much faster than people talk. We get way ahead of them, know what they are going to say, so we get bored and drop out. Or the subject may be dull, and we start thinking of something else.
- We have several things on our minds at once and tend to switch over to think about the most urgent one.
- While the skills of reading, writing, and speaking are taught in school, listening rarely is. We're just not trained in it.
- While someone else is talking, instead of listening we mentally rehearse what we're going to say in response.
- The speaker may present new ideas which make us feel uncomfortable, so we get busy thinking about why they won't work, instead of listening.
- We may not be sure what the speaker is talking about, either because he or she just can't get the point across well or uses too much technical language and jargon. We don't want to seem stupid and ask questions, so we look alert, nod, and think about something else.
- We may not like the speaker or believe him or her, so we don't pay much attention.
- We just plain may not be able to hear the message because the speaker doesn't talk loudly enough, there's too much noise, or the old ear drums are giving out.

With all those working against us, no wonder we can't listen. Do you have any of those difficulties? Chances are you do. But there are ways you can improve your listening. Most people don't know how little they listen, so just understanding you may have a problem is a big step toward improving your listening skills.

HOW TO LISTEN EFFECTIVELY

To listen well you must:

1. Be able to hear what's being said.
2. Actively focus your attention on what's being said.
3. Understand and accept what's being said for what it is, independent of your feelings about it.

4. Evaluate what has been said.
5. Give feedback.

Here are some thoughts about each:

1. How to Hear What's Being Said

Let's face it, if the words don't get into your noggin in the first place, there's no hope. Follow these suggestions:

Ask the speaker to speak louder if you can't hear.

Move closer to the speaker.

Remove distractions. Close doors or windows if there's commotion outside. Hold phone calls.

And, most important of all,

SHUT UP. You can't hear much when you're talking yourself. Don't talk. Don't interrupt. Be patient, give the speaker time.

If you still can't hear,

Have your hearing checked. Seriously. If you have a mechanical problem with hearing, you will never be a successful listener.

2. How to Focus Your Attention on What's Being Said

Listen for items that interest you, even in dull topics. They're in there if you concentrate and ferret them out.

Keep active. Take notes, key-word notes that will help you identify and remember the main points of what was said. Respond to the speaker: nod, say "uh huh," "yep," "I see," or look expectantly at the speaker. This keeps you involved and encourages the speaker.

Sit up, lean forward, and watch the speaker.

Don't give up if you find your mind wandering. You probably haven't missed much. Refocus your attention and pick up the train of thought.

Don't look through papers or try to read and listen at the same time. You can't do it.

Try to set aside your biases with regard to the speaker. If a brand new MBA is expounding on expense control, you may have trouble listening because you wonder if he or she knows anything about the real world. If you really want to listen and find out if there are some gems of wisdom there, you may have to set aside your feelings about new MBA's and let the content seep through.

Don't rehearse what you are going to say next. Rehearsing causes more lost listening than just about anything else. When the speaker is through, pause a moment. Think about what you'll say. Then respond.

Tell yourself you will paraphrase what is said later on. This will make you pay strict attention. Even if you don't have a chance to talk later with the speaker (for instance, if he or she is speaking to three thousand people in the Michigan State field house), plan to tell your spouse or a friend what was said.

When you start getting bored, mentally review and summarize what has been said so far and list points of interest to you.

3. How to Understand and Accept What's Being Said

Decide at the outset you will take whatever the speaker says, whether you like it or not, without interpreting it to fit your own ideas, and try to understand exactly what the speaker means. Stay loose and accept whatever comes along without becoming defensive, angry, or rejecting it out of hand. That's easy for me to say, hard for any of us to do.

Don't let the speaker's poor choice of words, bad grammar, offensive language, or misuse of words distract you from the main message. Keep listening for it and going after it. Also, don't get distracted by details or side issues the speaker brings up.

If you don't understand, ask questions. Ask questions to clarify, not to challenge. You're not ready to evaluate yet.

Listen for hidden meanings. Should you take what the speaker is saying at face value or are there deeper meanings? Watch for *nonverbal* clues (see below).

This doesn't mean you can't listen critically. It does mean there is a place for everything and, in the listening process, understanding comes before evaluating.

4. How to Evaluate What's Being Said

Again, make sure you understand first, before you evaluate.

Think of good points first before you tear into the bad ones.

Make your evaluation based on the content of what was said, not on *how* the speaker said it (don't reject ideas just because the speaker was a lousy presenter). Don't evaluate on whether you like the speaker personally or not.

Weigh all the evidence presented. Did it seem logical and valid—did it make sense? Was it complete?

Look for things the speaker said that could change your established opinions or beliefs, anything that could prove you wrong.

If possible, do homework on the subject before you listen so you can evaluate based on facts, not just your own opinions.

Decide what it is the speaker wants to have happen as a result of all this talking. Does he or she want you to:

Know more?
Make a decision?
Do something?
Or just be entertained?

Once you know that, or think you know, decide if you agree that that purpose is right or not, and then what you will do, if anything, about it.

5. How to Give Feedback

Restate the speaker's key points if you are in a situation where you can do that, like a one-on-one conversation or a small meeting. Add your own interpretations and opinions only after you have paraphrased, as exactly as you can, the speaker's original points.

Remember: The speaker has no way to know if you were listening well, or if communication took place, until you do this.

Tell the speaker what you intend to do, if anything, and why.

HOW TO GET OTHERS TO LISTEN

If you are trying to become a better listener, why not turn the tables and make others listen better to you? That's only fair, right? Here's how.

1. If you are speaking to a group, give a presentation that's so good they can't help listening. (See Chapter 6 on giving presentations.)
2. Be sure the listener can hear. Eliminate as many distractions as you can. Speak up. If you sense your listener is getting bored, change your pace, take a break, finish up quickly, or say something unexpected.

3. Focus your listener's attention. Start with a grabber that will get your listener's attention right up front and make him or her want to hear what's coming next. Use a startling fact, a statement that appeals to your listener's needs, or "Think what would happen if . . ." Tell your listener you'll want to discuss what you've said when you're finished and want his or her opinion and help.
4. Make sure your listener understands. Pause occasionally and ask, "Is that clear? Any questions so far?" Tell the listener why you feel as you do so that he or she doesn't have to puzzle about your motivation.
5. Help your listener evaluate. Ask, "Do you see some good points in that? What were they?" State clearly what you'd like the listener to do.
6. Ask for feedback. Ask, "How do you feel about what I said?" "What does it mean to you?" "What do you plan to do?" If what the listener tells you has little relation to what you said, go back and start over.

"Boss, I've got an idea how we can get the User Friendly account back."

"Huh? Get it back? What are you talking about? I didn't know we lost it."

"We did. They just called."

"They did?"

"Want to hear my idea?"

"Shoot, I'm all ears!"

•

READING THE OTHER PERSON

To really understand what the other person is feeling, you have to be aware of the total person and everything he or she says and does. This is true if you are the listener—you can tell how the speaker feels about what he or she is saying by observing how he or she says it—and it's also true if you are the speaker.

There's an old saying that goes, when speaking, listen carefully to what your audience is telling you. This is an important part of the communication process that many people overlook.

You may be lucky and have the person you're talking with tell you, "I'm ecstatic, I'll do it" or "I hate it." "You'll have to hang me by my thumbs for a week before I'll say yes," so you'll know. But often, responses aren't that clear, and you'll have to look for clues as to what your listener is thinking and how he or she feels.

Here are some important ones to watch for:

What to look for in the other person	What it may mean	
	LISTENER is receptive, agrees, likes. SPEAKER is honest, certain, enthusiastic.	LISTENER disagrees, dislikes, or is bored. SPEAKER doesn't know or is stretching the truth.
Posture	Sitting forward on edge of chair, leaning toward you. Arms loose and relaxed. Legs crossed naturally and relaxed.	Slouching, leaning back. Arms tense, folded across chest. Knees and feet together.
Hand Signals	Hands relaxed, easy natural gestures.	Hands clasped, holding on to chair or desk. Chopping or clenched-fist gestures. Fingers drumming.
Location	Moving out from behind desk, getting closer.	Moving behind desk, moving away from you.
Eyes	Looking at you.	Avoiding eye contact. Looking out window, studying papers.
Facial Expression	Smiling, looking attentive.	Frowning, looking disdainful, uncertain.*
Speech Patterns	Speech normal, calm Using supportive words and sounds. Tone sympathetic. Words precise, understandable, uses facts. Speaks directly to the issues. Uses "we" and "us."	Speech too loud, too fast (indicates tension). Silence, muttering. Tone sarcastic, biting, annoyed. Words vague, uses opinions rather than facts. Dances around the subject. Uses phrases like "to tell the truth," "frankly," or "to be honest with you." No evidence of partnership feeling.

* Be careful, some people just look that way normally.

Build your listening skills: Make sure you can hear what's being said, actively focus on what's being said, understand and accept it, no matter how you feel, then evaluate and finally, give feedback. Becoming a better listener will help you all day, every day to understand your team members better, motivate them and get them working together as a team. And that will help you be a better manager, and stand out from the crowd.

Harnessing the Organization

12. Importance of the Irrelevant: How to Deal with Nonwork Factors That Influence Your Career

Shirley: We've got to do something about Mac. His work isn't up to par.

Ed: Mac? His work is fine. Why, he's the first one here every morning.

Shirley: He is? Well . . . maybe I'm being too tough on him.

Organizations have personalities just like people. Understanding your organization's personality and its likes and dislikes can help you work within it more easily and accomplish more of what you want to.

What is revered and rewarded in one organization can be open invitation to unemployment in another. Some organizations, for instance, are fast-action pressure cookers where anything goes: gambles are taken, instant seat-of-the-pants decisions are made, people are fired, whatever, to get the job done. Being a hard-driving high roller is a real plus in a situation like that. The same high roller might look like a hyena in a library at a more deliberate, cautious organization, where risks are avoided, things move at a slower, less frenetic pace, and people are carefully nursed and cared for. There, being conservative, conventional, and thoroughly predictable is more likely to win respect.

Fitting the norm of your organization will help you be thought of as an insider, one who really belongs and can play a more and more important part in its management. Mavericks are fine, and a few of them do well. More often, though, they are thought of as peculiar, and everyone is a little hesitant to deal with them.

If you must be your own person, that's fine. Stick to your guns, do things your own way. But keep in mind, if you behave differently from others, especially those who are respected and admired in the organization, you will be hurting your own career momentum.

That may seem contrary to the whole idea of standing out from the crowd, which after all is what this book is about. But standing out because of your mastery of *Upward Bound* skills is one thing. Standing out because of what others see as weird behavior is something else again. Practice your pecadillos at home.

When you think about behavior that is highly prized and rewarded in your organization, you may be surprised to find that much of it has little or nothing to do with getting the work done. It is irrelevant. Even so, it is very important and can have a tremendous impact on your progress, because sometimes *how* you do something is more important than what you actually accomplish.

That's why, in this chapter, we'll look at a few common, high-impact irrelevants:

Dress	Messing around
Working hours	Tolerance for boredom
Vacations	Your office
Expense accounts	First impressions
Drinking	Smoking

As we go through these, first think of several people you consider to be successful in your organization. How do they handle the irrelevants? You can learn big lessons from them. Then, ask yourself, "How well does my behavior fit? Am I acting like a successful person would act or am I behaving in alien ways that will hurt my image and my career?"

You can't change your basic personality easily, but you can bend and modify certain habits a little, you can concentrate on practicing what's rewarded in your organization and avoiding what's not.

Let's think about our irrelevants.

DRESS

The number one rule on dress is that there is no one rule that applies to every organization. Sartorial splendor in one firm is a clown suit in another. Navy blue pinstripes are right in a bank, laughable in an ad agency where everybody wears jeans and sweatshirts.

Look at the people around you in your organization, especially the ones on a fast track to the executive suite. What do they wear? Don't worry if you don't like their taste. Get past that to *style* of dress, because that's what you want to copy.

Adopt the style of your organization. Don't wear orange clothes if everyone important is in dark gray. Don't wear sport coats if the other men dress in three-piece suits. Don't wear sweaters and skirts if the other women wear tailored fashions. Don't dress to get sniggers, dress to get admiring glances because you are capturing the organization's style and wearing it better than most.

WORKING HOURS

Some employers expect you to be there early in the morning; others expect you'll stay late at night; still others, unhappily, expect both.

What is the norm in your organization? Have you ever thought about it or have you just been going along working the "official" hours? If many high fliers are there at 7:00 A.M., show up once in a while at seven, too, and let people know you're there. Have a reason to contact one or more of them as soon as you get in. If someone suggests getting together tomorrow, say, "How about seven?"

Extend your working hours by carrying a briefcase. Never arrive or leave for the day without it, even if you only have your lunch in it. People may think you are working at home, and they'll never know for sure.

VACATIONS

The big question, besides when to go and what to do, is whether to take vacations or not. How is taking vacations viewed by management?

The only guideline on vacations is: Take them.

That may seem in conflict with other strategies we've discussed, especially if top people don't take their vacations, or all their vacations. But vacations don't come along that often and don't impact that much on your overall work pattern. Unless you are told outright, or put under much obvious pressure not to, you should take them.

In most organizations, there are people who take their vacations and those who don't. Think of some of each in your organization. Is there any difference in how well they are doing? Probably not.

When you retire and look back over thirty-five years of work, no matter how high up you are, how well you've done, and how rewarding your work has been, you will think, "I wish I had taken more time for fun, spent more time with my family, stopped now and then to smell the roses." Don't let all that get away from you.

Vacations are necessary for another very important work-related reason. Vacations, by giving you a chance *not* to think about work, will help you come up with all kinds of new ideas about your job and how to do it better. The more you don't think about it, the more ideas will keep popping into your mind. Then, when you come back, you'll be ready to tear the place apart.

EXPENSE ACCOUNTS

Expense accounts can't help you much, but can hurt you a lot. You'll never get rich on an expense account, or even recoup all your costs, but you can damage your image by charging too much to your account.

You know your employer's philosophy on expenses: Whether to fly first class and stay at the Ritz la Ritz, or sit in the back of the plane and bunk in a Ma and Pa's Cabins, and you probably follow that pretty well. But beyond that is a big open area for judgment. How many meals do you charge for? (On the last day of your trip, do you put down dinner? Even if your plane gets in at four o'clock?) How much do you put down? What your dinner actually costs or what it should have if you had not gone crazy and ordered the rack of lamb? How about cab fare . . . could you have taken a limo or bus? Do you charge tips, after-dinner carousing entertainment expenses? Car repairs? Where do you draw the line?

In some organizations it doesn't matter. In many others, struggling to control expenses, it does. If yours is one of the latter, don't let a buck here and there give people up the line the impression you are fast and loose with expense money. Somebody may decide you are spending too much in other areas, too, and want to perform surgery on your budget. Get what you are entitled to and that's it. Write off the rest as reimbursed business expenses and forget it.

DRINKING

Again, follow your organization's norm. But remember one thing. Attitudes and habits have changed. The era of the hard-drinking, stay-up-all-night executive has passed, even in sales. If entertaining clients is part of your job, you don't have to get zonked with them time after time. If they want to, fine. If you want to, that's okay too. But if you've got important work to do after a client lunch, or the next day after a client dinner, have a good time on something low octane. A glass of white wine at lunch is sociable and won't damage you much. Three martinis is also sociable, but can wipe you out for the afternoon.

The point is, you are not going to do your best work if you're half blitzed or hung over, and you don't *have* to be if you don't want to be. Your clients won't think less of you; in fact, they may have a new admiration for you.

MESSING AROUND

Equal opportunity may not have solved all the inequities, but it has brought more men and women together in peer relationships today than ever before. Men and women go to meetings together, make decisions together, travel together, drink together, go to restaurants together, and stay in the same hotels together. There are more temptations, more opportunities today for both sexes. So what? What you do with any of that is obviously your business. But there are some things to think about:

1. Messing around, no matter how discreet you try to keep it, is such juicy conversation, everyone in the office will know about it before you can say, "Your place or mine?"
2. Messing around has an element of sneakiness about it. Sneaky is not valued behavior.
3. Messing around is almost always seen as indiscreet by others, even those who are gross philanderers. They see it as forgivable for themselves, maybe, but not for you.
4. Everyone who has messed around will tell you it takes a lot of time and energy (that otherwise could be used for work). Since at least some of the higher-ups have messed around and know this, they'll assume, if you are messing around, you are not putting as much time and energy into your job as you should be.
5. There is still a double standard in regard to sex in the office. As questionable as it may be for men, it is deadly for women. Any woman who is even suspected of having an affair may find her career stalled, or at the very least will get snide comments about reasons for every promotion or raise she gets.

Yet, knowing all this, people still are people and become attracted to each other. My advice: Stay away from it at all costs . . . if you can't, have fun, but don't try to kid yourself about what you're getting away with.

TOLERANCE FOR BOREDOM

Watch successful people. Most seldom show boredom, even though they, like the rest of us, have to listen to boring people, boring speeches, sit through boring meetings, and read boring reports. Unfortunately, life is not a circus and there are lots of chronically dull people—or people who are wearisome at times (you and I included).

The trouble is, what's boring for you may be red hot for someone else, and often you have no way of knowing. Better to use lots of patience and pretend interest than to antagonize someone who is trying to present a favorite project while you're falling asleep, and have them suspect you aren't really interested in what's going on at work. Remember, you think broadly, think "corporate," and that means you are interested in everything. Even that sleep-inducing, no-importance drivel you have to suffer through now and then.

That doesn't mean you have to sit and smile through everything no matter how it is presented. Skim through Goliath reports to get to the bottom line. Ask people giving rambling reports to get to the point, but try to make it seem you are doing it because you can't wait to get to the bottom line, not because you are about to slip into a coma.

YOUR OFFICE

You may spend a lot of time in your office, but try to resist the temptation to turn it into a second home with pictures all over the walls, plants and trees crowding in like a rain forest, special furniture, a throw rug or two, and knick-knacks all over your desk. Comfortable as that might seem, it gives the impression you feel your office is permanent and that you'll be there forever. It's better to keep a sparse appearance: one picture, maybe. A plant. That's it. That shows you're not attached to your office and are ready to move on a moment's notice (to a larger office, of course).

That's true even if you are likely to be in your job for a long time, because

1. If a better office does become available, you won't be crossed off the list because you are "so attached to the one you have."
2. Being too settled in an office can make it seem like you are "comfortable" and settled in other ways too.

Also think about your office housekeeping. The chart below will help you.

Office Housekeeping Styles

Style	How it looks	Pluses & minuses (Gives the impression:)
Incredible Mess	Like your attic and garage combined. Papers, letters, folders, boxes, books, magazines, old sandwiches, and coffee cups piled everywhere.	+ You're handling a big workload. – You are disorganized, and can't find anything. – You are a slob in other things, too.
Compulsively Neat	Everything in its place, straight and orderly. One piece of paper in the middle of your desk.	+ You are neat and organized. – You don't have much to do. – You're structured to the point of being neurotic.
Medium Neat/ Messy	A few papers around, or books and folders open. Semi-neat during the day, usually put away at night.	+ You have all of the above pluses. + You have none of the above minuses.

Studied messiness is the way to go. Nobody respects a slob, and everybody wonders about a compulsive. Keep your style somewhere in between.

FIRST IMPRESSIONS

First impressions belong on our list of irrelevants because they can be influenced by many factors other than performance—and often are. Some, like dress, we've already discussed. Others we will look at here.

The important thing to remember about first impressions is that they shouldn't just happen. You can and should manage them to your advantage.

Even if you have been with your organization for years and know everyone from the president to the porter, you still have opportunities all over the place to make good "first" impressions: when you meet with someone you haven't worked closely with before or haven't worked with for a long time, when you welcome someone new into the firm, when you work with someone who has taken on new responsibilities, and when *you* take on new responsibilities.

In any of these circumstances, people form opinions very quickly about you. Those opinions may be hard to change later on. So it is important that you go into a new situation prepared and ready to manage the impression you create right from the very first minute.

Here's how.

1. Do your homework. Prepare for your get-togethers. Think through what you want to cover and how. Get supporting data. Rehearse. Anticipate questions and make up answers. Plan to get your main points in early before the discussion gets sidetracked onto something else. Do this for every encounter, even brief, casual ones, when you will be with someone who can influence your career. That's not only bosses. Lots of people can affect how you are seen in the organization. Word gets around.
2. Know your own area. Be prepared to discuss your operation in detail. Know your numbers: profit, sales, production, productivity, whatever is important. If you can't remember all the numbers, make up a notebook (your "Operation Book"). Keep your numbers in it and take it with you. Better yet, see Chapter 14 to develop memory skills. Vague answers about your own area make lousy impressions.
3. Know the organization. Be able to talk intelligently about the organization beyond your own department. Keep up-to-date on anything your organization publishes about itself so you can talk about sales, quarterly earnings, new policies, new ventures, and new systems.

   Also, check out the other person's department. Make up a couple of intelligent questions to ask. This will make you seem very perceptive—and will also be fun for him or her—people love to talk about what they do.

   The best way to find out what's really going on is to ask questions. That sounds silly, but lots of people are afraid to, because they don't want to admit they don't know something. That's nonsense. If you don't know, ask. And don't settle for surface answers or vague statements. Dig, paraphrase, ask again, until you are sure you understand.
4. Know the language. Part of knowing the organization is speaking its language and much of that is jargon: company organization terms, titles, names of departments, functions, processes, and products. Financial terms: ROE, EPS, ROI, gross profit, cash flow, IRR. Data-processing lingo: acronymns for systems, authoring languages, computer programs. Euphemisms: deviation from plan (really screwed up); got a minute? (I'm here, now listen); negative increase (we're going broke); lacks people skills (a real bastard).

If you are in a conversation that goes like this:

Linda: You mean the I/O?

Dan: Yeah.

Linda: Is it megatasked?

Dan: Of course, but interruptible with a channel on each side.

Linda: What about chains?

Dan: About the same as the 81M–10 or the AG 57.

Linda: How is that different from the UXM?

Dan: I think the canning vector handles the overplay for you.

You'd better be ready to jump in with . . .

You: It's like the Agrom 150 CXX.

Linda and Dan: Oh.

Keep up with jargon and use it when appropriate, not to confuse and mystify people who don't understand it, but to show you know what's going on with others who know and use the "in" terms.

Right or wrong, careers are influenced by first impressions. Make sure every one you give from now on is a plus for your career.

SMOKING

When you are with someone important who doesn't, don't.

PLAN FOR MANAGING IRRELEVANTS

Using the Irrelevant Table following, jot down those irrelevants in the left-hand column that are important in your organization. Use any we've discussed above or add others that are unique to your work environment.

In the middle column, describe how successful people handle them. Then, in the right-hand column, outline, as specifically as possible, changes you are planning to make . . . the way you handle each so that you can more closely fit what's highly regarded in your organization.

Remember to watch the irrelevants. They are important. Straying off the ranch into the land of pecadillos can hurt you a lot. Don't let little everyday appearances you can easily control slow you down. Follow the lead of the best people in your organization and use irrelevants to help advance your career.

Irrelevant Table

Irrelevant	How successful people handle	Specific adjustments you should make

13. **Managing Your Boss:** How to Get the Most Out of Your Boss

Genie: Master, you shall have your first two wishes: Ten million dollars and a gold-plated Rolls-Royce. What is your third wish?

Exec: I wish my boss would work for me for a week . . . just one week.

Do you think of your boss as someone who gives the orders and yourself as someone who carries them out? Do you think of your boss as an adversary who makes you do things you don't want to do and pushes you in directions you don't want to go? If so, you don't have a good relationship with your boss, and you are missing all kinds of opportunities to get more fun, satisfaction, career growth, and reward out of your job. You don't have to be enemies with your supervisor. And you don't have to sit around and take whatever comes from the boss. In fact, you should be giving your manager subtle but strong guidance and direction to make sure he or she is doing more of what you want, and becoming more like your partner than your boss.

You can manage your boss. And you should, so that he or she

- will give you more freedom
- will give you more important work to do
- will recognize and reward you for good work, and

- will do a better job, and get promoted faster, thereby getting out of your way.

Without proper management, bosses tend to wander off on their own and may not do any of those. Make sure your boss is getting the guidance he or she needs. It may be hard to believe, but the boss is human, too, just like everybody else. He or she has anxieties, insecurities, problems, and all the fears, foibles, and frailties you have been assuming up until now were reserved only for you. They may not be evident because the boss is not going to put them on exhibit or tell you about them, any more than you are about to hang a list of your weaknesses on the office bulletin board. But you can bet they are there.

Let's say you tell your boss, Albert, the Glitch Productions deal has just fallen through. Inside, he'll be screaming, "OH, NO! This is awful! How will I tell the V.P.? I'm ruined!" But if he is like most bosses, Albert won't tell you he's falling apart. Instead, he'll hide that by 1) yelling at you, 2) throwing things, 3) cursing the clods at Glitch or 4) saying something icily controlled like "Well, these things happen. Let's see what we can do to pick up the pieces and find something even better." Don't assume that just because Albert isn't a quaking puddle of flesh on the office carpet, he doesn't have the same inner gnawings you do. He probably does.

Bosses are in very unique and difficult situations. It is almost unnatural for anyone to fill the role of boss. For instance, the boss—any boss—is totally exposed every working day to subordinates. The boss can color and interpret things when describing them to his or her boss, but you see and feel the direct results of almost everything your boss does. You know more about your boss's behavior than anyone else's, except maybe that of your spouse.

For example, it comes as no news to anyone that bosses sometimes make mistakes and make lousy decisions. What happens when they do? Subordinates, even those who have been semicomatose for days, suddenly have a new cause for living. Hardly anything is more fun to celebrate than some bone-headed decision the boss made. People love to get something on their superiors. They'll grasp any mistake the manager makes and gleefully use it to liven up their workday conversations.

The boss may make a hundred decisions each week. Some are big ones. Canceling a contract or firing a marginal performer. And some little. Deciding whom to go to lunch with or how to word a memo. But in those hundred, there is lots of room for error. Even if the boss only makes ten mistakes out of a hundred and is batting .900, it's the ten goofs that people will center their coffee-break discussion around all week long. "You won't believe what the boss did!" "How could a guy in his position be so dumb?"

What can we learn from all that?

1. Being the boss is not always as much fun as a three-legged race.
2. Bosses are not superpeople. You can't expect perfection from a person just because he or she happens to be your boss.
3. Bosses need help and guidance, too, and will accept it from anywhere—up, down, or across the organization—if it is presented right.

"Presented right" is the key because your boss will only be receptive to your management if you do it in a way that turns him or her on.

The best way to find out what that is is to start keeping a log of what *seems* to please your boss. Watch carefully when you are working with your boss how he or she reacts to what's happening. For instance, does the boss often go back for more facts or details, assembling tons of information, or does he or she prefer a short summary on one piece of paper? Is the boss distant and conscious of status or does he or she try to be "one of the boys"? Does the boss like to take risks or play it safe? Does the boss like to plan things out to the last nit or does he or she prefer to go ahead and get on with it?

Pay attention to everything he or she says that reveals an attitude. Watch nonverbal reactions (see Chapter 11). Make notes every day for a few weeks until you feel confident you know your boss's likes and dislikes pretty well. Use the Boss Chart below to keep your log.

BOSS CHART

These turn the Boss on:	How to do more of them:
These turn the Boss off:	**How to avoid doing them:**

When you have made a bunch of entries in the left-hand column, think of each one in terms of your own behavior. Generally speaking, you should try to do more of what turns the boss on and less or none of what turns him or her off. If some of that is contrary to your normal style, you would have to work hard to do it. In the right-hand column of the chart, list specific actions you can take to provide the boss with more of what he or she likes and less of the dislikes.

You have probably noticed so far I have talked about you changing the way *you* approach the boss. Probably, you would rather have a surefire way to change your boss. As much as I would like to give you a magic formula for making your boss behave the way you want him or her to (and pocket the money you'd be willing to pay me for that), I'm afraid I can't. There is no formula. In fact, attempting to change your boss's behavior at all is a low-yield activity, AT LEAST UNTIL YOU HAVE DONE THE CHANGING FIRST AND SHOWN THE BOSS THAT YOU ARE WILLING TO MEET HIM OR HER MORE THAN HALFWAY.

Keep the Boss Chart handy. We will use it again pretty soon.

Now let's find out where your boss needs help. Look down the list below and decide whether your boss does each of these

A. Enough to suit you.

B. Sometimes, but could do more (Needs some guidance).

C. Hardly ever (Badly needs your help).

RATE EACH ITEM A, B, OR C.

Boss's Actions	Your Rating
Works with you to set goals so you know what's expected.	
Lets you know what's going on.	
Delegates responsibility and important work.	
Gives you freedom to run your own area.	
Accepts new ideas, new ways of doing things.	
Gives you feedback on how you are doing.	
Supports you and your programs—provides adequate resources.	
Recognizes and rewards good work.	

Now go back and pick out the one area that is most important to you, the one you want to work on first, then the second, and so on. To get your boss to change his or her ways, you will first need to plan how to approach the boss, using the Boss Chart, as we discussed earlier. Look at what turns your boss on and do plenty of that. Look at what turns him or her off and use none of that.

Next, go in, sit down, and talk to your boss about what it is you want him or her to do.

"TALK TO MY BOSS?! YOU'VE GOT TO BE KIDDING!!"

If that's your reaction, consider this. You can't manage your boss by wishing. You have to do something. Most bosses will be receptive to your interest in building a better working relationship if you:

1. Protect his or her ego. If you are trying to get the boss to delegate more important work, you wouldn't go in and say, "You're not doing those Jones proposals very well, why not give them to me?" Instead say, "You know those Jones proposals? They are very interesting to me and I would like to help you with them. Would you be willing to let me take a crack at two or three of them and see how I do?"
2. Don't threaten his or her security by giving the impression you want to take over his or her job. Always put the emphasis on helping him, her, or the department to perform better and get things done more easily.
3. Use good negotiating skills (see Chapter 8).
4. Don't show disappointment or anger if your first try doesn't work. It may not, but the worst that could happen would be for the boss to say No, and even if that happens, he or she will probably think more highly of you for asking and might keep you in mind for the future.

And there's always a good possibility that your strategy will work and the boss will do exactly what you want, demonstrating beyond any doubt that *you can manage your boss.*

Let's look at the various "Boss's Actions" you rated above and see how you can get your boss to do more of them. Work through this list in your priority order, starting with the area you ranked most important to you.

How to Get the Boss to Work with You to Set Goals So You Know What's Expected

Sometimes we race along, working feverishly, without really knowing exactly what it is we're supposed to do. More than one person has been floored at performance-appraisal time by a criticism that such and such had not been done, or had not been done fast enough, big enough, or whatever, when the poor appraisee had never been told what was expected in the first place.

If you feel uneasy about what your boss wants and you are not getting much guidance from him or her, it may be time to initiate a conversation.

Be especially careful of your boss's ego on this one. Bosses like to pride themselves on their ability to communicate in a crystal-clear manner and to set fair but tough goals for their people. So be careful to avoid implying that that wasn't done. "I don't know what the hell I'm supposed to be doing around here" is not a good opening.

Here's a better way.

Using your job description and your knowledge of the day-to-day work, make a list of your major duties and responsibilities. Alongside each put what you think your goals are: time, amount, quality of the end product, people to be involved, general approach, and method to be used. Use the What's Expected Chart below to help.

Go see the boss. Say you just want to take a few minutes to go over your job responsibilities again (implying you do that all the time with the boss) to make sure you are doing what he or she expects you to. Go over each duty and cover related projects you are currently working on. Run down your list of duties and, for each one, ask, "Am I doing this the way you want me to? How could I do it better?" When you have gone through the list, ask, "Is there anything else I should be doing that I'm not doing now?" Try to pin the boss down on specific expectations.

If the boss seems to be having a tough time getting down to specifics, help him or her by asking questions like:

- What is this project going to be used for? Why are we doing it and what do we hope to accomplish?
- Who else up the line is going to see what I've done, and what do these people expect?
- What department or company goals are we trying to support? Specifically, what should I be doing to support them?
- What do we hope our department to become a year from now, two years? What does that tell us about what I should be doing now?

When you are done, use the boss's views on each item to revise what you have noted in the right-hand "What's Expected" column.

WHAT'S EXPECTED CHART

Your Major Responsibilities	What Is Expected: Goals and Standards, Time, Amount, Quality, Etc.

How to Get Your Boss to Let You Know What's Going On

Your boss may not be giving you all the information you need because he or she

1. Doesn't have it.
2. Can't get it.
3. Doesn't know you need it.
4. Doesn't want you to have it.

Whatever you suspect the real reason to be, start out by assuming that just about any information is obtainable if there is a good reason for getting it. Make a list, using the What's Going On Chart, of all the kinds of information you need, but are not now getting. Be sure you

WHAT'S GOING ON CHART

Information You Need	Why You Need it	Benefits of Your Having It to You, Boss, Department	Possible Objections to Your Having It	How to Overcome

really need each item because you will find it hard to get anyone interested in giving you information that's just "nice to know."

Opposite each item of information you need, list why you need it. Be specific and indicate the part of your job it is needed for and what having it will do to improve your performance. Then list the benefits that will accrue to your boss and the department.

Before you go to your boss with the list, ask yourself if the boss might have objections to any item or items on the list, and think through how you will overcome those objections.

Discuss the list with your boss, emphasizing the benefits to the department, to him or her, and to your job performance.

If the boss cannot or will not get some of the information for you, at least you have done your best. And the boss will have a new awareness of your need for information (as well as your desire to do a good job).

And, too, there are other ways to get information. Friends around the organization may be able to help—anyone who has access to what you want. Going to them after you have struck out with the boss may produce other problems that you will have to evaluate. The point is, if your boss won't or can't get it for you, there are other ways.

One last thing, if you want more information flowing down, be sure enough is flowing up. Give your boss everything he or she needs to know about what you are doing and then some.

How to Get the Boss to Delegate More Responsibility and Important Work

Sometimes bosses don't delegate important work and decision-making power because they underrate the ability of their subordinates (to be fair, subordinates often overrate their capabilities at the same time). If you suspect you are underrated, the way out is to

a) find a way to demonstrate your superior abilities, and

b) let the boss know you are interested in using them.

Here are steps you can take to raise the boss's eyebrows and get him or her thinking, "I've got the proverbial eager beaver here . . . maybe I should see what this person can really do."

- Come up with a proposal, unsolicited and on your own, and present it to the boss on how to

  control costs

  market a new product

  automate work now being done by hand

GIVE ME MORE CHART

Work You'd Like to Do	Special Skills You Have to Do It	Benefits to the Boss	Benefits to the Department/Company

increase sales, market share
get work done faster, better
provide better service to your customers
or anything else that will make the boss look good.

- Ask to represent the boss when he or she can't attend a meeting.
- Go the extra mile. Always give the boss more than he or she asks for.
- Volunteer to take on work that's not being done.
- Talk with your boss about the best use of your time and talents, and how they could lead to more responsibility.
- Ask to help with the big new project that the boss is working on. Most bosses will involve you to the extent they feel you can help them do a better job. Try something like this: "Boss, you know the flexible-hours study you're doing? I think we should look at how some other companies are handling that. If you'd help me pick the companies you're interested in, I'd be glad to get in touch with them and make a report at the April staff meeting."

  Do a good research job and bang-up presentation, and your boss will more than likely think of you the next time some important work needs to be done.

  Use the Give Me More Chart to plan your approach.

Some additional hints:

- If your boss doesn't schedule them, initiate regular update sessions so you can fill him or her in on what great things you are doing, at the same time subtly stressing the fact that you are competent way beyond your present responsibilities, ready and eager to take on more.
- When you do get a new piece of work, no matter how small or insignificant, break your chops to do it well. Come up with original approaches, new formats. Be thorough, fast, and follow through to see that every detail is right. Plenty of people have gained new stature in the boss's eyes by doing a great job of running the department charity drive or coordinating agendas for staff meetings.

How to Get the Boss to Give You Freedom to Run Your Own Area

Some bosses just naturally turn people loose to do their thing, others have a strong need for control and will try to run everything, including work that subordinates can do perfectly well themselves.

If your boss is in the latter category, you've got a challenge, but one you can meet.

First, you have to establish a track record of successfully handling your area. Using the Freedom Chart, make a list of your most important duties in the left-hand column. If you have already filled in the What's Expected Chart, take your list from that. Then make a separate list of your successes and failures in accomplishing each one. When you are satisfied that you are completely capable (remember, if you can't do the job, there's some justification for the boss to jump in and do it for you), you're ready to strike. Look at each entry on the Freedom Chart and think about whose responsibility it should be. The second through fifth columns represent a gradation of possibilities running from "You do it all" to "The boss does it."

Specifically they mean:

Do on own:	You do the work and not bother the boss with it at all.
Handle by exception:	You do the work, but keep the boss informed of deviations (good or bad) from the plan.
Review by boss:	The boss reviews the work at various phases and makes suggestions. You still pretty much make final decisions.
Boss approves:	Same as above, but the boss has final okay.
Boss does:	It may be part of your job description but, for one reason or another, the boss wants to do it.

Set aside some time with the boss and explain that you want to talk about your job and make sure you both agree on how it should be done. Cover your chart and discuss each point, putting an X in the appropriate column. If the boss wants all the X's in the right-hand column, give him or her examples (from the list you made earlier) of your demonstrated competence in each area. Tell him or her that since you have shown you can do it (or similar work) in the past or have shown you can learn to do things just as difficult, the boss could save a lot of his or her time (and give himself or herself freedom to work on more important things) by giving that work to you and not being so much involved.

When you have negotiated how you will work together and have filled out the chart, make copies of the chart for the boss. If the boss continues to work the same as before (wait awhile and see; a few mistakes are common and backsliding is human), haul out the chart and have another meeting.

FREEDOM CHART

Duty	Do on Own	Handle by Exception	Review by Boss	Boss Approves	Boss Does

How to Get Your Boss to Accept New Ideas and New Ways of Doing Things

Your boss may not immediately fall in love with your ideas for revamping the department he or she has been running successfully for thirty years. In fact, most people are apprehensive about change, and your boss may not be immediately receptive to *any* new suggestions you have. That's normal, but an initial negative reaction often is only a delaying tactic to give the boss a chance to vent his or her apprehension and get used to the idea.

On the other hand, an initial "no" may be as enduring as the Great Wall of China. So you will have to determine what your own boss is up to. If you think the boss is stalling for time and will eventually say okay, wait it out. If he or she is the kind of person who resists anything new, you need more drastic action.

One of the best ways to make the boss more accepting is to show what great things your idea or suggestion will do for him or her, and for the organization as a whole. Use the Idea Chart. Make a list of them before discussing the idea with the boss. Try to anticipate any objections he or she will have, and work out ways to overcome them. One hint: Selling something new is usually more effective if you can relate your idea somehow to something the boss said or did in the past. Then it becomes at least partly his or her idea.

"Remember when you moved the sales department out to the annex? Well, I was thinking about our space problems, and when I realized what you did, that gave me the idea of remodeling the storage space in the annex and using it for our marketing people. That would get the two groups together again. I know how concerned you are about the bad communications we have now. That should really make everything run smoother!"

Here's something else to try. There's an old ploy that sales people have used for years: asking the customer to make little decisions instead of the one big one.

The TV salesperson doesn't ask you, "Do you want the set?" No. He asks, "Do you want the twenty-five-inch or the nineteen-inch?" "Do you want the mahogany finish or the oak?" "Would you rather we deliver on Thursday or Friday?" Pretty soon he or she has the sale signed, sealed, and in the cash register and has never actually asked if you wanted to buy anything.

You can do the same thing. "Boss, you know that storage area could have some great views. Do you think we should build the offices so they have a view of the woods or the front lawn?" Now, your boss has bought enough TV sets so that he or she will know what you're up to, but because

IDEA CHART

Your New Idea	Benefits for the Boss, Department, Company	Boss's Possible Objections	How to Overcome Them

making the little decisions is so much less stressful than making the big ones, the boss may not mind and will go along anyhow. "If we remodeled, I think we should face them toward the woods."

Giving alternatives (all of which are okay with you) is a way to make it easier for the boss to accept your ideas.

"Do you think October would be a good time to start or should we wait until after the holidays?" "If we shoot for October we will have everything settled by the first of the year."

Here are some other things you can do:

Offer to help the boss do whatever you suggest or do it yourself.

Cite examples of other departments or other outside organizations that have used the idea successfully.

Set up a meeting with someone who has used the idea and likes it, so the boss can hear it right from the horse's mouth.

Sell the idea ahead of time to someone you know the boss respects. Take that person with you when you go in to tackle the boss.

Give the boss lots of strokes every time he or she buys an idea, build his or her self-image as an open-minded person. Comment on that every once in a while even if you have to bite your tongue. Pretty soon the boss may start believing—and doing—it.

How to Get Your Boss to Give You Feedback on How You Are Doing

There are a couple things you should know about this:

1. Some bosses feel you are paid to do a good job, so when you come through and do what you are paid to do, they don't feel a need to hold a clambake for you. Whether that's good human-relations practice or not is beside the point. That's the way some bosses are.
2. One way to let people know how they are doing is through performance appraisal and some organizations have well-developed, elaborate appraisal programs. *BUT,* many bosses hate doing appraisals. It takes time away from running the department (many think of appraisals as special projects and not part of managing), appraisals are hard to do, and it is uncomfortable to sit down with someone face-to-face and give them criticism or even praise. So, many bosses will avoid doing appraisals or, if they can't get away with that, they will get through them as quickly as possible.

To get feedback if you don't get appraisals, make a list of what you feel you have accomplished in the last six months or so. Gather all the supporting facts. Outline your strengths and what opportunities you see for learning, growing, and improving in the future. Use the Feedback Form below. Then make an appointment with your boss. Try to get him or her to a quiet spot where you won't be interrupted.

FEEDBACK FORM

MAJOR ACCOMPLISHMENTS DURING THE PERIOD
FROM __________ TO __________ :

MAJOR STRENGTHS:

OPPORTUNITY AREAS FOR LEARNING, GROWING, IMPROVING IN THE FUTURE:

When you begin, remember your boss's ego is at stake. Be careful. Don't start out by saying, "You never let me know how I'm doing." Instead say something like, "You know, we've been working together for six months now and things have been so hectic, we really haven't had time to sit down and discuss how I'm doing. I've got some questions I'd like to ask you to make sure I'm on the right track." That puts the burden evenly on both of you, not just on the boss.

Then whip out your list of accomplishments and say, "Here are the things I see as my accomplishments over the last six months. Do you agree? Is there anything here that isn't accurate? Are there others that should be on the list and aren't? Are you happy with the way these came out? How could I have done better?"

End your conversation by saying something like, "I really want to do well and get ahead. Is there anything I could be doing more than what I'm doing now to speed that up?"

To get feedback if you have a formal appraisal system:

1. Early on, well before your appraisal date, get a blank copy of the appraisal form and instructions so you will know how you will be appraised and on what. If you can't get a copy, use the Feedback Form.
2. Fill out the appraisal form on yourself, being tough but fair. You may be pleasantly surprised in the actual appraisal to find your boss thinks more highly of your performance than you do. But, of course, you won't let the boss know that.
3. If it will help you feel better, fill out an appraisal form on your boss. Showing it to the boss is risky, but there are a few bosses who might be receptive and this could open up good dialogue about your relationship. If your boss is one of the exceptional ones who might look kindly on this, try it.
4. If you have had some noticeable failures or have some glaring weaknesses that will come up in your appraisal, practice your responses to what you suppose your boss will say. Make your responses nondefensive, constructive, and full of determination to do better in the future.
5. Make a list of what you hope to accomplish in the coming year: your work goals, what you want to learn, and how far you want to grow beyond what you are doing now. Growth could include additional responsibilities you'd like, new projects or committee assignments you hope your boss will give you, courses you plan to attend, and outside activities you hope to involve yourself in.
6. When you go to the appraisal interview, try to make it as easy as possible for your boss. If he or she says things you disagree with, point that out: "I understand your concern, but I'm not sure I agree with your comment on the Anderson situation, Fred. Here's how I see it." Then lay out the facts to support your opinion. Try to work out a statement for the appraisal form that is agreeable to both of

you. Use your rehearsed answers to respond to criticisms you feel are just.

Cover your list of accomplishments if it's different from the one the boss made up. Suggest comments from the appraisal form you filled out on yourself if you feel they will enhance your appraisal, and ask the boss if they shouldn't be on the real appraisal.

7. Keep your appraisal discussion focused as much as possible on the future. As soon as past accomplishments have been covered and appropriate strokes given, bring up your future goals and aspirations. Try to keep coming back to: "How can I do a better job for you and the company? What should I be concentrating on? How can I learn, grow, take on more responsibility, and get ahead faster?" Cover your list of next year's goals and get agreement on it.
8. If the boss wants to talk in generalities, gently try to pin him or her down. "Can you explain that a little more? Can you give me an example of when I did something like that?" Also, if he or she doesn't offer, try to get a bottom line. "How do you rate me overall, say on a scale of one to ten?"
9. At the end of the appraisal interview, even if it has been stormy and not overly pleasant, no matter what, say, "Thanks, boss. That was a good session. We may not agree one hundred percent on what's happened, but I appreciate your taking the time and trouble to do this and, believe me, it's been helpful to me. This gives me a good start on the next year. Thanks again." A little positive reinforcement like that can make your boss more eager to give you feedback in the future.
10. Always remember, even if the appraisal is typed and signed, it can be changed, and should be if it is not a fair reflection of your performance. Be careful here, though, because your boss's view of your performance and yours may be different . . . and he or she may be right. Avoid a confrontation on judgmental issues. Go to the mat on facts if they are wrong.

How to Get the Boss to Give You and Your Programs More Support and Provide Adequate Resources

Bosses can really come in handy when you are trying to get things done. They can, among other things, help you sell your programs to top management, help you get cooperation from "tough customers" elsewhere in the organization, and help you get more budget money, equipment, and staff.

SUPPORT CHART

Project: ____________________

Specific Things You Would Like the Boss to Do	How Boss's Support (and the Project's Success) Will Help Him or Her	How Support Will Benefit the Department and the Organization

Some bosses are naturally supportive and others have to be prodded. If your boss is a candidate for prodding, it may be because he or she

Doesn't know you need help.

Doesn't know what you are doing.

Doesn't think what you are doing is worthwhile.

Has different goals and objectives than you do.

Any of these problems can be attacked by using the following steps:

1. Use the Support Chart to write out the specific kinds of support you would like and what the success of your project would do to make the boss look good.
2. Outline your project and ask the boss for support. Just asking for assistance will make the boss feel important and make him or her like your projects better.
3. Cover in detail what you'd like the boss to do.
4. Show what the boss's help could do to improve your performance and how it would make him or her look like a star.
5. Make it clear you are asking for help, not trying to shove off work on the boss. You still will do the work. You will even do most of what you're asking the boss to help with if he or she will give you suggestions and clear the way for you.
6. Involve the boss on an on-going basis in your work. Give the boss updates, ask for advice and suggestions even when you don't need them. The more ideas the boss contributes to your work, the more ownership he or she will feel.
7. Use the boss's ego to help you. Make it clear you feel the boss has such status and power in the organization that he or she can get things done that you never could in a million years. Even if that's not true.

How to Get the Boss to Recognize and Reward Your Good Work

1. Make sure your work really is good enough to deserve recognition and reward. See "How to Get Your Boss to Give You Feedback on How You Are Doing" above.
2. Let your boss know about your triumphs and successes every chance you get. He or she will hear fast enough about your goofs so make sure he or she gets the positive side too. This is easier to do if you have opened up a continuing dialogue with your boss on work in prog-

ress. Send copies of anything that shows the quantity or quality of your work (including "thank you" letters) to the boss.

When you have done something you think is terrific, don't wait around for an appraisal that may be a year away. Go tell the boss about it. "What do you think about that?" "Looks like you did a good job." "Thanks."

3. Thank the boss for any tidbit of praise he or she gives and be sure the boss knows it's important to you to get recognition on a regular basis, not for any namby-pamby need for nuggies, but because you want to be sure you are on the right track, doing what the boss expects.
4. Don't be bashful about suggesting that what you have done should be recognized outside the department. "Should I write this up for the company newspaper?" "This would be a good thing to put on the bulletin board, don't you think?" "Top management would really be interested in this, wouldn't they? I could put a short report or presentation together, what do you think?"
5. Money is the sincerest form of reward and recognition. Don't wait around forever for the boss to decide to give you a raise. If you are in an organization with a highly structured pay system—such as civil service—there may not be much you can do to get more money until the magic time comes when everybody's pay is moved up—whether they deserve it or not. But if you are with an outfit where salary decisions are made at least to some degree based on merit, there may be more money waiting for you.

The way to get more money is to ask. But, because salary is such a high-charged, emotional issue, you should make your request in a very special way. Keep in mind you aren't the only one who wants more money. Everybody around you, including the boss, thinks the paycheck ought to be fatter. At any particular point in time, your boss may feel his or her own salary problem is bigger than yours. So you may have to divert the boss's attention from that problem to yours.

Here's what to do.

- Make sure your timing is right. Don't bring up a raise just when your organization has announced lousy third-quarter results and a belt-tightening campaign. Wait until things are going relatively well. Time your approach to follow some exceptional accomplishment of your own—something you know really pleased your boss.
- Have accurate information with you on what others in similar jobs inside or outside your company are making. Knowing that the average financial analyst with the same length of service as you have makes

eight thousand dollars more is powerful stuff. Again, before you lay that kind of thing on the boss, make sure the timing is right and you've just done something wonderful. When you ask for more money, there is always an implied possibility that you might quit and go somewhere else. If the boss doesn't think you're terrific, he or she may say, "Maybe you ought to try one of those other companies if they pay so much."

- Tie your salary discussion—unannounced—into a weekly update meeting, a project review, planning meeting, or other get-together where you and your boss are alone, discussing your work. Don't call a meeting to discuss salary. That raises red flags all over the place. Tell the boss you want to talk about your salary and he or she will turn into a turtle right before your eyes.
- Keep the discussion positive and work-related. Talk about how much you enjoy the job and how excited you are about all you've accomplished.
- Somewhere in there, tell the boss you had hoped by now some "salary action" would have been taken and that you sure would appreciate moving up in income. If you are a great Thespian, you might follow up by saying, "Of course, I like doing this so well I'd do it for nothing, but I've got to eat and pay the rent."
- Build up the boss's ego. Tell him or her, "You've been really fair to me in every area and I know you are the type of person I can talk about salary with." Bosses respond to positive feedback, too, and they'll try hard to believe it if it sounds halfway sincere.
- Each time you do get a salary increase, be sure you show your excitement (provided the increase is of decent size) and tell the boss, "Thanks, that's great. You know I'm really motivated by money and want to make a lot of it."

When talking rewards, don't ever:

- Threaten to leave. Most people don't react well to threats, and there's always the chance the boss will say, "Be my guest."
- Make it seem like money is the only important thing to you. Always sandwich money discussions in with other positive comments about the work, your progress, what a good relationship you have with the boss, and other upbeat stuff.
- Pester the boss with repeated requests for salary increases. You can do it once, maybe twice, with a boss; beyond that you are getting into dangerous territory. You can and should initiate discussions about your career now and then, and at those times you can make it known that, despite how much you like your work, you're still behind where you want to be in terms of income.

But there's a limit. No boss can respond to even the most convincing arguments in the world with an increase every month.

- Whine or make it seem like you are mistreated. You are bigger than that—if you really are mistreated, you ought to think about changing jobs or at least changing your circumstance within your organization. Don't talk about "deserving" more or being "owed" anything. That approach implies the boss has been unfair, less than perfect, and the last thing you want to do in this situation is to make the boss defensive by criticizing him or her.
- Come right out and use the phrase "I want a raise." You'll sound like Dagwood. And you know what happens to him every time he talks to Mr. Dithers about more money. The phrase is too worn out and has too many negative connotations. Try "salary adjustment," "something more in the paycheck," "monetary recognition," or similar euphemism.

Consider these final thoughts on managing the boss:

- Some bosses just cannot be managed. They are too stubborn, insecure, emotionally disturbed, frightened, or worried about you emerging as a competitor and will not respond to anything from anyone—even their bosses can't get them to change. If that is your situation, you can:

  Keep trying and keep hitting a stone wall.

  Grin and bear it—accept the situation and wait it out.

  Take action. (See Chapter 2 on career options.)

- Other bosses can be managed, but not easily. Tough bosses are good for you, though. A hard but manageable boss will be a challenge, keep you stretching, trying harder than you would otherwise. You can learn and grow a lot under a difficult boss. Look on it as going back to school.
- Most bosses, however, are ready and willing to be managed, provided you do it with common sense and keep their egos in mind. Try the strategies we've covered. You will be amazed at how much you can achieve if you do. There are bosses who have made 180-degree turnarounds in their styles, all because they learned so much from the people they were supervising.
- Be patient and persistent. We're talking about building a long-term relationship here, not a short, instant change. Most bosses won't roll over and let you rub their tummies any old time you feel like it. Remodeling takes time and continuing effort.

- And remember, just when you seem to be making progress, you will run into snags—times when you will be convinced your boss has reverted to monster status. But don't give up. Bosses are human and are victims of backsliding now and then. Backslides seem larger and worse in the boss, because we all want our bosses to be perfect.

Managing your boss takes some courage, but every person on the way up has some of that. Whatever you want your boss to do, you have to sit down with him or her and talk it over. Plan your approach around what you know the boss responds well to. Show how what you are suggesting will benefit the boss. Make it clear you are trying to do better and better work to make the department and the organization successful and the boss's help is necessary and valuable. Do this sincerely and confidently, and you will be surprised how well your boss responds to your leadership.

Doing It Right

14. I'll Think of It in a Minute: How to Remember What You Want To

"Mr. Fegley, I want you to meet the fellow who really helped us out on that real estate deal, Bob Simmons."
"Bob Simmons? I'm Ed Rukowski."

"I have a lousy memory. I can't remember names, I'm no good at details, and I never can think of the right thing to say until it's too late." Ever say that? Often? If so, you've probably convinced yourself that you do, in fact, have a lousy memory, and lo and behold . . . a self-fulfilling prophesy. Your memory seems to get worse.

You have a lousy memory? Not true. Nobody, except people with physical or emotional damage, has a lousy memory. Your memory may be unused, or underdeveloped, but there's nothing wrong with it.

Oh sure, some people seem to be able to remember much better than others, but even good rememberers forget some things . . . There is no such thing as photographic memory. Chances are, good rememberers have trained themselves (maybe without even knowing they were doing it) and have developed certain memory skills. Those skills involve the use of the simple but powerful techniques we'll cover in this chapter. If you use them well, you should be able to make dramatic improvements in your ability to remember.

Let's start by looking at five principles of memory:

1. Memory is not an absolute—it's not a case of remembering everything or not remembering anything. You may have partial memory; or be able to recall something now that you could not an hour ago; or have a name on the tip of your tongue, which means it is there in your memory somewhere, but you can't get it out.
2. Even if you are a good rememberer, you don't remember things exactly. The mind has a way of rearranging things to suit you over time, and usually allows you to remember things not as they happened, but as you feel they *should have* happened.
3. Bizarre, outrageous things tend to stay in your memory better than ordinary, humdrum things.
4. In a long list, or a long speech with many points, you will tend to remember items at the beginning and the end better than those in the middle.
5. Sometimes forgetting can be a blessing. You wouldn't want to remember everything that ever happened to you, and have all that junk clogging up your mind. In fact, there are probably several million things you are just as happy to forget anyhow, because they were grotty and would make you miserable to think of them. The mind has a way of forgetting bad things. That's wonderful and helps you keep a toehold on sanity.

WHAT IS MEMORY ANYHOW?

Remembering involves 1) obtaining information, 2) putting it in storage, 3) being able to get it out again. Think of it like earning money, putting it in a safe deposit box, and holding on to the key so you can get at the cash later on, when you want it.

When you don't remember, or forget, something has gone wrong with that process. Maybe you haven't obtained the information, either because you didn't listen, or because the information wasn't presented well, *or* maybe, even though you acquired the information you let it slip away before you locked it away in your safe deposit box; *or* maybe, even though you stored it away all right, you didn't work out a way to retrieve it. You never got the key to your safe deposit box.

Improving any of these, and preferably all of them, can cut down on the chances you'll forget.

HOW TO IMPROVE YOUR MEMORY

Let's look at how you can improve the way you acquire, store, and retrieve information.

1. How to Acquire Information

- Sort and select. We are all victims of information overload. With every new piece of information that comes at you, think, "Do I want to keep this? Will it do me any good?" If no, let it slide by. You can't remember everything. If yes, use these methods for acquiring information.
- Make sure you hear and understand the information. You can't store or retrieve material you haven't gotten in the first place. Work on your listening skills (Chapter 11), ask questions to clarify, paraphrase, and don't relax until you are certain you've gotten it. You must force yourself to stay one hundred percent alert when trying to acquire information. Ask yourself mental questions about the subject matter: What is the main message here? How can it be useful to me? How does it relate to what I already know, or believe? Then, as you are actively listening (or reading), check to see if you are getting the answers to those questions.
- Get involved. Studies have shown that people acquire information better if they actively participate in it while it is being presented. You are least likely to capture information, for instance, from a straight lecture. You are *most* likely to if you take part in discussing it or actually using it in some way or another. For instance, you attend a meeting on quarterly operating results. Someone from the accounting department gets up and reads off sales and profit figures for each of your company's divisions, and uses percentages to compare them with last year's. Unless you have a high interest in numbers, most of them will bounce right off your skull, and never get inside at all. If you took a test right after the meeting you'd lose your scholarship.

  However, if you write down the numbers you want to remember, ask a question or two about them, and then do something with them (like digging competitor's results out of *The Wall Street Journal* and seeing how you stack up) you'll be much more likely to get a hold long enough to put them in storage. Too much trouble? How important is it for you to acquire the information? You decide.
- Relate new information to things you know and like. Ask yourself, "What is this like that I know already? How can I relate the two?" You'll acquire information faster if you're familiar with it and interested in it. Try to think of a way you'll use it later that will be helpful to you.
- Break up the material you want to absorb into logical, smaller units. Acquiring individual bits can be easier than trying to wrestle with a whole glob. A telephone number thought of as (241) 328–8401 is easier to acquire than 2413288401.
- Give yourself a mental quiz once in a while to see how much you remember. If you know you're going to do this, you'll be more likely

to listen or read carefully and absorb the message. After all, you'd be embarrassed flunking your own quiz, right?

- Take a break now and then. Your attention span has limits, and after a point, data will just sail by your noggin and you won't acquire any of it.

2. How to Store Information

Scientists believe we have two kinds of memory, short-term and long-term. The short-term memory has a rapid forgetting rate—as fast as thirty seconds, and leaks like a sieve; while the long-term memory has a large capacity, and is mostly permanent, although it does have a few drips and a little forgetting does occur. Once you get information there, however, if you've transferred it properly, it should stay there waiting for you to retrieve it. So, the trick is to speed what you want to remember through the short-term into the long-term memory. Here are a few methods that will help you.

- Repeat the information you want to transfer. Say it out loud over and over. Explain it to everyone who will sit still and listen. Write it out. Overlearn it.
- Activate a few billion extra brain cells when you encounter something you want to remember. Use all five senses to stimulate your brain:

  Try to visualize the material you want to transfer. Images are good for storing objects and events. For most of us, pictures are easier to store and retrieve than words or numbers. Let's say you want to store numbers. Turn them into images. See the numbers in your mind, the shape and color of them. Think of them as three-dimensional. Feel their shapes.

  Exaggerate. Make them giant numbers, tall as the Empire State Building, so you can see them from miles away.

  Make them funny or outlandish. Imagine sales and profit figures in lacy Victorian valentine script.

  If what you are trying to transfer is an object, use many senses to surround it. Think how it smells, tastes, sounds, and feels, as well as how it looks.

  Turn concepts into objects. An investment decision can become a pile of bills, a new policy can be seen as the memos that will be sent out to communicate it; a study on where to open a new branch office can turn into a map with pins and flags in it.

- Organize material in your mind as you would in a file cabinet, and slip new information into it in the proper place. If you've developed a new sales forecast, actually think of it as going into the compartment in your long-term memory that has other sales information in it.
- Make items interact somehow, the more dramatically, the better. If you want to transfer the fact that Ed Jacobsen and Allan Schultz will be handling the dog-food account, picture them holding cans of dog food and being chased by hungry dogs. A bite here and there will help you make the transfer.
- Be sure to see the details. What are Ed and Allen wearing (and are their pants in shreds)? What kind of dogs are chasing them? Visualize the color and texture of the dog's fur. Motion is a great help—think of people and things in action.

  Long-term memory likes visual images (and impressions from the other senses), drama, motion, humor, and the bizarre.

3. How to Retrieve Information

Here are techniques that will help you get information back out of your long-term memory. Most of them you will have to put in place as you are transferring material from short- to long-term memory.

- Make up acronyms. For instance, if you have to remember to do a budget analysis, call Bob Adams, check on a delivery, speak to Fred about his lateness, and do your yearly productivity summary, think BADLY:

  *B*udget
  *A*dams
  *D*elivery
  *L*ateness
  *Y*early

  When you want to retrieve your list, all you will have to remember is your acronym, not the individual items on the list.
- Make a crazy story out of the facts you want to store and retrieve. If you can, tie it to some event that will trigger your memory and lead you right into the story.

  Let's say you are going on a trip with your boss. You want to tell him that orders are up forty-two percent in the St. Louis district, but Sam Smalley, district manager there, thinks demand will suffer later in the year because your competitor, Mega-Marketing International, is opening a branch in St. Louis. Also, deliveries to customers are running late by about twenty-one days and, Sam pointed out, there is no technical manual yet for the new 98–60–D enhancement and customers know that.

Okay, let's try a story. Use some event you know will happen as a trigger. Cocktails—when the stewardess comes around and asks, "Would you care for a cocktail?" imagine yourself ordering "A scotch and water—Mississippi River water of course." That then will trigger a story like: "Forty-two years ago, Sam Smalley was rafting down the Mississippi toward St. Louis. He was racing with another raft, which had a tattered flag that read Mega. Mark. Int. Sam was in the lead, and was sure to get to St. Louis first. The only problem was that his secretary, who was ninety-eight and wore a 60D bra, had lost the manual with the maps and other directions in it. That could make them twenty-one days late."

Put a happy ending on the story if you like, but whatever, be sure to get the images clear and vibrant in your mind. Hear the river, feel the dampness, smell the water, picture Sam's secretary, and hear that Mega. Mark. Int. flag fluttering in the breeze.

By the time you've thought of all that it will probably be too late to order a cocktail—the stewardess will be way up at the other end of the plane. You'll be thirsty, but your boss will be impressed.

- Form a chain. Make the first item interact with, or somehow associate with, the second item, and so on, through your list. This is a good technique for a shopping list, lists of things to do, and lists of keyword reminders.

  Let's say you have five pieces of information on the product you manage that you want to cover with senior officers when you see them. You don't know exactly when you will run into one or another of them and get a chance to talk, so it's hard to carry notes around. Instead you can form a chain.

  The items you want to cover are:

1. Dandelion-Be-Gone (your product) sales.
2. Weed-Zap (competitor) sales.
3. Marketing strategies.
4. Recommendations for a new ad agency.
5. Forecasts.

Sales, item 1, is easy enough to remember. So you don't need an aid. But it is the beginning of your chain. Sales, no matter how good they are, are never enough, never one hundred percent of the market, because you have competitors. That links you with number 2, Weed-

Zap. Weed-Zap is a tough competitor because they do a good job of marketing. That's your link with number 3. But you've got some ideas (strategies) to pep up your own marketing, and that links you with number 4, a new ad agency. Your new agency should help you build sales and share of market. What could be more natural than to slide right into what those figures will be next year—your link to number 5, forecasts.

- Hook key words to familiar locations you often encounter, in the order you come across the locations. For instance, think of what you see when you come home at night: mail box, door, hallway table, refrigerator, easy chair, TV. That gives you half a dozen anchors, but you could extend the number indefinitely as you roam through your house. Make sure your locations are very clear and distinct in your mind, that you use them in the order you normally encounter them, and that the items or ideas you want to retrieve interact vigorously with them.

  Let's say you are giving a report on market-research results and the first item you want to remember is customer confidence levels are up twenty-three percent on vitamin-enriched Collie Crunchies. Picture a collie jumping over your mail box, which has a giant 23 painted on its side. That you should remember. Next you want to remember that the tests came back on the dyes used in Collie Crunchies and they are thought to be not harmful. Picture your door, the next anchor on your list, slowly being covered with the Collie Crunchie dye, then have your door sprout a happy face, indicating it likes the dye.

  Next you want to talk about consumer preference for your packaging: fifty-two percent to forty-eight percent for your competitors. Picture your hallway table being wrapped in a big Collie Crunchie package with a giant 52% hanging over it. And so on through your anchors.

  This helps best for remembering items in order: lists, key points for discussions, meetings, and speeches. Try it. You'll be amazed how easily you will be able to remember.

Practice retrieving. The more you do it, the more confident you will become and the better you will be able to recall. There are memory exercises at the end of the chapter that will help. Use them.

SPECIAL CASES

1. How to Remember Names

This is a tough recall job. You may recognize someone's face, but you must then pull a name out of the air to go with it. And usually you have to do that quickly. If every person had a multiple-choice listing of names hanging around his or her neck, it would be easy to pick the right one. That's because recognizing is easier than recalling. But people aren't that obliging, so you have to use other methods to do this hard task. Here are some ideas.

- Make sure you get the name in the first place and get it right. Many names are complicated because they are unfamiliar and contain new combinations of sounds. But even simple names like Mary Smith can be forgotten instantly if you don't concentrate on acquiring them. Ask the person to repeat the name. Then say it out loud: "What was the name again?"

  "Mary Smith."

  "Ah, Mary Smith. Nice to meet you, Mary."
- Any time you meet someone, tell yourself, "I'd better get the name, I'll have to introduce that person to someone else pretty soon." In many cases you will.
- Call the person by name in conversation. As you say the first name, imagine the last.
- Focus on the person's face or body for distinctive features and try to hook the name to them. John Wiggins has nice hair—tell yourself it's John's wig. Rhymes often help in remembering names: Ed Jones has big bones. Bill Rose has a crooked nose. Many names have meanings of their own. Picture Sally Brewster stirring up a vat of your favorite suds, Ed Farmer picking your favorite vegies and so forth.

  But what do you do with Debbie Simon? "Debbie Simon met a pie man." Groan. The worse they are, the better you'll remember them.

  Try to build in action: George Emery—picture him speeding down the street in an Emery freight truck. Jane Santos—picture Jane in a Santa Claus outfit, ready to slide down a chimney.

  Make it a point to think of the association and recall the name (picturing the person as nearly as you can) several times during the first day and every once in a while after that. Have fun with names and faces and see how good you can get at remembering them.

2. How to Avoid Absentmindedness

When you're absentminded, mostly it's because you've not fixed what you want to do in your memory. Try these helpers.

- Picture an object and an event together in your mind. You want to remember to buy tickets at lunch. When you hang up your coat in the morning, visualize it as a giant ticket. See the printing all up and down it. Imagine how it would feel to hold a ticket that big. Then, when you go out at lunchtime and put on your coat, you will remember that image and head straight for the ticket window.

You want to remember that Al is seeing a client in Chicago this week (not so easy to do if Al and others in your office are all traveling a lot). Picture Al standing on the shore of Lake Michigan with the wind blowing his hair all over. If he's bald, have his hat sailing off in the Windy City breeze.

- Do something distracting to yourself.

You've got to call the boss at eleven o'clock. Move your wristwatch to the other arm. Every time you look at it all morning, you will remember the call.

You want to mail a letter as soon as you get to the airport. Put a folded sheet of paper or a three by five card in with your money. Think, "This is a model of that letter I've got to mail." When you go to pay the cab or limo driver, or to tip the baggage handler, you will notice it and remember the letter.

During a conversation, your boss asks you if you have the Benson Account file. A little thing. You don't want to make a big deal right then of asking for paper to write it down. Quickly picture your office chair with the file sitting on it. See the name typed clearly on the label and picture the file coming open and contents spilling out onto the seat of your chair. Think what it would feel like if you sat on the file. Chances are, when you get back to the office and see your chair, you will remember the file immediately.

AND SO, REMEMBER . . .

There isn't such a thing as a bad memory, only a memory that is untrained. The better you learn memory techniques and the more you practice using them, the better your memory will become. The improvement may be so dramatic it will startle you.

Give yourself plenty of positive self-talk ("I can remember that better than anyone.") and reward as your ability improves. ("I knew I could do it. I'm really making good progress. I'm getting a memory like a computer.")

Don't be discouraged if some things miss your safe deposit box and land on the floor. Even the best in the world forget some things.

Show off. Whenever you have an opportunity, be there with the facts and tell others what they are. They will be impressed and you will get even more reinforcement.

EXERCISES TO DEVELOP YOUR MEMORY MUSCLES

1. *Remember the names of the next five people you meet.*

Get the name right.

Repeat it out loud.

Find some distinctive feature about the face or person.

Associate the name with the feature; use outlandish images.

Practice recalling the name.

If you can still remember the names three months from now, you'll have mastered this. Use it every time you meet someone whose name you want to remember.

2. *Remember a list.* For example, things you have to do, questions to discuss with the boss, or items to buy in a store.

Make an acronym out of the first letters of the items, or

Make up a story involving each of the items, or

Make a chain: form an image of each item, then have it interact and associate it with the next item on your list, or

Write down your list, if you are not entirely confident. Take it with you and use any of the above methods to recall it. Don't look at it till you absolutely have to. If you can do this four or five times without peeking at the list, you've got it.

3. *Remember budget or operating figures.*

Write the numbers down.

Do something with them. Make a pie chart or graph, project them into the future.

Pretend they are your own dollars, or your own company's results.

Exaggerate them, make them funny.

Mention the figures to others as often as possible, without boring everyone into a stupor.

When you can recall key figures a half dozen times, you're getting good at this.

4. *Remember important information that is not very interesting to you.*

Ask yourself how you can use the information.

Break it into manageable parts.

Try to relate as much as you can to information that does interest you.

Practice recalling first the information that interests you, then the information you related it to.

When you are able to recall ho-hum stuff regularly, you know you're catching on.

5. *Remember important points you want to make in a speech, a meeting, or a discussion with somebody important.*

   Write down the points in the order you want to remember them.

   Pick familiar objects you see as you go through your office or home.

   Associate, using motion and humor, the points with the objects.

   Practice recalling them one or two times.

   When you are able to reel off your points confidently and without much hesitation, you will have this skill. (You'll also have fun doing it.)

6. *Remember random facts or ideas.*

   Sort and select only the information important for you to remember.

   Be sure you understand the information.

   Think of why it is important to you to remember.

   Say the information out loud.

   Use motion, outlandish images, and humor to dramatize the information.

   Use acronyms, chains, or locations to associate items in a series.

   Discuss the information with your spouse, business acquaintances, or anyone who will listen.

   Test your recall occasionally.

   When you can recall a dozen or so random facts and pieces of information, you will have mastered this.

Space out these exercises over time. Don't try to do them all at once. Tell yourself you will check to see if the information has really been transferred to long-term memory after one month, after three months, and after six months and a year. If you follow the steps as outlined, you will find—wow—it's there and you can retrieve it when you want.

Everyone will be impressed with your new skills. People who have good memories are respected because others feel confident of them. Using a few simple tools to acquire, store, and retrieve information will help you build a great memory.

15. But My Horoscope Said . . . How to Solve Problems, Make Decisions

Boss: Damn it, Sid, we've diddled around long enough with this. We've got the facts we need, let's make a decision. Right now!

Subordinate: I'll buy that, Ken. I wanted to do it yesterday.

Boss: Right. Ah . . . where's Ferguson? We ought to find out what he thinks.

Conversation overheard at International Anomaly, Inc.

This chapter is about solving problems and making decisions. You know something about them already because you handle lots of them every day, on and off the job. Some are little: what to wear to work, what to have for dinner; and some of them are big: which proposal to choose, how to calm an irate client, which person to hire, what to do about a subordinate's slumping performance. If you're like most people, you're not always ecstatic about dealing with problems and decisions. That's because they

- Take you into the future, the unknown. Scary.
- Leave you vulnerable. People can say you did the wrong thing. And maybe you did.
- Tamper with your security. Part of the reason you are with your organization is that it provides security for you. The best way not to endanger that security is to sidestep doing anything you could be criticized for.
- Make you uncertain. You can never be one hundred percent sure of a solution. You may think and think about it, but you will never think enough. You may get plenty of information on it, but you will never get enough. In the final analysis, you won't know how your solution will turn out until you've implemented it. Then, it's too late.

Many folks, even when they overcome all those insecurities and do go to work on a problem or make a decision, don't do a very good job of it. That's because:

- They don't get the facts right or get them and don't use them. Or they misinterpret them by not listening and not asking questions or by allowing their prejudices to distort what they find.
- They tend to take the safe route and think of things as they are rather than using a little creativity to look beyond what exists and come up with new and original alternatives.
- They are under a lot of pressure to find solutions, so they go for them right away . . .

  "What's the problem?"

  "The zucchini machine is down—second time today."

  "Darn. It's probably the retroactive integrator. Call Ace and get them to rush one over here right away."

  They go for the first fix they think of before they know what the problem really is and certainly before they've had a chance to look for alternative solutions.

Let's take a look at these two difficult *Upward Bound* skills, problem solving and decision making.

A problem is a train off the track. Something that has not gone the way it was planned and expected to. Problem solving is getting it back on the track—or finding an even better track for it to run on.

A decision is a choice from among alternatives. There may be a dozen ways to get the train back on the track and selecting the one that is best for the particular circumstance is what decision making is all about.

Decision making, then, is part of the process of problem solving. We'll see how they fit together in a minute.

Problems can be solved and decisions made by guessing, using intuition, flipping coins, checking your horoscope, using hunches, or relying on experience. At times, any of these can be useful. Mostly though, you will want to use a more systematic approach (which still may involve guessing, intuition, and any of the rest).

Let's look at a seven-step problem-solving system put together from the best of many that are around today. It goes like this.

1. Gather information.
2. Define the problem.
3. Determine probable causes.
4. Determine what you want to happen.
5. Generate alternatives.
6. Decide.
7. Implement and evaluate.

1. Gather Information.

Gathering information is a critical part of the problem-solving process, since it's the basis for defining the problem and determining its causes. If you can do those well, you will cut down on uncertainty (but not eliminate it), and reduce risk (but not eliminate it), and get closer to finding an answer.

Find out:

What difficulties the problem is causing.
Who is involved.
How long it has been going on.
How big it is.
Where it happens.
How often.
When it happens.
Why it happens.
What the future of it may be.

The trick is to find out as much about the problem as you can—within reason. There's a limit to the amount of information you can and should go after.

First, there are costs involved. Let's say you are working on introducing a new product. You can run up a good-sized bill doing too many market-research surveys, for instance, waste time and lose a lot of sales, while your competitor is selling similar products by the ton and grabbing off a big piece of the market.

Second, after a while you won't be coming up with much new information—just repeats of what you already have, stated in slightly different ways.

Third, in today's world you can stir up tidal waves of information without even half trying. Just crank up the computer and let it run all night. By daybreak it will have produced facts, figures, and analyses on everything in the immediate world remotely related to your problem and will have generated enough paper to fill your office from floor to ceiling and spill out all the way down the hall to the elevator. You will be worse off than when you started.

Fourth, new information may uncover new problems which makes your job even tougher.

When you have enough information to define the problem and take a good, informed guess at its causes, stop. Don't get any more. The importance of the problem will tell you how much digging to do. If it doesn't amount to much, you won't have to work all that hard getting information about it. If it's a whopper, you will.

When you're getting information, remember that opinions are important as well as facts. People's experiences and judgment give them views on problems that can help you. It's good to know the difference, though, between opinions and facts, because people often state opinions as though they were facts. Opinions will differ from person to person, facts will stay the same.

Once you ask a person for his opinion on a problem, you take on a sacred obligation. To listen. Even if you think the opinion you're getting is completely crazy, listen. Be sure you understand the meaning of what he or she is telling you. Don't shut off and discard opinions just because they're different from your own.

Watch out who is giving you opinions. Jean may be the best chemist in the lab, but when she starts giving you advice on marketing, she may be out of her field. Or she may be out of her field but still have good advice. You will have to decide. The point is, just because she's a crackerjack at chemistry doesn't mean she's great at everything.

In the course of information gathering, you should get insights into what the problem really is and be able to begin to define it. But before you go any further, now that you know something about the problem, you should stop and find out if it's a problem worth working on. Ask yourself:

How big is this problem and how big is it likely to become? What will it do that's so bad? Who's concerned about it?
Can I really do anything about this problem? Do I have the power and authority? What are my chances of really changing anything?
Is this really someone else's problem? Whose?
What will happen if I do nothing?

All of that to assess your relationship to the problem and whether or not you should take it on or pass it on.

As a general rule, if the problem is worth working on, and it's within your sphere of influence, go get it. If it's not, forget it. Don't waste your time working on things that don't matter or struggling to handle events you can't control.

If you decide the problem is worth your time, go on to Step 2.

2. Defining the Problem

- Write out a definition of the problem. That may not be as easy as it seems. Some problems are very hard to reduce to words on paper. But the act of doing that will help you understand more precisely what the problem is.
- Be careful not to settle for symptoms. Symptoms help you see that a problem exists, but aren't the real problem. Don't use them as definitions.
- Be specific: Include any facts and figures that help pinpoint the problem including what, when, where, and how much.
- Don't worry if the problem seems to change as you work on it. Problems often do change. You may have to write a new definition halfway through the process. There's nothing wrong with that—it just shows you are learning more about the problem.

Here is an example of a problem definition. Let's say you're over budget and trying to decide what to do about it.

> Problem: The department is 18 percent over budget as of October 31 and tending toward an overage of 22 percent at year-end.

3. Determining Causes

When you've defined the problem, use the definition and the other information you've gathered to take a look at what got you into the mess in the first place.

- List every possible cause you can think of. Look for many, because problems almost always have multiple causes. Few have only one.
- When you've listed your causes, rank them in terms of how important they are. That ranking will help you determine which cause to work on first. Remember, it's easier to deal with "thing" causes than "people" causes.

Here are some causes for our budget problem, with rankings:

Possible causes	Rank
Increase at midyear in printing costs.	1
Lack of close control by Bob Rollins.	3
Increased number of trips to clients.	2
More use of overtime.	4
Not enough money in the budget to begin with.	5

4. Determine What You Want to Happen

Ask yourself, "What would be a reasonably good outcome for all this?" That will give you a goal to shoot for, and some direction. And, later, after you have solved the problem, you can compare the actual results with those you wanted at the outset. If they are the same, or just as good, you will know you've done a good job.

In putting together the outcome, you should think in specific terms about your criteria for a good solution:

- Exactly what do I want to happen? (Use numbers if possible.)
- How fast (when)?
- Within what cost?
- With what risk to me and the organization?
- Using what type and amount of equipment, money, people?
- What side effects do I want to avoid?

Criteria should be measurable; if not, at least observable. Some may have a range ($3,000–$6,000), and some will be criteria you *must* meet (as opposed to others that might be good to meet or nice to meet).

Here's what criteria for the budget problem might look like, with *must* criteria indicated with an (m).

WHAT I WANT TO HAPPEN (Criteria of Good Solution)

(m) • Reduce budget overage to 0.
(m) • By December 31.
(m) • Without cutting pay or terminating employees.
(m) • Without sacrificing service to clients.
• Without calling too much attention to the problem by involving too many others.

Now we're going to look at generating alternatives. You will measure your alternatives against those criteria—the alternative that satisfies most of them is the one you will probably decide to use.

5. Generate Alternatives

This is part of the problem-solving process that you will be tempted to skip, going right to finding a solution. When you're under pressure to act, you don't want to sit around coming up with alternatives, because you want to be a dynamic executive, not some kind of a philosopher. Heroes on television and in the movies make confident, instantaneous decisions, they never generate alternatives, and they are always right.

And you'd like to be like them. But the truth of the matter is there aren't any hero decision makers in the real world. Peter Drucker, speaking at a symposium in 1982, stated that the forceful captain of industry probably doesn't exist. "Leaders," he said, "don't so much make decisions as understand issues, ask people what they think, and consider alternative ideas. Deliberation is what goes on, not decision making."

Alternatives are what make problem solving work. They make the difference between real problem solving and just picking something to do—like the first thing you happen to think of.

Here's how to do a good job developing alternatives:

- Find a lot. Don't just stop at a few—and never only two, which gives you just an either/or choice. All problems have more alternative solutions than that, often more than you dreamed possible. The more alternatives you come up with, the better chance you will have of finding one that will work.
- Don't generate only safe, conventional alternatives. Even if you are using an analytical, scientific system to help you decide, stay loose and let your mind mess around a little. See if you can think of weird, impractical ideas that you could later turn into usable ones. Ask questions like:

If money were no object, what would I do?
What else is this problem like and how did that get solved?
What's a solution that would get me fired? Thrown in jail?
If I just inherited Uncle Albert's fortune and didn't need this job, what would I do?

Ideas that come from those questions may contain seeds that can be nurtured and brought along to workable solutions. Always look beyond the problem and its immediate environment for possible solutions. Always look beyond "what is today." See Chapter 4 for more on creative thinking.

- When you can, get a group together to generate alternatives. If you handle it right, a group can come up with more alternatives than you can on your own. You will also get a greater buy-in and they will all feel more ownership in the problem and its solution. If you use a group, be sure to include at least some people who will implement the solution after it's decided on.
- If you have generated alternatives, but don't see any that meet enough of the criteria in Step 4, develop some more.

Remember, doing nothing is almost always an alternative. Especially if solving the problem would be too difficult, too costly, and more than it's worth.

Here are some alternatives for our budget problem:

ALTERNATIVES:

A. Find new, cheaper printer.

B. Use less expensive bindings, paper, less color work.

C. Ask clients to print their own.

D. Cut trips to clients. Use telephone, letters more.

E. Ask clients to travel to us.

F. Ask clients to postpone orders for the rest of the year.

G. Train Bob Rollins.

H. Fire Bob Rollins.

I. Steal the money and put it in our budget.

J. See if the customer service department is under budget and if they're willing to absorb our overage.

Note the following about the alternatives:

- Not all of them are sane. Stealing the money (I) is probably not in the best taste. But "off the wall" ideas are good because they trigger other ideas. In this case, I triggered J, transferring the overage to someone else's budget, which may be workable.
- There are alternatives for all the probable causes we developed earlier, starting with the most important. Ideally, this would be a longer list, with more alternatives for the more important causes. You could have fifty or seventy-five alternatives for a complex problem.

6. Decide

Now, what do you do with alternatives? First, if you have dozens, you will have to narrow your list down by picking those that seem most workable. Then use the simple method below to stack them up against the criteria and decide which is best. List your criteria on the left and the alternatives across the top. Check off each box where the alternatives meet the criteria. I've filled in the chart below using criteria and alternatives from our budget problem. I weeded out alternative I, stealing the money, since it did not seem practical.

	Alternatives								
Criteria	A.	B.	C.	D.	E.	F.	G.	H.	J.
(m) Reduce overage to 0	x	x	x	x	x	x			x
(m) By Dec. 31	x	x	x	x	x	x			x
(m) Without cutting people	x	x	x	x	x	x	x	x	x
(m) Without sacrificing service	x	x				x	x	x	x
Without calling attention		x					x		

The chart makes it pretty easy to see that alternatives A and B, having to do with reducing printing costs, meet all of the "must" criteria. So there's a tie. Alternative B, however, meets an additional nonmust criterion (A does not, since changing the printer might get phones ringing all over the organization) and that might be reason for picking B, although both are good choices. Alternative J, asking another department that may be under budget to absorb the cost, which was a spinoff from I, stealing the money, meets as many criteria as A and might also be a good choice.

When you have compared alternatives, you still may not have a clear-cut winner (as in the example above, where there are two or three). If you don't, you can

Generate more alternatives (always do this if none of them meet all or most of your must criteria).

Modify and improve the ones you have.

Use your judgment and experience to pick one that you feel is best.

If you are in doubt about an alternative, even though it comes out the winner, test it by asking these questions:

Will it work? Will it fix the problem?

Will people go along with it? Will it create more problems?

If your answers are yes, yes, yes, and no, go ahead with it.

Remember, there are no perfect decisions. There are flaws in any course of action. Few important decisions are 75 percent/25 percent, many are 51 percent/49 percent. So, if your judgment tells you that an alternative has a slight edge, even if you don't know exactly why, choose it. You are only going to do one of the alternatives—the one you choose. You won't use the others so you will never know if you picked the best one. Neither will anyone else.

Here are some other key points on making decisions:

- There are many "scientific" ways to make decisions, including decision trees and probability theory. If you work on difficult, complex decisions all the time, you will want to use them. All the analytical methods are based on assumptions made at the outset. You must be confident of your assumptions or you will be wasting a lot of time and trouble crunching numbers that will lead you to doubtful answers.

  If you have an operations research unit in your organization, check with them to see what expertise they have in decision methods. Or study one or more of the books listed at the end of the book.

- Whatever system you use, you will still come back to judgment—your experience, prior knowledge of the problem or similar problems, and even your intuition. Those, and the courage to use them, are the stuff that good decision makers are made of.

- Sometimes when you have made your decision, it is good to test it before you let it out of the cage. You can do that by taking the opposite view and thinking up all the arguments you can against it. If you can't think of too many strong ones, you probably have yourself a good decision.

- The right decision may not be what you want to have happen, it may not make you popular, it may not be what you expected would happen before you began problem solving, and it might not be fun. It can be right, nevertheless. It also may not be what your boss wants—but that's another problem.
- The main thing is to decide. Major league baseball umpires are trained to make a call, right or wrong. When a guy slides into second on a close play, the umpire has to call him out or safe, even if he was looking out into the centerfield bleachers at the time. You usually have more time than umpires do, but don't take forever. Decide. Keep some pressure on yourself to do it.
- Deciding is not so risky as you think it is. A friend of mine who works for a defense contractor tells this story:

> I'd made a decision that went bad. Of all the alternatives, I must have picked the worst. I didn't think I was picking the worst, but that's the way it turned out and it was costing us a bundle. The vice president came in and he was steaming. I got read out for twenty minutes. I agreed with everything he said, because it was a bad decision, what could I say? Then he said, "Okay, Brad, let's put this behind us now. I've said my piece. You make lots of decisions and most of them are good. This one stunk and I wanted to be sure you knew it." That was my punishment. Twenty minutes of chewing out. What risk is there in that?

You may expect the rack if you're wrong, but maybe you won't get it. You will have to analyze your own situation. What's happened in the past? Is the boss really rough on mistakes or does he or she let them pass with a little lecture? Bosses make mistakes, too, and they know it. Many will be tolerant, especially of someone who usually makes good decisions.

7. Implement and Evaluate

When you've made your decision, it's time to take action. Depending on the enormity of the decision and how much time you have, you may want to test the action—try it out in a small area of the organization first—or you may want to just go ahead and implement it full-scale.

A simple way to plan and communicate your decision is to make up an Action Plan showing what, when, and who, and get it out to everyone involved. Here's one filled out for the problem we worked on above.

Action Plan

What is to be done	By when	By whom
1. Get price quotes on cheaper paper and bindings (20% below what we're using now)	11/1	Charlie
2. Make spot calls to see how clients would react to less color. If acceptable, cut color use 15%.	10/15	Ann
3. Take a look at packaging and shipping to find potential savings, try for $3,000 between now and year-end.	11/1	Gene
4. Follow up with year-end budget to see if it all worked.	12/31	Frank

Everyone on your Action Plan should have been involved in the problem-solving process somewhere along the line . . . usually during alternative generation and when you're putting together the Action Plan. If one wasn't involved, be sure to cover what you are doing and why with him or her, and get agreement before putting names on the chart.

Part of your implementation plan should provide for evaluating results against the criteria developed in step 4. In this case the proof of the pudding will be:

Has the overage been reduced to 0?
By 12/30?
Without cutting salaries or staff?
Without reducing services?
Without calling attention?

When the results are in, go back and review your problem-solving/decision-making process: Where did you do well, where could you have done better? Where did it help you most? Least? What have you learned and how can you do better next time?

Here's what the entire analysis of the budget problem looks like:

1. Gather Information

The boss is angry about 18 percent overage—would be livid over 22 percent at year-end. Standard is to be on budget or slightly under. Bob Rollins has direct responsibility . . . Printing costs increased by 20 percent in July . . . We had no prior warning . . . Travel expense is up 8 percent over budget.

2. Define the Problem

The department is 18 percent over budget as of October 31 and trending toward an overage of 22 percent by year-end.

3. Determine Probable Causes

Determine Probable Causes	Rank
Increase at mid-year in printing costs	1
Lack of close control by Bob Rollins	3
Increased number of trips to clients	2
More use of overtime	4
Not enough money in the budget to begin with	5

4. Determine Criteria of Good Solution: (What You Want to Happen)

(m) Reduce budget overage to 0.

(m) By December 31st.

(m) Without cutting pay or terminating employees.

(m) Without sacrificing service to clients.

Without calling too much attention to the problem by involving too many others.

(m) = must criteria

5. Generate Alternatives

A. Find new, cheaper printer.

B. Use less expensive bindings, paper, less color work.

C. Ask clients to print their own.

D. Cut trips to clients. Use telephone, letters more.

E. Ask clients to travel to us.

F. Ask clients to postpone orders for the rest of the year.

G. Train Bob Rollins.

H. Fire Bob Rollins.

I. Steal the money and put it in our budget.

J. See if the customer service department is under budget and if they will absorb our overage.

6. Decide

Criteria:	Alternatives								
	A.	B.	C.	D.	E.	F.	G.	H.	J.
(m) Reduce overage to 0	x	x	x	x	x	x			x
(m) By Dec. 31	x	x	x	x	x	x			x
(m) Without cutting people.	x	x	x	x	x	x	x	x	x
(m) Without sacrificing service.	x	x				x	x	x	x
Without calling attention.		x					x		

7. Implement and Evaluate

Action Plan

What's to be done	By when	By whom
1. Get price quotes on cheaper paper and bindings (20% below what we're using now).	11/1	Charlie
2. Make spot checks to see how clients would react to less color. If acceptable, cut color use 15%.	10/15	Ann
3. Take a look at packaging and shipping to find potential savings. Try for $3,000 between now and year-end.	11/1	Gene
4. Follow up with year-end budget to see if it all worked.	12/30	Frank

Evaluation 12/30

Was overage reduced to 0?	Yes
By 12/30?	Yes
Without cutting people?	Yes
Without sacrificing service?	Yes & No—some cut-back on quality of printed material, client visits.
Without calling attention?	Yes & No. Boss got a couple of calls about quality.

All in all, a good solution. We could have done better by generating additional creative alternatives. Do that next time.

Here are some final thoughts on problem solving and decision making:

You don't have to deal with every problem the moment it comes up. Although problems have an abrasive way of demanding attention right now, most of them can wait. You do have time, usually, to go through a problem-solving process.

Problem solving and decision making are developmental. They should be done at the lowest possible level in the organization so people can learn from them. If people work for you, they will try to pass problems and decisions up to you—after all, they're only human. Pass them back down. Show them a problem-solving process like the seven-step one above. Ask them to use it. Even let your people make a few mistakes. They'll learn from mistakes. No one ever forgets a mistake.

The best way to improve decision-making ability is to practice it on the job. It's an expensive way to learn, because it can lead to a lot of errors, but it is the best way. That's true for you as well as for your people.

Remember that most decisions affect other people. Involve them in the process, especially in developing alternatives and designing the Action Plan, as described above. You can use the process and make a terrific decision all by yourself, but if you try to impose it on others, they may not like it. Usually where there is involvement there's buy-in, and that makes implementation easier and faster.

Good problem-solvers and decision-makers are relatively rare commodities. They are respected and sought after. The seven-step approach will help you become one of them.

16. **Is It Five O'Clock Already?** How to Make Time Work for You

". . . tick . . . tick . . . tick . . . tick . . . tick . . . tick . . . tick . . . tick . . . tick . . . tick . . ."

Big Ben

Ever since the caveman found he had more to do than time to do it in, people have been trying to find ways to save time. "Time management" today is big business with all sorts of books, seminars, and films on the market to help people with time. Of course you can't really manage time. You can't do much of anything with time. It's there—twenty-four hours every day—always moving along. What you *can* do is manage yourself and your work so that you get the best use of the time available.

In this chapter we'll look at ways to do that. First, here are a dozen tenets of time you should know:

Time is very fair. We all have the same amount each day. Time is the closest thing we have to equal opportunity.

Some people use their equal share of time better than others.

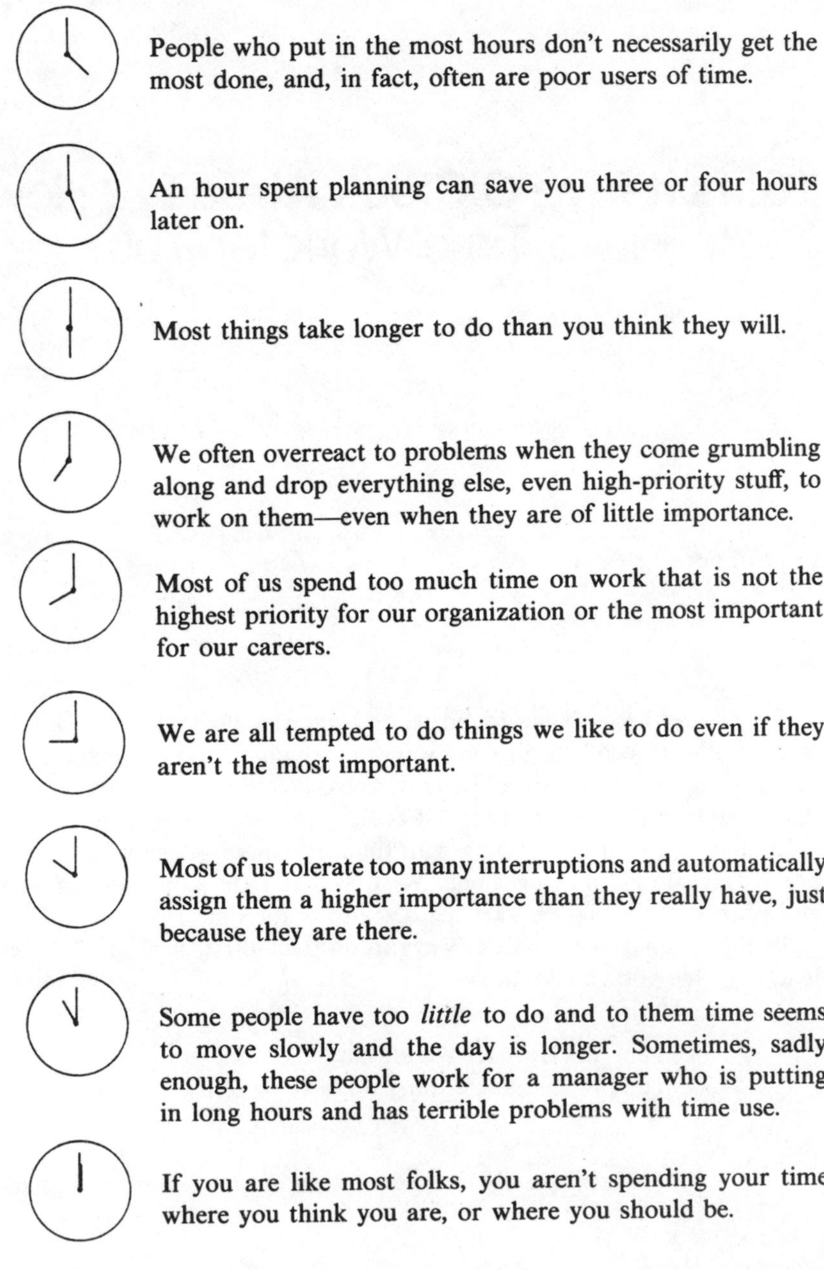

Many people see time as an enemy—something that is rushing by too quickly, as if to punish them, and that causes all kinds of stress.

People who put in the most hours don't necessarily get the most done, and, in fact, often are poor users of time.

An hour spent planning can save you three or four hours later on.

Most things take longer to do than you think they will.

We often overreact to problems when they come grumbling along and drop everything else, even high-priority stuff, to work on them—even when they are of little importance.

Most of us spend too much time on work that is not the highest priority for our organization or the most important for our careers.

We are all tempted to do things we like to do even if they aren't the most important.

Most of us tolerate too many interruptions and automatically assign them a higher importance than they really have, just because they are there.

Some people have too *little* to do and to them time seems to move slowly and the day is longer. Sometimes, sadly enough, these people work for a manager who is putting in long hours and has terrible problems with time use.

If you are like most folks, you aren't spending your time where you think you are, or where you should be.

And that gives us a good place to start. If you are going to learn to use your time better, it will be good to know how you're using it now. The Time Use Chart below will help you find out.

Most time-management courses start out with some sort of time log. Some logs are very complicated and take hours to fill out. And many folks, especially those worried enough about time to take a course in the first place, are too busy to keep up the time log and, therefore, don't get much out of the course. This one is simple. It will take you ten minutes a day for ten days. That's an hour and forty minutes. Do you have that much time to invest in improving your use of time? You have to decide.

Draw something that looks like the Time Use Chart on an eight-and-a-half-by-eleven-inch sheet of paper. Make ten photocopies of it.

Pick a "normal" week, if there is such a thing in your life, and a week that looks like it will be out of control. Fill one chart for each day of those two weeks.

Don't add to time problems you already have by spending hours fooling with this chart. Write in the major activities that take up chunks of time each day. Don't try to log in every time you go to the coffee machine or the bathroom. You may want to update the chart as you switch from one task to another during the day, or set aside a few minutes just before you leave at night to review your day and make your entries.

Fill in column A. List the activities that took up major blocks of time during the day. Then draw a line. Beneath that line, list all the work that you should have done during that day if you had had the time, work that was of high importance, that would have helped you do your job better and be more valuable to the organization.

In column B enter the approximate number of hours you spent on each activity.

In column C enter the percent of total time spent on each activity. Divide the hours used for each activity in column B by the total hours you worked during the day and multiply by 100.

$$\frac{\text{Hours Used}}{\text{Total Hours}} \times 100 = \%\ \text{total time}$$

Note: The percentages in column C will not add up to 100 because you did not account for every little activity.

When you have done all that, check the level of interruptions for the day at the bottom of the chart.

Now put aside this chapter until you have filled out your Time Use Chart for the two weeks. Then begin below.

TIME USE CHART

Day ________ Date ________

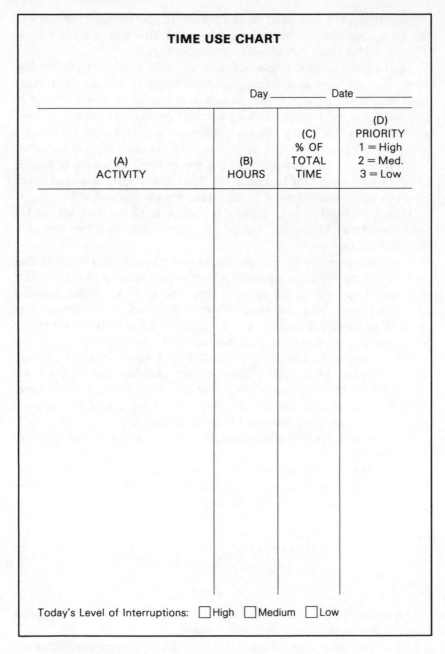

(A) ACTIVITY	(B) HOURS	(C) % OF TOTAL TIME	(D) PRIORITY 1 = High 2 = Med. 3 = Low

Today's Level of Interruptions: ☐ High ☐ Medium ☐ Low

Now that you have kept your Time Use Chart for two weeks, let's see what it means.

Review the ten sheets, looking at where and how you have been spending your time, then ask yourself these questions:

Time Analysis

Finding	Analysis
1. What percentage of your time did you spend planning and setting priorities? ________ %	If you aren't spending at least one hour a week (2–3%) of your time planning, and deciding on priorities, you are not using your time as well as you should be.
2. What percentage of your time are you spending on high-priority work? Work that helps you accomplish your job successfully and is important to the organization? ________ %	If that figure is below 65–70%, you aren't doing justice to your job, or to your career for that matter.
3. What percentage of days did you have "high" and "medium" interruptions? ________ %	Any day with high or medium interruptions was a day you were sidetracked from your work too many times. But let's face it, some interruptions are bound to happen. If more than 2 or 3 of your days out of 10 had high or medium interruptions, that's probably too many.
4. What percentage of your time did you spend in meetings? ________ %	If you spend more than 25% of your time in meetings, you are probably depressed. If you spend 50%, you're probably ready to take gas.
5. What percentage of your time did you spend traveling? (Estimate for a six-month period if the weeks you picked do not represent normal travel) ________ %	What did you think of that percentage? Did you make trips you really didn't have to?
6. What percentage of your time did you spend waiting? This may not be easy to tell from your chart, but think back over the two weeks and try to remember: time spent waiting for information, waiting to see people, waiting to get into a meeting to deliver your presentation, etc. ________ %	Any percentage is too high, especially if you didn't have anything else to do while you waited.

Time Analysis (*Continued*)

Finding	Analysis
7. Estimate the percentage of your time you spent goofing off: reading nonwork material, throwing the bull with co-workers, taking long lunch hours, flirting, etc. ________ %	I can't say what the right percentage should be for you, but 90% is too high. How do you feel about the amount of time you spend frittering?
8. What percentage of your time did you spend on work you shouldn't be doing? Low-priority work or work that could have been done as well or better by others: someone who works for you, a peer, someone in another department, a secretary, or even your boss. ________ %	Anything more than 0% is too much and is taking away from time you could spend on other work.
9. Count the times the buck got passed to you. How often did you agree to do something and then later think, "How did I get saddled with this, it's really not mine to do?" Estimate the percentage of time it took to work on these things. ________ %	Once or twice may be okay, but if you find 10% or more of your time is being taken up by people giving you their work to do, you're being had.
10. What percentage of your time did you spend looking for things you couldn't find? (You'll probably have to estimate this as you think back over the week.) ________ %	Any percentage is too high. This is time use that doesn't do anyone any good. You may as well have gone down to the lounge and watched the soaps on TV.

Time Analysis (*Continued*)

Finding	Analysis
11. What percentage of your time did you spend doing paperwork? ________ %	I can't give you even a fuzzy guideline on this because jobs vary in the amount of paperwork involved. Many people, however, feel they do too much. How do you feel about the time you spent on paperwork?
12. What percentage of your time did you spend redoing things you should (could) have done right the first time? ________ %	Again, any percentage is too high.
13. What percentage of your time did you spend reading? ________ %	How do you feel about that percentage? Do you spend too much time reading?

How did you make out? Are you beginning to see where the problems are? Okay, let's look for some solutions. As you read this next section, keep your Time Use Charts in front of you. You'll want to refer to them as you discover a variety of things you can do on the job to use time better.

Before you begin, keep this in mind. Stop thinking of time as an opponent that races by before you get your work done and your deadlines met. Think of time as a resource, like money or people. It is an asset, if put to good use, and can help you achieve whatever you want to. And, unlike money and people, it's free and it doesn't talk back.

I have spoken with many managers about getting on friendlier terms with time. Most of them told me they would feel more loving toward time if they could:

Make time last longer, or
Make the work shorter.

Silly as it sounds, these two are possible.

SEVEN WAYS TO MAKE TIME LAST LONGER

You can make time last longer by improving the way you handle the areas covered in questions 1 through 7 in your Time Analysis above: planning; working on priority stuff; avoiding interruptions, meetings, and airplanes; using waiting time; and goofing off wisely.

1. Plan Your Time

If you are a real go-getter, you probably see yourself storming into the office in the morning, coffee in one hand, briefcase in the other, and wading right into that pile of work. The phone rings all day, people rush in and out, and in the evening you stagger home, shot, but satisfied you had a hell of a day. You probably did. Somehow, sitting around planning your time doesn't quite fit in with that image, does it? It's like a goalie filing his nails in the middle of the Stanley Cup playoffs. Who has time for that?

But, remember. An hour spent planning can save you three to four hours later on. You should spend at least an hour a week planning. That doesn't have to be one solid hour, all at once. It can be a few minutes each morning to get organized and think through what you have to do for the day. However you do it, planning will help you make time last longer.

The best way to start planning is to set priorities on your work. And that leads us to number 2 . . .

2. Focus on High-Priority Work

Take your Time Use Chart to your boss and review it with him or her. Ask, "Is this the work I should be doing?" "What are the priorities as you see them?" "What is most important to the organization?" "Where should I be spending my time to make the best possible contribution?"

After your discussion, set priorities in Column D: number 1 being the highest priority; number 2, medium; and number 3, low. Make up your mind right now that you are going to concentrate on doing work that will help you be *Upward Bound,* that you will get high-priority work done and done well before going on to medium- or low-priority work. Do high-priority work even if it is not the easiest and not your favorite. People who work on number-one priorities are seen as leaders. People who work on number 3's are seen as clerks. It's as simple as that.

Where are you spending your time? Go back and look at the percentages of total time and the priorities in columns C and D of your Time Use

Chart. Are you spending most of your time on high-priority work? Here's how to be sure you are.

- At the beginning of each year, do your overall planning. Get yourself a good planning calendar. Not a three-by-five-inch day-at-a-time calendar, but a big one you can write on that spreads out a whole month in front of you and has big squares for each day.

  The one I use is about two feet by a foot and a half and covers half of my credenza. If I didn't have a credenza, I'd nail it to the wall, it's so useful. A calendar that big gives you a clear picture of what you are up against in terms of time. At the beginning of each year, go through all the months, mark off holidays and vacations, trips you know are coming up, and pencil in standing meetings and lunches. You can also plot out tentative times for regularly recurring events such as budgeting, performance appraisals, and reports. Then block out time for your number-one priorities, lifting them from your Time Use Chart.
- Each Monday, take a long view of the week. Revise and adjust your calendar so you can carve out time to spend on high-priority work. Even if other activities have tried to crowd them out, you must protect some time each week to work on number-one priorities.
- Each day, when you first get to work, make a list of all the tasks you have to do that day. Then look at your list in terms of priority work. Tasks that are related to number-one priority should be done first. If there's time, do some related to number-two priority. The number 3's you should delegate or not do at all. Adjust your calendar accordingly.
- When you come across a high-priority, urgent task that you hate doing, schedule it first so you can get it over with. Otherwise, you'll spend a lot of time worrying about it while you're trying to do other things.
- Pick your best time of day to do the tough jobs. For example, if you do your best thinking in the morning, schedule thinking tasks then. If you do people things better in the afternoon, do them in the afternoon. Find your own best times.
- Grouplike tasks. Mark off segments on your calendar for making phone calls, answering correspondence, and writing reports. Doing a bunch of similar jobs in a row is easier than doing one here and one there.
- When making time estimates, remember, everything takes longer than you think.

Look back at your Time Use Chart. Where could you have saved time by planning and setting priorities? How much time could you have saved?

Did you list planning anywhere? Probably not. Add it to your calendar and be sure you do it.

3. Avoid Interruptions

Interruptions keep you from making time last longer. They come from everywhere, but among the most common are the telephone and drop-in visitors. Here's what you can do about them and other interruptions.

- Stop thinking of all interruptions as legitimate, that you always have to stop what you are doing to handle them. Few of them need to be dealt with on the spot. When you allow yourself to be interrupted, you not only lose the interruption time but also the time it takes to get yourself back into what you were doing in the first place. Change your thinking about interruptions. Always ask yourself, "Is this important enough for me to put aside what I'm doing?" If not, don't allow yourself to be interrupted.
- Set up a "quiet hour" each day, put it on your calendar and tell everyone about it. That's your time to plan, catch up, and get organized. Ask others to stay away, except for emergencies. Once everyone knows and it gets to be a habit, you will have at least some time each week to yourself.
- To help everyone get into the habit, keep your door closed during quiet hour. Put a "quiet hour" sign on it. If you don't have a door, tie a string across the front of your space with a sign on it saying "door."
- If you feel weird about doing that, find a hideaway, an empty office, conference room, porter's closet, anywhere that's quiet—and go there regularly.
- Have your secretary, if you have one, screen calls and visitors. Lots of things people want to talk to you about can be handled just as well by your secretary.

  Nothing is more urgent than a ringing phone. You should arrange to have someone pick it up when you don't want to be interrupted. I know, it might be the chairman calling you. Then again, it might be a wrong number.
- Learn to say no. When you're deeply into a high-priority, urgent project and Charlie sticks his head in and says, "Hey, Fred, want to talk about the Consolidated Bean Bag contract for a minute?" say (tough as it might be), "Charlie, I'm really on a roll with this report. Can you catch me after lunch?" When someone comes in with that granddaddy of all interrupters, "Got a minute?" say "Sorry, not right now." Most people will respond well. They know what it's like to be interrupted themselves.

- Don't interrupt yourself unintentionally. Keep a reasonably clean desk. A messy desk is full of distractions that can catch your eye and interrupt your ongoing thoughts. If you are congenitally messy, at least put everything in one big pile before starting a new project, or get a side table to pile the mess on so you can keep your work place clear. Limit it to one project at a time.
- Assume you are going to have some interruptions. When the chairman does phone you, you will probably agree to take the call. You can't avoid all interruptions. But as you think back to the days covered by your Time Use Chart, how much wear and tear on your hide could you have saved if you had handled most interruptions differently? Start thinking right now about how to deal with the ones you can and should avoid and do it.

4. Avoid Meetings

Meetings are hardened criminals in the world of time. They steal horrendous amounts of time every working day. There are too many of them, they last too long, and don't accomplish half of what they should.

Stay away from meetings as often and as long as you can. Find reasons not to hold meetings. Suggest other ways to get the job done.

For meetings you absolutely, positively can't get out of, find ways to make them shorter and more productive. See Chapter 7 on getting the most out of meetings.

Go back to your Time Use Chart and look for meetings you could have shortened, improved, or avoided altogether.

5. Avoid Travel

By the time you get ready for your trip, get to the airport, wait for your plane, fly, circle, land, wait for your bags, find a limo or cab, wait for the desk clerk to find your reservation, toss and turn all night in a strange bed, conduct your business, reverse the process to get home, and then recover, you will have wasted plenty of time, some of it your own. Even dedicated goofing off in the office probably can't waste more time than traveling does.

Here are some thoughts on travel:

- Look at the trips you are planning for the next few months. Are they all really necessary? Could some of the work be done just as well by phone or letter or by someone who is in that area anyhow? Probably you can eliminate some trips just by looking at your objectives critically.

- Sometimes you may want to take a trip because:

  It's to a nice place like San Francisco.

  You need a few days away from the office or away from home.

  There's someone there you want to visit.

  Your taste buds are on strike and you crave airline food.

  If you take a trip that isn't absolutely necessary just because you want to, fine. Have fun. But do it knowing that travel will not make your time last longer.

- Bunch your trips together. While you are out, you might as well be out. Instead of three short trips in a month, schedule them all together. Then at least you'll get ready and recover only once instead of three times.
- Explore teleconferencing as an alternative to travel. Teleconferencing, which includes phone and video communications, will someday save millions of hours now wasted traveling.
- If you have to go, work on the plane. Take a report or a troublesome memo to work on in the air. There's not much room and there are lots of distractions, but somehow at thirty thousand feet, with a gin and tonic, you can be very productive. Try it.

Go back to your Time Use Chart and look at where you could have combined trips, shortened them, or avoided them altogether.

6. Use Waiting Time

Don't spend time staring at the ceiling while you're waiting to see someone, waiting to get into a meeting, or waiting for someone or something to show up. Anticipate waiting time—you know pretty much when it might happen. Take something along to work on. Of course, you can't do a giant, high-priority project during a fifteen-minute wait, but maybe you can do a little piece of it. Or maybe you can spend that time planning, or writing short memos you will have to do sooner or later anyway.

7. Goof Off Wisely

Goofing off wastes time. That's what it's for. So when you do it, do it with that in mind. Goofing off can also help you to work faster and better when you finally get around to getting back to work. That's a therapeutic goof off.

The trick is to find the right balance. Have your coffee break, take a long lunch once in a while, gossip with the folks in the hall, walk over to say witty things to that attractive person in the next department—and do these often enough to keep yourself refreshed and ready to work all day long. Anything past what you need is wasted and will not help you make time last longer.

SIX WAYS TO MAKE WORK SHORTER

You can make work shorter by improving the way you handle the areas covered in questions 8 through 13 of your Time Analysis above: delegate, watch what's being delegated to you, get organized, declare war on paper work, do it right the first time, and read less.

1. Delegate

Look at your Time Use Chart. I'll bet half of the things on it you could have—and should have—delegated. Check them off. If you can't find that many, wait till you finish reading this section, then go back and look again.

Delegation is powerful medicine. It frees you up to work on high-priority stuff that will make you more important. And it can help those you delegate to gain new experiences. Also, delegating will keep you from going bananas.

Don't ever do work that someone or something else can do. Get rid of it. Here's how:

- Help your subordinates learn and grow. If you have people working for you, you have unlimited opportunities to dump work. Think about them and their capabilities—and potential capabilities. Think of what each can do now and what each could *learn* to do. Go back to your Time Use Chart and find jobs you could have passed on. Look for routine tasks, work you don't really have time for, number-three priorities, old responsibilities you're sick of, and *also* work that is challenging but would help others grow. Don't delegate high-priority stuff, lousy jobs like firing people, jobs that are really yours to do, or work way beyond anyone's potential ability.

  When you do delegate:

  Give support: provide instructions, training, budget money, or whatever is needed.

  Follow up to see how things are going.

  Provide recognition for good work.

- Don't forget your peers. Was there work on your Time Use Chart that peers could do and would like to do? Let's say you had to hold an important meeting that required a lot of research and hard thinking. Maybe someone you work with would have been delighted to prepare a chunk of it in exchange for running part of the meeting. Sometimes that other person is more qualified to do it anyhow.
- Give responsibilities away. Are there things you are responsible for that another manager would like to take over? Probably there are and probably you've been fighting attempts by that manager so you won't lose any of your empire. Think a minute, though. What would happen if you gave that responsibility away? Would it lower your status or pay, or hurt your ability to get things done in the organization? Would it harm the operation of your department? No? Would it free you up to work on more number-one priorities? Why not do it?

  Pick out activities on your Time Use Chart you could give away permanently.
- Procrastinate. Procrastinating is an important part of delegating, especially when it comes to paperwork. In this case, instead of delegating to a person, you will be delegating to the wastebasket. Here's how it works.

  Every day you get a big pile of memos, reports, articles, and other assorted junk you don't quite know what to do with. Maybe you get nervous that all that paper is accumulating and rush around trying to get rid of it, piece by piece.

  Don't do that. Pile it on the side of your desk (the side nearest the wastebasket). Let it age a bit. After it has seasoned for about a week, riffle through it and pull out anything that still seems important enough to keep. Then slide the rest over the edge. Just because papers appear in your in-basket doesn't mean they're important or that you have to do anything with them. Get lazy. When you pick up something that falls into the "Why did this land on my desk?" category, quickly lapse into a catatonic stupor, long enough for the urge to do something with it to pass. Then toss it on your procrastinating pile.
- Don't do anything. Even better than procrastinating is not doing anything at all. Usually when folks look at work they think of alternate ways of doing it: "I could do it this way or I could do it that way." One option most forget is not doing it at all. Always ask yourself, "What would happen if I didn't do this?" If the answer is "Nothing," don't do it. Think how a few don't-do-it's could make time last longer.

  Go back and look at your Time Use Chart once again. Are there things on it that didn't need to be done at all?

- Feed the computer. Anything you work on that is routine or clerical probably can be automated. Don't do anything that can be done for you by a machine.

  If you can avoid it, don't automate anything through your company's data-processing department. That usually involves too many meetings, too much staff time, and too much expense. Instead, get a personal computer or arrange to share one with other people in your department. Little computers can be a joy to run and can make your time last much longer.

  Probably you are already sneaking a look at your Time Use Chart. Go to it. What do you see that could be automated?

- Involve your secretary. If you are lucky enough to have a secretary or share a secretary, you have someone who can really help you make work shorter.

  Look at your Time Use Chart and ask yourself, "Could my secretary do any of this work?"

  Ask your secretary what part of your job she would like to do and feels she could do well. Go over the Time Use Chart with her.

  Ask your secretary for ideas on how you could organize your job better.

  Make her part of your management staff. Include her in meetings of your managers, if that will help her keep up with what's going on and give her ideas for making your work shorter.

  Have a planning meeting with her once a week to discuss upcoming work and priorities. One ground rule for this meeting should be: She can ask any question about the work without feeling silly about it. You'll be amazed at how many things you assume are familiar to her (because you're close to them yourself) that are not.

  Give your secretary background on on-going work. Explain what it is, why it's being done. Decide if she can do some of it.

  Be sure she is completely informed on what her responsibilities are. Her job should include screening, sorting, reminding, prioritizing, organizing, scheduling, and informing as well as typing, filing, and answering the phone.

  Don't:

  Interrupt her while she is working.

  Ask your secretary to get coffee, run to the Xerox for single copies, or go out and buy presents for your spouse.

Ask her to do work that could be done by the word-processing department or by a computer.

Try to design her work or filing systems for her. Let her do it.

Ask her to take dictation when a dictating machine would do just as well.

2. Watch What's Being Delegated to You

Stuff from the boss or high-priority work, okay. But when someone who works for you or a peer comes in and says, "We've got that same problem with accounting. Could you call Ann (you know her so well) and get it straightened out?" think a minute before you say, "Okay." Is this really your problem or are you being used? Don't do work a lazy person wants to give you. Pass the whole mess back on the spot. Say something like, "This is a great chance for you to get to know Ann better. Why don't you call, say we've discussed it, and ask if you could get together with her to work it out."

If a subordinate gives you a report that needs work, don't rewrite it. Give your suggestions and let him or her revise it. If a subordinate is in danger of missing tomorrow morning's deadline and comes to you for help, don't grab the work and finish it yourself. Say, "Sorry, Bob. I'll help you through the problem areas, but it looks like you'll be up all night finishing this one."

Look at anything and everything that comes your way with the thought in mind, "Can I pass this back?"

3. Get Yourself Organized

It's hard to make work shorter if you can't find it in the first place. Not being able to find things bugs a lot of people. You may use cross-references, color-coded files, and desk-top organizers and still not be able to find things. Maybe you are subconsciously trying to give yourself an ulcer, but if you really want to change, here are three things that will help:

Take a day to set up files. If you have a secretary, let her do it. Unless you have extraordinarily complex filing, put them in straight alphabetical order.

Put everything away in the files at night before you leave or give everything to your secretary half an hour before quitting time.

Store anything you can in your microcomputer and throw away the paper.

4. Declare War on Paperwork

- When you pick up a piece of paper, don't put it down until you've done something with it. Delegate, write a response, or put it in your procrastinating pile, but do something with it.
- Store big projects that generate lots of paper in loose-leaf binders rather than files. Then, instead of having papers and files loose and falling out all over, you will have them secure in one place.
- Look at reports and forms critically. "What are they used for?" "Are they needed?" "What would happen if I didn't fill this out for a month or two? Or stopped writing this report? Would anyone ask for it?" Do away with every report, every form, every piece of paper that doesn't have a real purpose.
- Have your secretary handle as much paperwork as possible before it gets to your desk. She should throw out junk mail, write answers to routine letters, and fill in forms for you.

  Think about the two weeks covered by your Time Use Chart. How much could you have shortened work if you had been able to find things and if your paperwork had been under control?

5. Do It Right the First Time

Going back and doing things over doesn't exactly shorten work. Doing them right the first time can.

Ask questions, listen, dig, make sure you understand what you are supposed to do. Do your homework, get the facts, check in periodically with others involved to make sure you're on track. Then go ahead and do it right. Whatever you are doing, keep it short and keep it simple. That will make it easier to do and easier to do right.

6. Read Less

Reading is a great time consumer (and waster) for many managers and tends to make everyone's work longer. "I just can't keep up" is a common complaint and every mail delivery brings in another load.

Here are some tips for making the best of your reading time:

- Don't feel you have to read everything that comes your way. Sort and prioritize reading material just as you do your work.
- When you read anything for its message, go for the heart. For instance, in any piece with bullets, go right to the bullets. You could have skipped the opening paragraph above, for instance, dropped down to the first bullet, and still gotten the message.

- Take inventory of the newspapers and magazines you get. Can you drop some? Could you substitute digests like the Kiplinger Letters? *Dun's Business Month?*
- Learn to read on buses, trains, and airplanes.
- Ask all your subordinates, including your secretary, to clip and highlight articles that would be of interest to you and others in your group—then just scan the highlights.
- Before you read anything, look over contents, headings, and chapter titles to see if it's worth reading.
- Discipline yourself to give it one shot, get the message the first time. Don't let yourself go back and reread while you're reading any line or paragraph. Push along on down the page.
- Have your eyes checked once in a while.
- Just because you've started something, doesn't mean you have to finish it. If it isn't pertinent, interesting, or if it's superficial, chuck it.
- Ask to be given exceptions—deviations from plan, good and bad—not entire reports.
- Set a limit on the length of reports and memos your staff sends you. At least one company, Procter & Gamble, still tries to hang on to their tradition of not allowing any memo or report to be longer than one page.
- If you are still having trouble, take a speed-reading course.

Here are some final hints on use of time:

Change old habits. To use time more effectively, you must change old habits and adopt new ones. Like giving up cigarettes, it's not easy.

Remember, nothing is perfect. Don't waste time trying to make things 100 percent perfect when 90 or 95 percent will do. The extra effort and time involved probably isn't worth the small improvement.

Create your own deadlines. That will help you concentrate and keep you motivated to use your time to get work done. Reward yourself later when you've met your deadline.

Don't "reinvent the wheel." Before you plunge into a project, find out if someone else has done it. Ask around. Call other companies to see what they've done. Chances are, some work has already been done for you. Use the organization. We all think we can do it best, but chances are you can get lots of expert help if you ask for it.

That's about it. Wow, look at the time. I've got to get going . . . and you do too. Manage yourself so that you concentrate on those number-one priorities. That's the right thing to do.

Keeping Cool

17. Ulcer City: How to Deal with Stress

"Just being here in the office raises my blood pressure twenty points. Oh, oh . . . here comes the boss . . . up another 20."

Jim Benson, systems analyst,
Interactive Dynamics, Inc.

Stress is here to stay. It is as much a part of life for most people who work as alarm clocks at dawn and coffee at ten o'clock. For some it crops up once in a while, others live with it every day on the job. Chances are you experience stress, too, and maybe you would like to handle it better.

Stress is estimated to cost U.S. industry over $17 billion a year in lost time and productivity, mistakes, and bad decisions. How anybody arrived at that figure, I'm not quite sure, but even at half that amount, it's impressive.

Just reading figures like that can convince you in a hurry that stress is all bad. It isn't.

First Rule of Stress: Stress is normal and, channeled right, can help you. It can make you more alert, give you more energy, and enable you to work better than you do in ordinary, ho-hum situations.

On the other hand, uncontrolled stress can be anywhere from annoying to downright disabling. It can be as mild as feelings of nervousness or worry, or so severe that it causes a lot of unhappy symptoms including headache, nausea, knotted muscles, indigestion, chest pains, and panic.

People under unmanaged stress may find themselves working harder than seems necessary to get things done, having difficulty making decisions, worrying too much, flying off the handle, and having feelings of worthlessness or inadequacy. Eventually: Burn-out or even worse. People under runaway stress for too long a time may even develop physical diseases such as arteriosclerosis, hypertension, heart problems, and migraine headaches. Some estimates show that fifty to eighty percent of all diseases are related to psychosomatic or stress-related origins.

All that cheerful news can be summed up in:

The Second Rule of Stress: While stress can be good for you, it can also knock you off.

There is a third rule of stress, which I'll slide into with this story:

Sam Sanderson, a friend of mine, tells of the first time he gave a report to the board of directors of his company. "The report was in good shape," Sam says, "I'd worked on it for weeks, but I was nervous anyhow. Tossed and turned all night . . . you know how those things are. Anyhow, on the day of the report, I got up early to make sure I had plenty of time, looked out the window and saw it had snowed during the night. Oh, oh. I could feel the anxiety starting to grow. Out on the highway, traffic was slow and stopped altogether in some places. I kept checking my watch. Stop and go. Tick, tick.

"Finally, I got to the city. Just enough time to make it. The streets had been salted and were wet. I raced out of the parking lot right into a wall of water splashed up by a passing taxi. I got to the office steaming mad, tried to clean off my pants as well as I could, grabbed my report, and sprinted up three flights of stairs to the boardroom. I got there, heart pounding, mouth dry, out of breath, and went inside. Twenty-two guys sitting there around the table wondering where I'd been and why I was wearing a suit with spots on it. How did they get there? Didn't it snow on their streets?

"The president started to introduce my report and, as I opened my folder to look at my notes one last time, I almost shot through the ceiling. I'd grabbed the wrong report."

Third Rule of Stress: There is a perversity out there that tends, when something goes wrong, to pile five or six other problems on top of the first like a logjam in a stream, the effect of which is to raise your stress level to painful heights.

What is stress? Stress is how you react physically and emotionally—how you behave—under pressure.

If you could measure stress, it might look something like this:

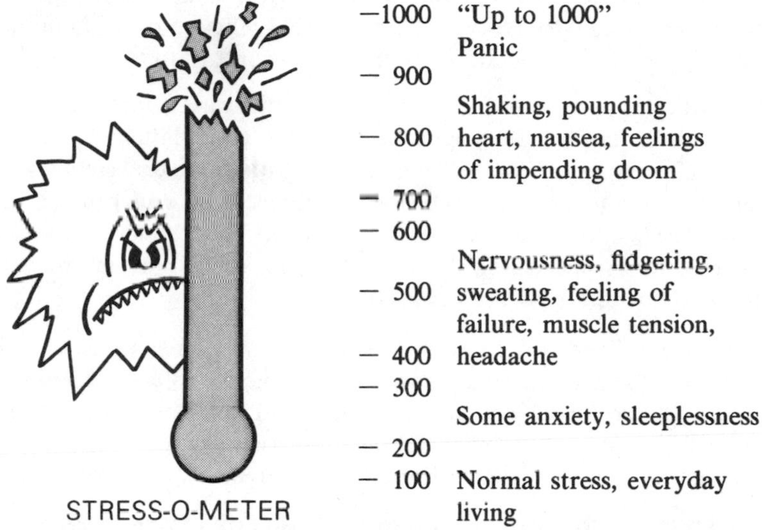

STRESS-O-METER

While the stress-o-meter is not a scientific instrument, it can help you look at your stress and defuse it. We'll use it from time to time as we go along.

What causes stress? Just about anything and everything. For our purposes in this chapter, we will concentrate on work related stress and its five interrelated causes: work situations, people, change, personal habits, and imagination.

Work situations. Not surprisingly, the type of work you do can have a lot to do with your general stress level. The National Institute for Occupational Safety and Health came up recently with a list of high-stress occupations. Among them are nurse, musician, lab technician, teacher's aide, computer programmer, and public relations. Other studies have identified secretarial work as a high-stress area.

Where you are in the hierarchy of your organization can also influence your stress-o-meter readings. Oddly enough, folks who are very high up in organizations, making those giant, multimillion-dollar life-and-death decisions are likely to be under less stress than the middle managers reporting to them. My friend Sam Sanderson was under much more stress than the board members—and not only at that one meeting, but probably on a day-to-day basis also. They had made it and he hadn't yet.

There are a number of other on-the-job factors that can cause stress, many of them related to what you do in your day-to-day work: firing someone, speaking in front of groups, working on your *Upward Bound* skills and trying super hard to improve, having too much (or too little) work to do, commuting, taxes, unclear responsibilities, telephones, interruptions, mistakes, getting a performance appraisal (good or bad), disagreement on who does what, travel, and being told what to do without being asked your opinion—to name a few. I get tense just thinking about them.

People. People cause a lot of problems with stress-o-meters. Conflict, confrontation, stealing ideas, spreading rumors, not fulfilling agreements, goofing off, passing the buck, blaming you, criticizing, backstabbing, not giving recognition for a job well done, taking credit, and general SOB-ishness. Bosses cause a lot of stress. Even good ones. Some people don't relate well to anyone telling them what to do, even in a nice way. For them, just having a boss can cause stress.

Change. Change is constant—as soon as you have adjusted to the last one and things are settling down, another change rolls in. Reorganizations, new bosses or co-workers, mergers, being promoted (or not being promoted), getting a new office, automation, relocation, or new policies, directions, or procedures can all send your stress-o-meter skyrocketing.

Personal habits and attitudes. These can boil your stress-o-meter too: drinking too much coffee or booze, smoking, taking drugs, eating too much sugar, salt, getting overtired, being pessimistic, worrying about your career, taking everything personally, dwelling on past failures, and using negative self-talk.

A big stress producer is what I call the "one-hundred-percent factor." Many of us strive too hard for perfection and are disappointed if we fall short. Which means we are always upset. You spend an hour talking with the big boss. In the course of your discussion you get one fact wrong and he corrects you. You leave thinking, "I blew it." During the hour you gave the boss one hundred facts. You got one wrong. Ninety-nine but not one hundred percent. You dwell on that one mistake, upset because you were not perfect.

Imagination. Imagination can cause plenty of stress, certainly more than it should. Believing others are making more money than you are (a universal belief, often true) or are getting all the breaks, anticipating problems that never happen, thinking of bad possible outcomes rather than good ones, and reading the worst into a new situation can all lead to unnecessary stress.

HOW TO DEAL WITH STRESS

So far we have looked at what stress is and what causes it. What can you do, short of having a frontal lobotomy, to handle stress?

Fourth Rule of Stress: Stress can be managed like anything else in your life. To do it requires determination and practice.

There are three ways to manage stress: 1) Attack the outside factors that are causing you stress; 2) change your own habits; and 3) improve the way you react to stress.

1. Attack the Outside Factors That Cause Stress

This is the best way to reduce stress because it involves going after the source rather than treating the symptoms. Here are some examples.

Having it out with the boss. If you believe your boss is annoyed at something you have done and you are not quite sure what, go and ask. Instead of stewing about it, go find out. "Boss, there's something I'd like your help with. I may be mistaken, but I have a feeling something has been bothering you this past week and wonder if there's anything I should be doing to get whatever it is straightened out?" That sounds ridiculously obvious, but it is amazing how many people never do it. They never go after the cause but live with the anxiety it causes. For more on having it out with the boss, see Chapter 13.

Attacking change. "What can I do?" you ask. "Somebody else decides the change and then tells me about it." That may be true, but there are still things you can do to attack change so it will not burst your stress-o-meter.

The very best way to attack change is to go after it before it happens. Try to anticipate what changes will be coming up. Look at trends inside your organization and at what's happening outside—in business, science, government, technology, and people's lifestyles. Write down possible changes you see and skills you may have to develop to cope with them or to capitalize on them.

Next, think of past changes. What was your reaction? What could you have done to handle the change better and reduce stress? Was the change as bad as you initially thought?

Then, when change comes along, find out everything you can about the change. Why did it come about? What do others think of it? What is good about it?

Discuss the change with your boss. Ask how he or she sees it. State how you feel about it. First, see Chapter 3 on attitude.

Find out what the change will do to you. Will it change your job, status, pay, responsibility? Then after you have gotten over your initial emotional response, go back and ask yourself, "What will this really mean to me?" Then think of all the ways you could make the change help you.

Think of how you can be involved in the change. Can you help implement it? Can you offer ideas and suggestions to improve it?

You may not be able to stop the change, but by taking some active role in relation to it, you will be able to use the change to your advantage. Or, at the very least, you will feel better about it.

Handling conflict. If it is conflict that is causing you stress, here's how to deal with it.

First, take a break and defuse your anger. Anger doesn't lead to good rational thinking. When you have calmed down, talk to the person with whom you're having the conflict. Treat him/her with respect (hold the putdown), listen till you experience his or her side of the issue, then state your views, needs, and feelings. Focus on "I" not "you"; that is, state "I feel upset when you". . . (that's hard to argue with), not "You make me sick" or "You always . . ."

With that behind you, choose a strategy.

If the issue isn't really important, forget it, do nothing.

Smooth it over if maintaining the relationship is more important than winning.

Pull rank when you are in a position to do so, when there is not time to use other methods, and when you can tolerate the problems this creates.

Negotiate, compromise, collaborate, when it is important that you both win.

Like change, conflict tends to become less of an irritant when you actively do something about it.

There are other things you can do to attack the causes of stress and many of them are covered in other chapters of ***1000 Things You Never Learned in Business School.*** Skills you acquire through this book will help you reduce stress because you will be more confident and able to cope better. Just think how much calmer you will feel next time you speak in front of a group, knowing you will be terrific; think how your stress-o-meter will go down when you tackle a touchy subject with the boss, confident you know how to handle him or her; imagine how good you will feel when you have planned your time and know you are using it in the best possible way.

2. Change Habits That Cause Stress

I always felt smoking cigarettes and drinking martinis were about as relaxing an activity as I could find, that is until I learned that, if overdone, these can actually produce more stress. Whenever there is something that's fun, somebody comes along and figures out why it's bad.

I know you are not going to stop smoking, drinking, or using drugs just by virtue of reading this. But at least if you didn't know it before, now you are aware that they can play havoc with stress-o-meter levels.

I won't even suggest that you quit. But, I do want to give you one hint that will help if you are worried about your habits causing you stress and sincerely want to change. And that is to set some modest goals for yourself. Few people can give up cigarettes, coffee, and ice cream all at once and make all that last more than a day. It just doesn't work. "Habit is habit," Mark Twain once said, "and not to be thrown out the window by any man, but coaxed down the stairs one step at a time."

Cut down a little at a time on smoking, drinking, eating, or whatever you are doing too much of *while at the same time replacing that habit* with small doses of exercise or meditation or whatever you find helps to calm you.

Habits that reduce stress. I've had good success with running, hard tennis (not pitty-pat), and skiing. I still haven't been able to get much out of meditation, although many people swear by it. If it works for you, by all means use it.

Other relaxation techniques include using self-suggestion (sort of self-hypnosis) to relax muscles and calm heart rate; alternately tensing and relaxing muscles; emptying the mind of all thoughts for a period of time; deep breathing and visualization (imagining you are on the beach or listening to a summer rain). If you want to get fancy, you can even try biofeedback where machines will monitor your body activity and will help you learn to turn on your inner relaxation switch.

If you are interested in developing any of these techniques for yourself, there are books that deal with them in depth (see reading list at the end of the book).

And finally, harness your imagination. Promise yourself you will not spend time worrying about eventualities. If you cannot find out the facts, don't invent them, especially if you are prone to invent bad ones. It is absurd to do this, so stop it. Save your energy and your stress-o-meter peaks for problems that really exist.

Something like meditating is goofing off. I'd recommend it. Set aside time every day to stop achieving and have fun. Take time for liberal arts—books, plays, music, art, hobbies—activities that have nothing to do with work. People who cope have many outside interests and pursue them. This goof-off time should be pure fun. If you have a hobby that, deep down, you know bores you, find another. If you start a book and don't like it, can it and pick up another.

3. Improve the Ways You React to Stress

Responses to stress are learned. You are not born with them and you aren't stuck with the same old responses for life. You developed your responses by trial and error (each time you got kicked around, you tried out a response), without expert help, and maybe they aren't the best.

To do better in the future, try these positive reactions to stress:

1. Accept the fact that stress is out there—a yard full of feisty cocker spaniels ready to nip you every time you step out the door. There's no way to avoid it.
2. Remember that stress is not all bad. It can get your juices flowing and actually make you perform better. Stress can be good.
3. Convince yourself you are a good stress manager. Build your own self-fulfilling prophesy of stress: Predict positive outcomes, do it over and over until you believe it and eventually it will happen (sometimes—after all, this is the real world). Think of past stressful events and how you reacted. In what ways did you handle stress well? Can you use those again in dealing with future stress? What are your strengths? Did you use them? Begin telling yourself that you can use these strengths to deal with stress.
4. Ask yourself if you've handled similar situations before and how you went about it. Think of how you would successfully manage those parts of the situation you can control. Forget about the parts you can't control.
5. Tell yourself it will be over soon. It is not the worst thing that could happen. Tell yourself, "I can do this. I can handle it all right. I've done it before, or things just as tough before, and come out all right. Any anxiety I feel is normal and will help me."
6. Remember, tension, anger, desire to leap out of your skin, are your responses. They're not done to you—you do them. There is nothing in the stressful situation itself that can make you feel that way. It's how you decide to feel. You must practice not responding physically to outside irritants.
7. Don't be so hard on yourself. Nobody's perfect. Quit dwelling on past mistakes. If you made a good half-hour talk, quit focusing on the couple sentences or words you tripped over.
8. Have images ready to divert you from focusing on the stress. Use them immediately when the old stress-o-meter starts to rise. Describe things around you. Look for beauty in everyday objects. Keep a mental file of favorite scenes or activities: beaches, songs, restaurants, bars, your dog, a hammock, a warm August day, the first snow of winter,

tennis, skiing (those are a few of mine). Reach in and pull one out. Concentrate on it. Feel it, hear it, smell it. Practice and practice this technique until it begins to work for you. It can really help.

9. Tell yourself the whole tension level in society is absurd. A year from now—or maybe even a week from now—what you're upset about won't be remembered. Even you won't be upset by it. It's not that important.
10. Remember, everyone else feels stress. All those calm, confident people you see at the office—they have anxiety, too, and are afraid they won't measure up.
11. Admit your stress to others—it helps to share the burden. Also talk with others about how they cope.
12. Ask yourself: "What's the worst thing that could happen? How would I feel? Would that be life and death or could I handle it? How likely is it to happen? How can I reduce the chances of it happening?"
13. Write everything down. Label your stress zero to 1,000 using the stress-o-meter. Somehow, when you describe and label your stress it goes down fast.
14. Decide on a course of action. Knowing that you will do something and what that is are very positive ways to reduce stress.
15. To help you with 13 and 14 above, use the Stress Analysis Chart (SAC) that follows. When the cocker spaniel nips, whip out an SAC and go to work. You will feel better in no time.
16. After you have gotten through a stressful situation, reward yourself. Go buy some new clothes, go out to a nice restaurant, buy a bottle of fine wine or a new record. Something. And tell yourself beforehand that that's what you will do.

    Reinforce yourself with positive thoughts. "See, I did it. I knew I could." "Here's what I learned and here's what I'll use next time." If you have some setbacks, that's okay too. You're only human. But be ready to bounce back quickly.

People on the way up place themselves under extra stress. Remember to attack the cause of stress, change your habits that cause stress, and improve the way you react to stress, and you will be able to handle whatever comes along. May your stress-o-meter never rise above 500.

STRESS ANALYSIS CHART

WHAT'S BOTHERING ME	HOW I FEEL RATING ON STRESS-O-METER:

WHAT I'VE DONE SO FAR

WHAT I SHOULD DO

To Attack the Cause:

-
-
-
-
-

To Change Habits That Cause Stress:

-
-
-
-
-

To Improve the Way I React:

-
-
-
-
-

The Last Word

It has been fun sharing these thoughts with you and I hope you've enjoyed reading them. More than that, I hope you will profit from learning and using the skills and they will make your life richer, both materially and in satisfaction and pride.

Since we've covered all this ground together, I can't resist repeating one last piece of advice because it's so important. Be patient. If you are really intent on improving your work and your life, you will have to work at it over a period of time. You will not be able to develop all your *Upward Bound* skills in a week or a month. Don't try—you will only get discouraged and drop right back into your old routine. Work on one skill at a time. Practice it until you begin to see progress, until the new skill becomes natural to you, until you do it without thinking and it becomes part of your style. Then go on to another.

If you do that, building one skill, then another, and staying with it—making learning and growing as much a part of your life as eating and sleeping—you will find

1. You'll build lasting improvement in your skills.
2. You'll progress quickly.
3. You'll become addicted, because seeing yourself improve, knowing each day you're doing better than the day before, is one of the great joys of life.

Good success in getting out ahead of the pack and staying there.

WILLIAM N. YEOMANS

Books, Articles, and Other Sources of Additional Information

Chapter 1: STARTING UP

Deal, Terrence E., and Kennedy, Allan A. *Corporate Cultures.* Reading, MA.: Addison-Wesley Publishing Co., 1982.

Types of cultures within companies and how they help or hinder success.

Fox, Joseph M. *Executive Qualities.* Reading, MA.: Addison-Wesley Publishing Co., 1976.

By a former IBM executive, this book spells out qualities an effective executive should have.

Naisbitt, John. *Megatrends.* New York: Warner Books, Inc., 1982.

Ten trends that will shape our future.

Peters, Thomas J., and Waterman, Robert H., Jr. *In Search of Excellence.* New York: Harper & Row, 1982.

An important work on what makes organizations great. If you haven't read it, you should be ashamed of yourself. Go do it.

Chapter 2: UP, UP . . . AND AWAY (Career Options)

Bolles, Richard N. *The Three Boxes of Life.* Berkeley, CA.: Ten Speed Press, 1981.

A detailed workbook and planning guide to help you move out of the box you may find yourself in at any point in your life and career.

Gale, Barry and Linda. *Discover What You're Best At.* New York: Simon & Schuster, 1982.

Aptitude and interest inventories, and other helpful information on career planning plus descriptions of over one thousand careers.

Hagberg, Janet, and Leider, Richard. *The Inventurers.* Reading, MA.: Addison-Wesley Publishing Co., 1983.

Fun to read and to do the exercises. A guide to sizing up what you want out of life and making changes to get it.

Schwartz, Dr. Lester, and Brechner, Irv. *The Career Finder.* New York: Ballantine Books, 1983.

Career questionnaires and profiles, along with information on fifteen hundred entry-level jobs.

Sheehy, Gail. *Passages.* New York: Bantam Books, 1977.

A popular paperback outlining some of the crises people often meet at various stages of their lives.

Chapter 3: ATTITUDES ANONYMOUS (Positive Attitudes)

Schwartz, David. *Getting What You Want.* New York: William Morrow, 1983.

How to gain more wealth, influence, and happiness through positive attitudes.

Chapter 4: IT'LL NEVER WORK (Creativity)

Albrecht, Karl. *Brain Power.* Englewood Cliffs, NJ: Prentice-Hall, 1980.

Fun to read. Lots of jokes and anecdotes, also good information and ideas.

Edwards, Betty. *Drawing on the Right Side of the Brain.* Los Angeles: J. P. Tarcher, Inc., 1979.

A delight to read, with a good method for getting "noncreative" people to use the right brain more. Contains a concise and lucid explanation of right brain, left brain.

Perkins, D. N. *The Mind's Best Work.* Cambridge, MA.: Harvard University Press, 1981.

Written by a Harvard philosopher, this book looks at creativity in new ways. The last chapter is all you need to read.

Prince, George M. *The Practice of Creativity.* New York: Collier Books, 1970.

A classic. You can't read this without saying over and over, "Boy, he's so right."

Springer, Sally P., and Deutsch, George. *Left Brain, Right Brain.* San Francisco: W. H. Freeman & Co., 1981.

A little deep as far as anatomy of the brain is concerned, but fascinating to read, and a complete survey of the left brain/right brain work that's been done to date.

Workshop:

Synectics, Inc.
17 Dunster Street
Cambridge, MA 02138

George Prince, who wrote *The Practice of Creativity* and other works mentioned elsewhere in this book, is the chairman of Synectics. The Synectics Basic Course will give you training and practice in creative problem solving. After a week at Synectics, you will look at ideas in entirely new ways.

Chapter 5: WHAT DID HE SAY? (Writing)

Bly, Robert W., and Blake, Gary. *Technical Writing.* New York: McGraw-Hill, 1982.

A snappy little paperback on technical and business writing. Well done.

Roman, Kenneth, and Raphaelson, Joel. *Writing That Works.* New York: Harper & Row, 1981.

Written by two advertising executives, this book provides good advice on how to write memos, letters, reports, speeches and (if all that fails) resumes. Informative and fun to read.

Strunk, William, Jr., and White, E. B. *The Elements of Style.* 3rd Ed. New York: Macmillan, 1979.

Originally written by Strunk, a Cornell professor, in the early 1900s and revised several times thereafter by White, his student. This book is a classic. Clear and concise, it covers style, composition, use of words, and much more.

Zinsser, William. *On Writing Well.* New York: Harper & Row, 1980.

Not strictly on business writing, but important to read if you really want to go all out to improve your writing.

American Heritage Dictionary of the English Language. Boston: Houghton-Mifflin, 1981.

Roget's International Thesaurus, Fourth Ed. New York: Thomas Y. Crowell, 1977.

Chapter 6: I HOPE THE EARTH WILL SWALLOW ME UP (Speaking)

Hilton, Jack, and Knoblauch, Mary. *On Television!* New York: ANACOM, 1980.

This covers appearances on television, mainly how to handle antagonistic interviewers on "investigative" shows, but contains many good suggestions on presenting yourself and your message on or off television.

Kenny, Michael (for Kodak). *Presenting Yourself (A Kodak How-To Book).* New York: John Wiley and Sons, 1982.

Paperback, attractive and interesting to read. Good information on presentations, especially the audiovisual aspects.

Leech, Thomas. *How to Prepare, Stage and Deliver Winning Presentations.* New York: ANACOM, 1982.

A big book, complete and thorough. Sound advice on all phases of presenting.

Lewis, David V. *Secrets of Successful Writing, Speaking and Listening.* New York: ANACOM, 1982.

Using good communications to gain understanding, get what you want, improve your image, and further your career.

Mause, L., Jr. *Mastering the Business and Technical Presentation.* Boston: CBI Publications, 1981.

Paperback. A quick read; good reference.

Vardaman, George T. *Making Successful Presentations.* New York: ANACOM, 1981.

A complete guide to making successful presentations of all kinds, with samples of presentations by top business executives.

Chapter 7: THERE GOES THE AFTERNOON (Meetings)

Hon, David. *Meetings That Matter.* New York: John Wiley and Sons 1980.

How to run task-oriented meetings.

Jay, Anthony. "How to Run a Meeting." *Harvard Business Review,* March–April, 1976, pp 43–57.

A droll, but oh so true look at what happens in meetings. Must reading. Be sure to dig this article out.

Prince, George. "Creative Meetings Through Power Sharing." *Harvard Business Review,* July–August, 1972, pp 47–54.

George Prince has spent years studying meetings and covers some of what he's learned in this article, along with suggesting some creative new ways to make meetings better.

Schindler-Rainman, E., and Lippitt, Ronald. *Taking Your Meetings Out of the Doldrums.* La Jolla, CA.: University Associates, 1977.
Suggested for pepping up meetings.

Chapter 8: HOW MUCH? (Negotiating)

Cohen, Herb. *You Can Negotiate Anything.* New York: Bantam Books, 1982.
A very popular paperback, describing negotiation practices including a chapter on how the Russians negotiate. How to get what you want in everyday life and the win-win style.

Fisher, Robert, and Ury, William. *Getting Into Yes.* New York: Penguin, 1981.
A quick read, with a good chapter on how to handle tough opponents who pull dirty tricks.

Karass, Chester. *The Negotiating Game.* New York: Thomas Y. Crowell, 1970.
Karass summarizes research done on winning and losing negotiations and outlines negotiation strategies.

Nierenberg, Gerald L. *The Art of Negotiating.* New York: Cornerstone Library, 1968.
A lawyer, author, and lecturer, Nierenberg describes methods of negotiating for all situations, with emphasis on detecting what the other person wants and needs, and negotiating for mutual satisfaction.

Chapter 9: TELL ME ABOUT YOURSELF (Selection and Training)

Drake, John D. *Interviewing for Managers.* New York: ANACOM, 1982.
A clearly written "how to" book by a guy who has spent a working lifetime interviewing people.

Fear, Richard A. *The Evaluation Interview.* New York: McGraw-Hill, 1978.
A training program on how to interview. Can be purchased with or without cassette tapes. See Chapters 3 through 6.

Stockard, James G. *Career Development and Job Training.* New York: ANACOM, 1977.
A wealth of information on training and development and managing the growth of people.

Chapter 10: OVER THE TOP (Motivation and Teamwork)

Blanchard, Kenneth, and Johnson, Spencer. *The One Minute Manager.* New York: Berkley, 1983.

This expensive little book has a message about people that may make it worth the price. It covers how to manage in an organization or a family in a way that will motivate people through one-minute goal setting, one-minute praising, and one-minute reprimands.

Dyer, William G. *Team Building.* Reading, MA.: Addison-Wesley Publishing Co., 1977.

A dynamite little book on getting people to work together effectively.

Hill, Norman C. *Increasing Managerial Effectiveness.* Reading, MA.: Addison-Wesley Publishing Co., 1979.

Paperback. A well-done, common-sense approach to management and motivation. Worth reading.

LeBoeuf, Michael. *The Productivity Challenge.* New York: McGraw-Hill, 1982.

Practical methods for improving the workplace so people can do their best. See Chapters 5, 6, and 10.

Rosenbaum, Bernard L. *How to Motivate Today's Workers.* New York: McGraw-Hill, 1982.

Good overview of motivation theory and techniques.

Shonk, James H. *Working in Teams.* New York: ANACOM, 1982.

A short, practical guide to improving teamwork.

Chapter 11: HUH? (Listening)

Cooper, Ken. *Body Business.* New York: ANACOM, 1979.

How to read other people's nonverbal signals and to control your own.

Fast, Julius. *Body Language.* New York: Pocket Books, 1970.

A short primer on sizing up what people's postures mean.

Malandro, Loretta, and Barker, Larry. *Non-Verbal Communication.* Reading, MA.: Addison-Wesley Publishing Co., 1983.

Complete, nicely illustrated, and enjoyable book covering all types of nonverbal behaviors and what they mean.

Montgomery, Robert L. *Listening Made Easy.* New York: ANACOM, 1981.

Easy read, complete with cartoons. Some good information on increasing your ability to listen.

Nierenberg, Gerald L. *How to Read a Person Like a Book.* New York: Cornerstone Library, 1981.

What to look for in the other person's behavior and what that behavior means. By a skilled negotiator who has had much experience sizing up the other guy.

Chapter 12: IMPORTANCE OF THE IRRELEVANT

Golding, Charles William. *What It Takes to Get to the Top—and Stay There.* New York: Putnam, 1983.

Many ideas on how to handle irrelevants, as well as developing other success skills.

McCaffrey, Paradis and Shea. *The Language of Business.* Cambridge, MA.: Cambridge Business Research, Inc., 1980.

Chapter 13: MANAGING YOUR BOSS

Anthony, William P. *Managing Your Boss.* New York: ANACOM, 1983.

How to use the power you have (more than you think), shape your image, open up communications, and build a new relationship with your boss. Complete with case studies and exercises.

Fallon, William K. *Leadership on the Job.* New York: ANACOM, 1973.

See Chapter 21 by Peter Drucker on "How to Manage Your Boss."

Hegarty, Christopher. *How to Manage Your Boss.* Mill Valley, CA.: Network, Inc., 1982.

How to transform what can be an adversary relationship into one of cooperation and teamwork. Putting yourself in the boss's shoes and understanding his or her needs.

Chapter 14: I'LL THINK OF IT IN A MINUTE (Memory)

Albrecht, Karl. *Brain Power.* Englewood Cliffs, NJ: Prentice-Hall, 1980.

A good section on memory in Chapter 12. Many other ideas on making yourself more alert.

Higbee, Kenneth L. *Your Memory: How It Works and How to Improve It.* Englewood Cliffs, NJ: Prentice-Hall, 1977.

Good information on memory-improvement techniques.

Chapter 15: BUT MY HOROSCOPE SAID (Problem Solving, Decision Making)

Moody, Paul. *Decision Making.* New York: McGraw-Hill, 1983.

Moody covers the waterfront on decision making and even throws in PERT and quality circles, which are really on the fringe, but his book is enlightening and easy to read.

Ulschak, Francis, et al. *Small Group Problem-Solving.* Reading, MA.: Addison-Wesley Publishing Co., 1981.

As the title indicates, a look at the group in problem solving with a comprehensive review of group techniques.

Chapter 16: IS IT FIVE O'CLOCK ALREADY? (Time)

Agardy, Franklin J. *How to Read Faster and Better.* New York: Fireside, 1983.

A short paperback by the president of the Evelyn Wood Reading Institute covering some of the principles taught by that well-known firm.

Januz, Lauren R., and Jones, Susan K. *Time Management for Executives.* New York: Charles Scribner's Sons, 1981.

Well done, wide-ranging coverage of the topic.

Lakein, Alan. *How to Get Control of Your Time and Your Life.* New York: Signet, 1973.

A paperback packed with helpful approaches to using time better. The Lakein system is widely known and used by managers.

MacKenzie, R. Alec. *The Time Trap.* New York: ANACOM, 1972.

Practical and usable. Good information on working with subordinates and secretaries to use time better.

Also in paperback: McGraw-Hill, 1972.

Winston, Stephanie. *The Organized Executive.* New York: W. W. Norton, 1983.

How to get your office, your files, and yourself organized, and more.

Chapter 17: ULCER CITY (Stress)

Albrecht, Karl. *Stress and the Manager: Making It Work for You.* Englewood Cliffs, NJ: Prentice-Hall, 1978.

One of Albrecht's many informative books. He does a good job of explaining the causes of stress and how to use stress to your advantage.

Girdano, Daniel A., and Everly, George S., Jr. *Controlling Stress and Tension: A Holistic Approach.* Englewood Cliffs, NJ: Prentice-Hall, 1979.

A mind-body approach to relaxing, reducing frustration, and improving self-esteem. Includes helpful checklists and exercises.

Herman, G., M.D. *Stress and the Bottom Line.* New York: ANACOM, 1981.

A very thorough look at stress. Good if you would like to dig into the subject in detail.

LeShan, Lawrence. *How to Meditate: A Guide to Self-Discovery.* Boston: Little, Brown & Co., 1974.

A practical guide that describes several methods of meditation, and takes some of the mystery out of the subject.

Levi, Lennart, M.D. *Preventing Work Stress.* Reading, MA.: Addison-Wesley Publishing Co., 1981.

A small, quick reference in paperback.

Selye, Dr. Hans. *Stress without Distress.* New York: Signet, 1982.

How to use stress effectively. Written by a physician who has researched and written extensively on this and other subjects.

Toffler, Alvin. *Future Shock.* New York: Random House, 1970.

A classic. Why change is making us all nervous.

Yates, Dr. Jere E. *Managing Stress: A Businessperson's Guide.* New York: ANACOM, 1981.

A concise, complete description of what causes stress in business and how to deal with it.

Index

ABOUT THE AUTHOR

William N. Yeomans has over twenty years of human-resource management experience and is currently manager of training and development for one of the nation's largest corporations.

He is a recognized authority on career development and management. He is the author of a series of books on job hunting and career planning for college graduates, the latest of which is *JOBS 82–83*. His work has also appeared in *The New York Times* and in *Career Insights, The Graduate, Glamour* and *Mademoiselle* magazines, *The Training and Development Journal* and in *The Journal of General Psychology.*

He has spoken at numerous colleges and universities and has conducted workshops and seminars on management subjects for organizations such as the American Management Associations, the American Society for Training and Development, and the National Retail Merchants Association. He has been a featured speaker at numerous major national conventions and on a recent television series, *Where the Jobs Are.*

Mr. Yeomans has an MBA from Cornell University and graduated with honors from Hamilton College. He lives in a two-hundred-year-old home in northern New Jersey.